Alessio Buscemi, Daniele Proverbio

Leading with AI in the EU

Also of Interest

AI Ethics and Governance
Historical, Cultural, and Regulatory Perspectives
Manuel Wörsdörfer, 2026
ISBN 978-3-11-224594-1, e-ISBN (PDF) 978-3-11-224595-8, e-ISBN (EPUB) 978-3-11-224596-5

Artificial Intelligence
Shaping the Future of Innovation
Alfred Essa, 2025
ISBN 978-3-11-158238-2, e-ISBN (PDF) 978-3-11-158354-9, e-ISBN (EPUB) 978-3-11-158411-9

RAG Artificial Intelligence
Retrieval-Augmented Generation in Generative AI
Saloni Garg, Amit Sagtani, Kamal Kant Hiran, 2026
ISBN 978-3-11-222677-3, e-ISBN (PDF) 978-3-11-222678-0, e-ISBN (EPUB) 978-3-11-222679-7

Digital Trust
Online Safety, Identification Models, Ethical Digital Environments
Pascal Muam Mah, Mahmoud Ahmed Nasr, 2026
ISBN 978-3-11-222974-3, e-ISBN (PDF) 978-3-11-222975-0, e-ISBN (EPUB) 978-3-11-222976-7

Alessio Buscemi, Daniele Proverbio

Leading with AI in the EU

Governance, Practices, and Compliance

DE GRUYTER

Authors

Dr. Alessio Buscemi
Luxembourg Institute of Science and Technology
Av. des Hauts-Fourneaux 5
4362 Esch-sur-Alzette
Luxembourg
alessio.buscemi@list.lu

Dr. Daniele Proverbio
University of Trento
via Sommarive 9
38123 Trento
Italy
daniele.proverbio@unitn.it

ISBN 978-3-11-225409-7
ISBN 978-3-11-225410-3 (PDF)
ISBN 978-3-11-225411-0 (E-PUB)
DOI https://doi.org/10.1515/9783112254103

Library of Congress Control Number: 2026940610

Bibliographic information published by the Deutsche Nationalbibliothek
The Deutsche Nationalbibliothek lists this publication in the Deutsche Nationalbibliografie; detailed bibliographic data are available on the Internet at https://dnb.dnb.de.

De Gruyter and Walter de Gruyter GmbH are part of De Gruyter Brill.
www.degruyterbrill.com

Questions about General Product Safety Regulation: productsafety@degruyterbrill.com

Cover illustration: Blue Planet Studio / iStock / Getty Images Plus

Contents

Preface

Generative AI has moved rapidly from a specialized technology to a general-purpose capability embedded in everyday organizational activity. Language-based systems now support writing, searching, summarizing, designing, coding, and decision preparation across functions. More recently, these systems are evolving into agent-based configurations, capable of planning tasks, invoking tools, coordinating across steps, and operating with increasing autonomy within defined boundaries. Together, generative AI and agentic systems are reshaping how knowledge work is organized, executed, and governed.

In 2025, MIT surveyed more than 300 generative AI projects implemented by large and mid-sized companies around the world [1], finding that only 5 % of the projects generated measurable return on investment. Importantly, the limiting factors were rarely technical. Models generally performed as expected in controlled environments, data was available, and compute constraints were manageable. The differentiator was organizational readiness. Where leadership struggled to articulate success criteria, teams operated in silos, governance structures were informal or absent, and employees lacked understanding or trust, promising initiatives were terminated to scale.

In Europe in particular, the AI transformation unfolds under conditions that introduce a set of distinct and cumulative difficulties for institutions and businesses. Adoption takes place within stringent data protection regimes, dense sector-specific regulation, strong labour and social protection frameworks, and heightened expectations of accountability toward workers, consumers, and public institutions. At the same time, the EU has about 30 % more AI professionals per capita than the US and three times than China [2], yet it struggles to retain them.[1] While AI accountability frameworks exist globally, European regulations distinctively emphasize external, stakeholder-facing justification. As a result, European organizations are often required to demonstrate not only that a system performs effectively, but *why* it is used, *how* it influences decisions, and *who* remains accountable when outcomes are contested. Yet despite these structural challenges, in 2025, 32.7 % of people aged 16–74 in the EU used generative AI tools on average, with significant variation between member states, roughly aligned with US adoption rates and superior to China, suggesting that the capacity to compete remains intact if governance and institutional barriers can be addressed [4, 5]. These conditions do not reduce the relevance of generative AI. They define the environment within which its use must remain legitimate, defensible, and sustainable.

Beyond regulation, European organizations increasingly face the challenge of digital sovereignty. Much of the generative AI ecosystem is currently controlled by non-European actors, spanning foundational models, cloud infrastructure, development

1 Note that three out of four European international AI PhD students at American universities move and stay in the US for at least five years [3].

https://doi.org/10.1515/9783112254103-203

platforms, and data-processing pipelines. This creates structural dependencies that go beyond procurement choices. Decisions about where data is processed, how models evolve, under which jurisdictions systems operate, and how failures are handled are often shaped by external providers whose incentives and governance structures do not necessarily align with European legal obligations or societal expectations.

Recent empirical indicators illustrate the magnitude of this dependency and its consequences. Annual AI venture investment in the US reaches €50–60 billion, compared to about €6–7 billion in the EU, while the US maintains seventeen times Europe's AI supercomputing capacity [6]. In 2025, three US hyperscalers held 72 % of the European cloud market [7]. At the same time, while European organizations remain heavily reliant on non-European cloud and AI providers in practice, interviews with senior technology leaders consistently indicate a preference for European public cloud offerings, sovereign-certified infrastructures, or on-premise private cloud solutions when hosting AI systems. Estimates suggest that reducing this dependency through sovereign AI infrastructure and capabilities could unlock approximately €480 billion in economic value for Europe [8]. This contrast highlights a structural mismatch between preferences for control and accountability, and the realities of the current AI supply chain.

For teams operating in Europe, digital sovereignty is therefore not an abstract policy objective, but a concrete managerial concern. Dependence on externally governed AI systems can complicate compliance with data protection and sectoral rules, limit transparency and auditability, and reduce the overall capacity to adapt or constrain systems over time. It also raises questions of resilience and continuity: how organizations maintain control over critical processes, knowledge assets, and decision-support functions when core components of their AI stack lie outside their direct governance.

These challenges are particularly acute for generative AI and agent-based systems. Unlike traditional IT tools, these systems are deeply embedded in organizational workflows and interact directly with knowledge workers through natural language. They influence how information is produced, interpreted, and acted upon, often in ways that are difficult to fully specify in advance. As autonomy increases, so does the importance of retaining meaningful control over data flows, decision pathways, escalation mechanisms, and accountability structures. In the European context, adopting generative AI therefore requires balancing innovation with the need to preserve legal certainty, coherence, and strategic autonomy.

From a managerial perspective, this creates a growing sense of urgency combined with a lack of orientation. Leaders are increasingly exposed to compelling demonstrations, early productivity gains, and competitive pressure to act. At the same time, guidance is fragmented. Technical teams focus on models, architectures, and performance. Legal teams concentrate on compliance and liability. Innovation units run pilots and proofs of concept. Vendors promote tools, benchmarks, and rapid deployment narratives. What is often missing is a coherent managerial framework that connects these perspectives into a single decision-making structure aligned with European legal, social, and institutional responsibilities.

As a result, organizations may face two opposing but equally unsatisfactory outcomes. Rapid, opportunistic deployment of generative AI in isolated use cases can increase the risk of governance gaps, unclear accountability, vendor lock-in, and scaling failures once systems become business-critical or subject to scrutiny. Conversely, excessive caution driven by uncertainty around regulation, sovereignty, and long-term implications may lead to paralysis, leaving companies and institutions unable to move beyond exploratory discussions while competitors advance. In both cases, the core difficulty is rarely technical capability. It is the absence of a structured approach for making informed, defensible choices about where generative AI fits and how it should be governed over time.

This book addresses that gap. It provides a coherent foundation for understanding, integrating, and governing generative AI in European organizations, offering a comprehensive view of the modern AI ecosystem through a managerial lens. The focus on generative AI is deliberate: unlike many AI applications confined to specialized functions, generative systems cut across team boundaries. They shape how organizations write, analyze, communicate, and decide, and they form the foundation for more advanced agentic systems that further challenge traditional notions of control and accountability. It is precisely this transversal nature that makes generative AI both a strategic opportunity and a governance imperative.

The framework presented here brings together perspectives that are typically treated in isolation: productivity and impact, operational risk and compliance, ethical and social considerations, and strategic questions of control and sovereignty. While each of these dimensions is well covered in existing literature, they are rarely integrated into a unified framework grounded in European realities. What follows is not a catalogue of tools or a checklist for rapid deployment. It is neither a legal manual nor a purely abstract reflection on Artificial Intelligence. Instead, it develops a structured framework for understanding generative AI and agent-based systems as strategic resources. The focus is on how value is created, how responsibility is allocated, how risks are monitored, and how systems remain aligned with legal, social, and institutional expectations as they evolve.

Throughout, generative AI is approached primarily as an organizational and governance challenge rather than a purely technical one. Models are treated as components within broader socio-technical systems. What matters is how they are embedded in workflows, how AI-supported decisions are reviewed and escalated, how errors and failures are handled, and how explanations can be provided to internal and external stakeholders. The central issue is not speed of deployment, but the capacity to integrate generative AI (and its legacy AI agents) into decision-making structures that already carry legal and institutional responsibility. The most significant risks and benefits do not arise from the models themselves, but from the choices that govern their use.

The chapters that follow guide the reader through the key dimensions shaping generative AI adoption in European organizations. Early sections establish a concise technical foundation for non-specialists. Subsequent chapters examine value creation and risk across operational, social, regulatory, and strategic domains. A substantial part focuses on leadership and governance, proposing structured approaches to use-case selection, lifecycle management, evaluation, accountability, and sovereignty-aware deployment choices. Rather than fixed recipes, what emerges are reasoning principles and governance models designed to remain robust as technologies and regulatory interpretations evolve.

Ultimately, this book aims to equip leaders operating in Europe, as well as those engaging with the European market, with the analytical frameworks and decision-making discipline required to adopt generative AI with confidence and restraint. The objective is not merely effective deployment, but sustainable adoption: enabling teams to integrate generative AI and agent-based systems in ways that remain economically viable, institutionally legitimate, strategically autonomous, and resilient over time within Europe's regulatory and societal context.

Navigating this book

The chapters follow a coherent progression, while the book is designed to support flexible reading paths. Readers already familiar with AI fundamentals may move directly to the chapters on adoption, governance, and regulation. Others may prefer a sequential journey, progressing from conceptual foundations to managerial application. This flexibility reflects a simple reality: organizations approach generative AI from different starting points, yet they share a common opportunity to develop clearer judgment, stronger capabilities, and more confident decision-making over time.

Case studies and use cases are woven throughout the book as analytical anchors, not as prescriptive models. They are used to connect abstract concepts to concrete decision contexts and dynamics, illustrating how choices unfold in practice. Rather than offering templates to replicate, the book invites critical examination of real situations. It deliberately avoids fixed recipes in favor of frameworks, distinctions, and reasoning tools that support context-sensitive judgment. This approach recognizes both the diversity of organizational environments and the rapid evolution of AI technologies. Accordingly, the book moves from established practices that are already delivering value to emerging approaches and forward-looking perspectives that invite experimentation within a structured managerial framework.

Chapter 1 establishes a shared technical and conceptual baseline. It traces the evolution of Artificial Intelligence from early symbolic systems to contemporary generative models, explaining why AI has moved from a specialized technical field to a pervasive force shaping business, policy, and society. Key concepts such as prompt engineering, fine-tuning, retrieval-augmented generation, and AI agents are introduced in accessible language, consistently linked to their managerial relevance and practical implications.

Chapters 2 and 3 turn attention to value creation. They explore how generative AI can be applied across contexts, the strategic choices involved in selecting models, tools, and deployment approaches, and the conditions that enable sustainable impact. Topics such as shadow AI, cost structures and operational dependencies are discussed to help leaders translate innovation goals into viable and scalable initiatives grounded in reality.

Chapters 4 and 5 deepen this perspective by focusing on decision discipline as a source of advantage. They examine how use cases can be identified and prioritized, how potential returns can be assessed under uncertainty, and how the full lifecycle of a generative AI system can be managed effectively. From problem framing and pilot design to scaling, monitoring, and eventual system retirement, these chapters emphasize that consistent value creation emerges from clear governance and thoughtful execution as much as from technical capability.

Chapter 6 introduces a more reflective perspective by examining what happens when systems operate at scale. Drawing on documented breakdowns, it shows how generative AI can fail through hallucinations, data leakage, biased outputs, or inadequate crisis handling. These cases are presented not as warnings against adoption, but as learning opportunities that have shaped best practices in testing, monitoring, and safety. The chapter highlights how organizations that invest early in these capabilities are better positioned to deploy AI with confidence and resilience.

Chapter 7 situates AI-related choices within the European regulatory environment. It explains the logic of the EU AI Act as a product-based, risk-oriented framework and clarifies the roles of providers, deployers, and other actors. Instruments such as regulatory sandboxes are discussed as spaces for learning and collaboration. Rather than treating regulation as a constraint, the chapter frames it as an enabler of trust, market access, and long-term competitiveness in Europe.

Building on this foundation, Chapter 8 turns to leadership and governance. It explores what it means to lead in environments where algorithmic systems shape decisions and outcomes, and how accountability, ethics, and culture can be embedded into AI development and oversight. Responsibilities across boards, executives, compliance, data, and business teams are examined, highlighting leadership as an active capability: aligning ambition with responsibility and turning complexity into coordinated action.

Chapter 9 adopts a forward-looking perspective focused on preparedness and adaptability. Innovation, regulation, and societal expectations will continue to evolve together. Rather than predicting specific technological trajectories, the chapter emphasizes the importance of building capacity to adapt with discipline, legitimacy, and institutional resilience.

Chapter 10 broadens the lens to Europe's AI ecosystem as a whole. It examines Europe's distinctive approach to AI development, including infrastructure, energy considerations, industrial policy, and governance models, and shows how regulatory leadership and institutional coordination are increasingly being leveraged as sources of technological strength and economic resilience.

The closing chapter returns to the central theme of the book: generative AI as a strategic capability shaped by managerial choices and execution. It reinforces the idea that preparedness, accountability, and Europe's distinctive operating context are not limitations, but foundations for durable value creation.

Acknowledgment

The authors would like to thank all people who helped reviewing and validating the content of the book: M. Bernardi, C. Caivano, G. Gariani, E. Pallaro, P. Pino, E. Vaniglia, D. Pagani, G. Castignani. They also thank the numerous colleagues and friends who helped with their discussion, motivation, and feedback, as well as the editorial staff for their professional support.

https://doi.org/10.1515/9783112254103-204

1 Understanding artificial intelligence

Artificial intelligence has moved from a technical specialty to a strategic concern. Decisions about AI now influence cost structures, risk exposure, regulatory obligations, and organizational capabilities across sectors. Yet much of the public discourse remains polarised between inflated promises and abstract fears. For leaders, neither extreme is useful. What matters is understanding what AI actually is today, how it reached this point, and which assumptions continue to shape its capabilities and limits. Artificial intelligence has different meanings, depending on the disciplines and use cases. Originally, it is associated with the academic endeavour of understanding and reproducing human-like intelligence with a combination of computer science, linguistics, philosophy, biology, and more. At the same time, its meaning migrated into technology and business, as a label to identify computational solutions aimed at solving non-trivial tasks in automated and unsupervised manner. For the purposes of this book, we follow the second meaning; in this chapter, we briefly survey its history and evolution, to gain a better understanding of what we are talking about and to give some context, so as to pave the way to the next chapters focusing on value creation, challenges, and actionable strategies.

1.1 The three booms of AI

The history of AI has not followed a linear trajectory. It has evolved through alternating waves of enthusiasm and stagnation, often described as booms and winters. Figure 1.1 illustrates this wavy pattern across three main eras, each defined by distinct assumptions about what intelligence is, how it can be replicated, and which technologies could make that possible.

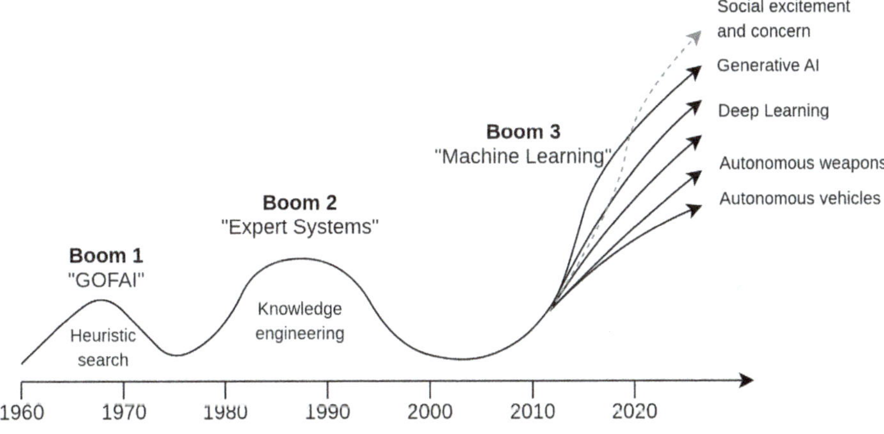

Figure 1.1: The three AI booms.

https://doi.org/10.1515/9783112254103-001

The first boom, during the 1950s and '60s, is often referred to as the era of "Good Old-Fashioned AI" or GOFAI [9]. This was the age of symbolic reasoning, when AI pioneers believed that intelligence could be represented through logic and explicit rules. Early procedural programs, like the General Problem Solver [10] and the Logic Theorist [11], attempted to mimic human reasoning by manipulating symbols according to well-defined principles. The core assumption was that cognition could be decomposed into a sequence of logical operations ("procedures", from which the term "procedural programming"), much like mathematics or language grammar. Technologically, these systems relied on heuristic search and production rules, and they achieved remarkable results in narrow domains such as games and puzzles. However, they struggled to scale. Real-world problems proved far more ambiguous and unpredictable than formal logic could handle, and computing power at the time was too limited to manage complexity. As expectations exceeded performance, funding and confidence declined, leading to the first AI winter in the 1970s [12].

The second boom, in the 1980s, was driven by expert systems and the rise of knowledge engineering. The idea was to focus not on general intelligence but on domain-specific expertise. If a computer could reproduce the reasoning of a specialist doctor or chemist, then intelligence could emerge from accumulated knowledge. So-called "expert systems", like MYCIN [13] for medical diagnosis and DENDRAL [14] for chemical analysis, illustrated this principle. They operated through a knowledge base of human-authored rules and an inference engine that applied those rules to new cases. The approach assumed that intelligence resided primarily in explicit, codified knowledge, and that reasoning could be formalized as rule application. In practice, however, knowledge extraction was slow, maintenance was difficult, and systems became brittle when facing uncertainty or exceptions. As costs rose and flexibility remained limited, enthusiasm faded once more, bringing about the second AI winter in the early 1990s.

The third boom began in the 2000s and is even more accelerated today. It is grounded in a different philosophy: that intelligence is more closely associated with statistical task fulfillment than with formal logic, and that it can emerge not only from explicit rules but also from learning patterns directly from data. This is the era of Machine Learning (ML) [15]. Instead of encoding reasoning step by step, systems are trained to identify statistical relationships between inputs and outputs. With sufficient data and computational power, they can infer structure from experience.

Advances in hardware, particularly Graphics Processing Units (GPUs) [16], made it possible to train large-scale ML models, while the explosion of digital data, or Big Data, provided the raw material for learning. Neural networks enabled the rise of Deep Learning, a branch of Machine Learning relying on layered representations, which allowed machines to recognize images, translate languages, and eventually generate text, code, and media. These achievements marked a shift from narrow prediction tasks to systems capable of creative and adaptive behavior.

Still, it is uncertain whether this period represents a lasting transformation or simply another phase in the historical cycle of AI enthusiasm and disillusionment. The level of investment and adoption is unprecedented, but so are the risks and limitations. ML systems remain opaque, data-intensive, and energy-hungry, and they introduce new ethical, organizational, and regulatory challenges. Even the range of tasks initially thought to be addressable by large-scale models is now increasingly recognized as bounded.

A useful parallel can be drawn with the dot-com boom of the late 1990s. While the speculative bubble eventually burst, the underlying technology did not disappear. On the contrary, the collapse filtered out unsustainable business models, while more structured and resilient companies not only survived but became dominant actors in the global economy. The internet itself did not fade away; it became foundational infrastructure.

A similar dynamic is likely for AI. Even if financial enthusiasm cools or expectations are recalibrated, AI systems are now deeply embedded in industrial processes, digital platforms, scientific research, and everyday services. This structural integration makes a third AI winter, in the classical sense, increasingly unlikely. Rather than disappearance, a phase of consolidation appears more plausible, in which weaker applications are abandoned while robust, well-governed systems endure and expand.

Another important feature distinguishing the current wave from earlier eras is diversification. The field is no longer dominated by a single paradigm but by multiple approaches evolving in parallel. Symbolic reasoning, probabilistic inference, reinforcement learning, generative models, knowledge graphs, and agentic AI pursue different goals and assumptions. This plurality increases resilience: if one approach reaches technical or economic limits, others continue to progress.

Finally, the red curve in Figure 1.1 represents not only technical capability but also social attention, excitement, and concern. AI has moved from research laboratories into business strategy, public policy, art, and everyday discourse. Fascination with its potential is now matched by anxiety about its risks, including bias, job displacement, misinformation, and environmental cost. Whether the current phase leads to consolidation or renewed cycles of disappointment remains uncertain. What is clear is that AI has become an enduring force shaping economies, institutions, and culture.

1.1.1 Zooming into the '00s

The third "AI boom" started around the '90s, but only within the next decades, we have witnessed several waves of hype, media attention, and digital transformation claims covering different aspects of "Artificial intelligence" and the "Digital era" in general. Let us zoom in the last about thirty years to put things into perspective, and show that nowadays AI in nothing else than the most recent development of a long-lasting trend, for which even the most conservative companies may better be equipped.

Figure 1.2 depicts the major digital technologies that have succeeded since the last '90s up to now. From the internet and the digitalization era, we progressed into the Big Data hype, followed by Machine Learning and Neural Networks, up to AI as we know

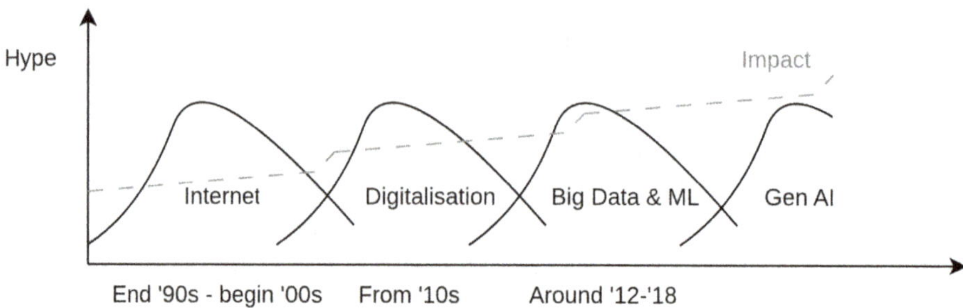

Figure 1.2: Hype cycles of the latest digital technologies, versus their impact on businesses, industries, and societies. Impact is shown linearly increasing for simplicity; in most cases, it is even exponential.

today. Each concept has been framed around a hyped narrative, promising to bring disruption in businesses and societies – and they did! However, while the financial, mediatic and consulting hype has somehow faded to give space to the "next big thing", their impact persisted and accumulated.

In fact, each digital and automated technology is a prerequisite of the next, and each newer technology builds upon the previous and likely anticipates a following one: Big Data became possible thanks to the digitalization propelled by internet diffusion, and without Big Data, the earlier Machine Learning algorithms could not have scaled into the neural networks and modern AI we know today.[1] Even the "current AI", which many identify with Generative AI,[2] can be already subdivided by its "agentic" offspring, which is anticipating even greater developments in the future. As such, the impact of each technology does not fade but accumulates.

The consequences for organizations are twofold. First, those that invested in previous digital technologies can usually harvest the greatest impact from the newest. As we will discuss later in the book, having a proper data management pipeline is essential to deploy the most impactful AI solutions, and having literacy built upon Machine Learning allows faster adoption. Second, that following hype cycles only risks to bring excitement and disillusion without benefiting from the underlying impact, and without being prepared for future developments. Instead, recognising the fast dynamics associated with digital technologies, identifying the long-lasting trends, and building a resilient and adaptive digital culture, would pose leaders in the advantageous situation of making the best of every emerging new "Artificial intelligence".

1 The technical details will be further surveyed later on in this chapter.

2 See next sections for details.

1.2 Learning from history

The three booms of AI are not only milestones in technological progress; they are mirrors reflecting how ambition, capability, and context shape one another. Each cycle has left behind technologies that we still use and embed in our devices: computer operating systems (OS) were conceived during the first wave; most apps work using principles defined during the first and second waves; expert systems from the second wave are still vastly used in factories automation programs. Also, each cycle has left lessons for today's leaders.

The first boom showed that intelligence cannot be detached from the complexity of the real world. Logical systems were elegant but brittle: they performed well in controlled environments but failed in messy, human ones. Intelligence remains inseparable from context. Modern predictive models succeed only when grounded in domain knowledge. AI amplifies human expertise, it does not replace it.

The second boom, driven by expert systems, revealed that codifying expertise is not enough if systems cannot adapt. Rules captured knowledge but not evolution. When conditions changed, systems broke down. The lesson is adaptability: AI must evolve with its environment.

The third boom, the age of Machine Learning, has taught us that scale alone is not intelligence. With enough data and computation, systems can infer extraordinary patterns, but without clear objectives, they can also optimize for the wrong things. Models that maximize clicks may spread misinformation; those that minimize risk may discriminate. The managerial lesson is alignment: technology is only as effective as the clarity of the goals it serves.

Companies such as NVIDIA [17], TSMC [18] and ASML [19] illustrate that progress depends not just on innovation but on anticipating constraints in computing power, energy, and materials. Similarly, European AI leaders such as Mistral [20], ElevenLabs [21], and DeepL [22] embody innovation grounded in openness, multilingualism, and ethical design.

For leaders outside the tech sector, the message is clear: it is not necessary to build AI to benefit from it. What matters is understanding where intelligence creates leverage: optimizing production lines, improving safety, reducing waste, or enhancing customer experience. Whether in an Italian vineyard, a German car plant, a Danish energy grid, or a French hospital, advantage will come from combining domain mastery with data-driven insight.

History tempers technological exuberance without negating progress. Previous AI waves slowed when expectations advanced faster than the supporting infrastructure and the maturity of teams. The current cycle faces similar structural realities, from energy availability to regulation and supply chain resilience. Yet these forces do not signal an impending slowdown. They act as filters, favoring organizations and regions able to align innovation with sustainable infrastructure and clear governance. For European leaders, this moment represents a window of opportunity: to scale Generative AI responsibly, invest in durable capabilities, and convert regulatory clarity into long-term competitive advantage.

The AI market may be cyclical, but its progress is cumulative. Each boom leaves behind infrastructure, talent, and lessons for the next. The leaders who thrive are those who build capacity in times of enthusiasm and maintain discipline when the cycle cools. To learn from history is not to predict the next winter, but to ensure that, whatever the season, organizations remain intelligent, adaptable, and aligned with human progress.

1.3 A brief taxonomy of modern AI

Through the three booms, we have seen that Artificial Intelligence as a broad field of automated task-making is composed of many philosophies and approaches. In this book, we mostly focus on the most recent Machine-Learning-based approaches. Figure 1.3 provides a simplified overview of how the main concepts of AI relate to one another. It does not aim to be exhaustive or perfectly rigorous from a technical standpoint. In fact, it mixes technological approaches such as neural networks with functional capabilities such as Generative AI. Nevertheless, it serves as a useful reference to clarify the terminology that will appear throughout the rest of this book.

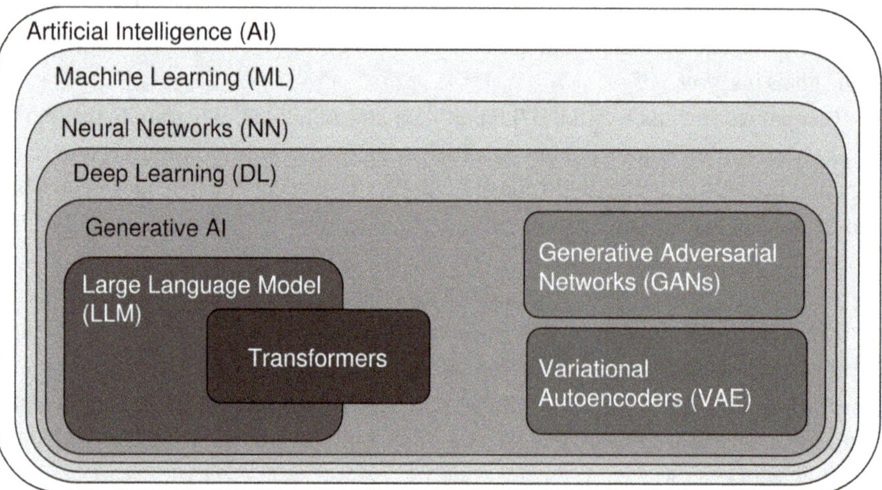

Figure 1.3: Taxonomy of AI.

At the broadest level, AI refers to any system capable of performing tasks that, if done by humans, would require intelligence. This includes reasoning, perception, planning, language understanding, and creativity. As we have seen in Section 1.1, AI is therefore an umbrella term encompassing a wide range of methods and applications, from symbolic reasoning to statistical learning, and from deterministic rules to adaptive neural networks.

The notion of intelligence in machines has evolved with each technological generation. In the early decades of research, many believed that once a machine could defeat a human at chess, it would have reached true intelligence. That milestone arrived in 1997, when IBM's Deep Blue famously defeated the chess world champion Garry Kasparov [23]. At the time, it was celebrated as a defining moment in the history of AI, a sign that machines had surpassed one of the highest symbols of human intellect. Yet, with hindsight, it is clear that this victory did not signal the arrival of super intelligence. Deep Blue did not "understand" chess; it computed millions of possible moves per second, following pre-programmed evaluation functions – and debates still exist as of whether chess is the apex of human intelligence, anyway.

Today, there are chess engines that no human can defeat, yet we rarely consider them AI in the modern sense. They have become just another category of software. This illustrates an important point: what we call AI changes over time. Once a task becomes routine, it often stops being labeled as intelligence. Optical character recognition, route planning, and spam filtering were all once seen as examples of AI. Today, they are considered standard features of digital systems.

In this sense, AI is a moving target. It continually redefines itself as technology progresses and as our understanding of what counts as "intelligent" evolves. Each generation of innovation resets the boundary between what is perceived as automation and what is perceived as cognition. The goal of this book is to help readers navigate this evolving boundary and understand where genuine intelligence, artificial or human, adds value, creates risk, and reshapes how organizations operate.

Within this broad field lies Machine Learning, the AI subdomain focused on algorithms that learn from data, which have introduced in Section 1.1. Instead of being explicitly programmed, these systems improve their performance through statistical inference and experience. ML includes diverse methods [24, 25] such as decision trees, regression models, clustering, and, more recently, Neural Networks (NN) [26]. NN are very loosely inspired by the structure of the human brain: they consist of layers of interconnected nodes that process information by adjusting the strength of their connections.[3] This approach is particularly effective at recognizing patterns in large datasets and lies at the core of most recent advances in AI. A further refinement within NN is Deep Learning (DL) [27]. DL models contain many layers that extract increasingly abstract features

3 We recall that this mapping is as loose as saying that airplanes are inspired by birds in how they fly, as both have wings and some sort of propulsion. Despite both artificial systems eventually work as intended (planes fly, and NN can reproduce an array of cognitive tasks), their similitude with the original natural system (bird of brain) stops here.

from raw data. This approach has enabled breakthroughs in speech recognition, computer vision, and natural language processing, providing the basis for the current wave of AI innovations.

Within DL we encounter Generative AI (genAI), a family of systems designed not merely to analyze or classify data but to create new content such as text, images, code, or audio [28]. Generative AI relies on specific architectures that learn the underlying structure of data and reproduce it in novel ways.

This layered structure illustrates that modern AI is not a single technology but a family of interconnected methods that build upon one another. For the purposes of this book, this diagram provides a shared vocabulary. Readers do not need to master every technical detail, but they should grasp the basic relationships: AI as the broad discipline, ML as its data-driven branch, DL as its most powerful architectures, and Generative AI as the current frontier transforming how machines interact with human creativity.

Although simplified, this overview captures the essential progression from intelligence to learning, from learning to representation, and from representation to generation. This is the trajectory that defines much of today's AI landscape and serves as the foundation for the discussions that follow. Note that, for marketing purposes, "AI" may also refer to the "next-gen" technology, to label the very new models as they progress in complexity and capabilities. As such, "AI" often addresses genAI only, at least in the marketing discourse. In this book, we will try to be as precise as possible, but some industry-based examples may use "AI" in this second, sloppier sense, to be more consistent with that industry's trends in communication.

To appreciate how AI systems operate, it is essential to understand how they learn. Learning is the process through which machines improve their performance by observing data, identifying patterns, and adjusting internal parameters. These adjustments are guided by algorithms designed to reduce the gap between prediction and reality. Over time, the system becomes better at making accurate inferences. In practice, there are three main paradigms of Machine Learning: Supervised Learning, Unsupervised Learning, and Reinforcement Learning. Each reflects a different way of relating experience to action, and each has its own advantages, risks, and implications for management and governance.

1.4 Where Generative AI comes from

Generative AI represents the most recent stage in a long continuum of learning paradigms that have progressively expanded what machines can infer, represent, and create. Its foundations lie in three complementary forms of learning paradigms: supervised, unsupervised, and reinforcement. Understanding these roots clarifies both the potential and the limits of today's generative systems.[4]

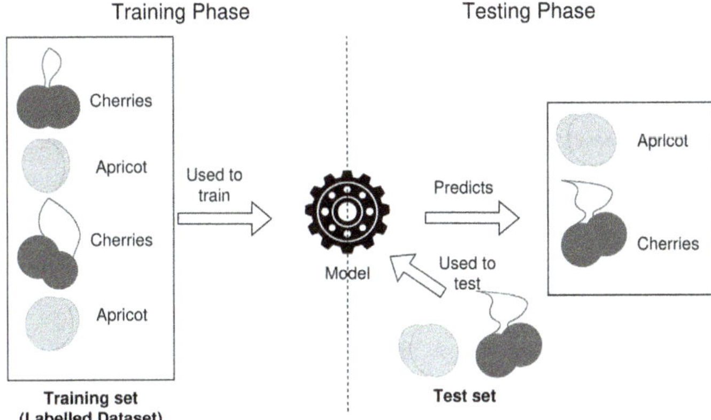

Figure 1.4: Illustration of the supervised learning process. A model is trained on some data representative of cherries and apricots, and when provided with test data, it becomes capable of labeling correctly cherries and apricots.

Supervised Learning is probably the dominant paradigm in industrial AI. As illustrated in Figure 1.4, it operates on "labeled" data, that is, data that are paired with a corresponding output (e. g., a series of apple images, plus the label "apple" attached to them). Here, the AI algorithm's task is to infer the mapping (i. e., the statistical rule) between the two. Technically, such inference is performed by tuning "weights" (or "parameters")" of a mathematical function;[5] such tuning is made by adjusting the weights' values each time the algorithm makes an error, until the predictions converge toward the correct answer. Mathematically, the training process is a mixture of statistical inference and optimization – not some dark magic, but "brute force" statistical processes. Conceptually it mirrors apprenticeship: the model learns by correction. In the business realm, this approach works best when the objective is clear, performance is measurable, and historical data are abundant: fraud detection, predictive maintenance, and medical image recognition all exemplify its maturity. Yet the method remains bound by its data; the model severely struggles to go beyond the examples it has been shown [29].[6]

4 This slightly more technical section aims at providing a non-expert overview of the technology behind AI models. It is by no means exhaustive, but aims at presenting some basic vocabulary of concepts that can be useful to interact with programmers, developers at large, and CTOs.

5 This is why models are "bigger" when they have more weights, e. g., the newer GPTs exceeding trillions of weights. As another example, the Gemini family currently offers models of different sizes. The number of weights vaguely correlates with the model capabilities in being flexible, but also with their cost.

6 Which is why Big Data are foundational for modern AI: they provide trillions of examples.

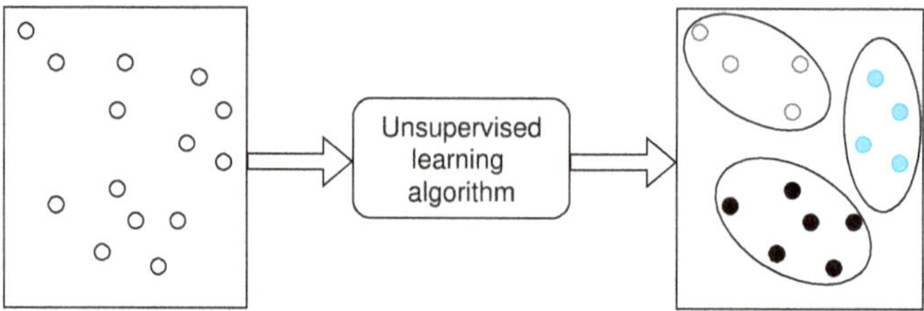

Figure 1.5: Illustration of the unsupervised learning process. A model learns structures in the data until it is capable of splitting a pool of data into 3 clusters.

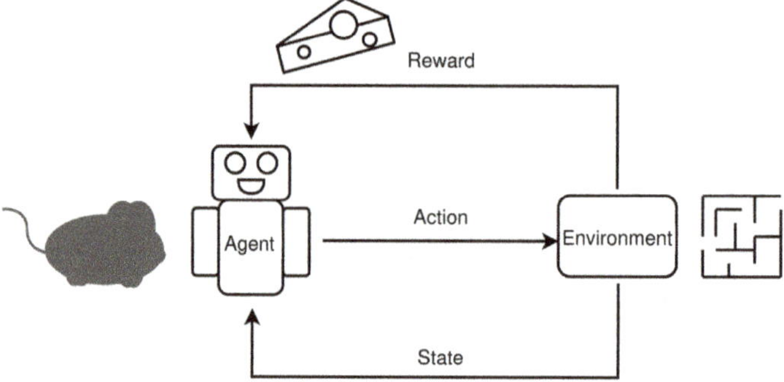

Figure 1.6: An AI agent behaves like a mouse in a labyrinth, it explores it and receives a reward when it solves it.

Unsupervised Learning is used when data are available but no predefined categories exist. As illustrated in Figure 1.5, instead of being trained on examples, the system explores the data to identify recurring patterns, groups, or relationships on its own [30, 31]. In practice, this supports tasks such as customer segmentation, anomaly detection, and the identification of emerging trends. These techniques help companies and institutions to make sense of complex information and highlight structures that would be difficult to spot manually. Importantly, unsupervised learning does not make decisions by itself. It surfaces patterns and signals that must be interpreted, validated, and acted upon by human decision-makers.

Reinforcement Learning introduces a temporal and interactive dimension. Instead of passively learning from fixed datasets, an agent interacts with an environment, taking actions, receiving rewards or penalties, and gradually developing strategies that maximize cumulative outcomes (see Figure 1.6). This is the logic behind systems that learned to master games like Go [32] or complex control problems such as autonomous driving and logistics optimization. Reinforcement Learning's strength lies in adaptability (an algorithm learns by doing) but it also demands caution, as poorly designed reward functions can produce unintended or unsafe behavior [33].

All paradigms find widespread applications in numerous industries. Supervised Learning is the underlying workforce of image recognition, automatic segmentation of textual and visual data, identification of patterns in time trends (such as financial fluctuations, price predictions, and more). Unsupervised Learning powers simple applications, such as the identification of coins in vending machines, up to market segmentation, clustering of clinical data or customer segments, and more. Reinforcement Learning is increasingly employed in robotics and manufacturing.

Moreover, these paradigms can be embedded into AI algorithms of increasing complexity in the number of parameters, but also in the way their adjustment is performed, through different "architectures". In simple ML, an "architecture" corresponds to simple mathematical functions which, to mirror "Artificial Intelligence", are called "neurons". Complex architectures (going from ML to NN and DL) are defined by how simpler functions are linked, so as to form complex ones. The more neurons are linked, and the more clever an architecture is designed, the more an AI model is capable of gradually abstracting features from raw data [27]. In shallow networks, where relatively few neurons are simply connected, this enables the recognition of basic patterns such as shapes or written characters. In deep neural networks, which consist of many neurons organized in hierarchical and more complex architectures, successive layers extract increasingly abstract representations. Early layers may detect edges or textures, while later layers combine these signals into objects, concepts, or semantic patterns relevant to language and behavior. Advances in network architectures have significantly expanded the range and reliability of tasks that AI systems can perform in practice. For instance, the most modern models are powered by the Transformer module [34]: an algorithmic gimmick associated with "attention", i. e., the capability to assign more importance to some data rather than others during the training phase, which enabled learning more nuanced relationships across vast and complex contexts.

From this lineage emerged Generative AI: systems designed not only to recognize patterns in data, but to generate new content consistent with the structures they have learned. While grounded in the same mathematical foundations as earlier supervised and unsupervised approaches, generative models shift the focus from classification and prediction towards synthesis. This shift marks a qualitative change in how AI systems are developed, experienced, and deployed in practice.

1.5 Generative AI

We are living through one of the most intense technological booms in recent decades. The emergence of Generative AI has transformed Artificial Intelligence from a capability largely confined to research laboratories and R&D departments into a mainstream societal phenomenon. In just a few years, these systems have moved into businesses, markets, and everyday life, reshaping communication, creativity, education, and business strategy. This moment represents a genuine inflection point: AI has become visible, tangible, and directly accessible to a broad public.

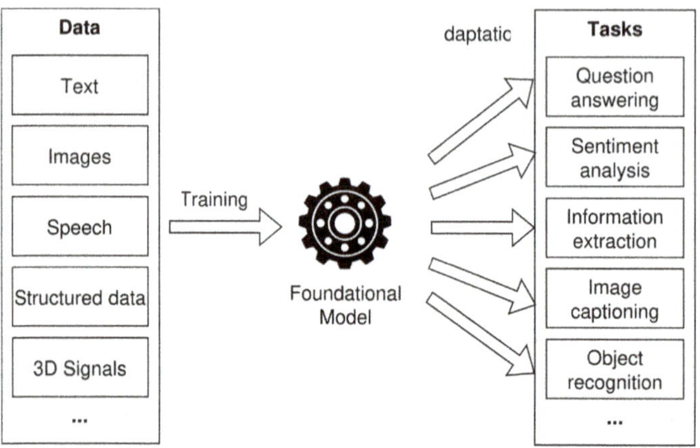

Figure 1.7: Generative AI can get diverse input and perform a number of tasks.

For many users, interacting with a language model or an image generator is the first time a computer appears to "understand" and "respond" in natural language. Although the underlying mechanisms remain statistical, the outputs often feel creative and intentional. This perception has profoundly altered how people relate to technology. AI is no longer an invisible optimization tool operating in the background, but a visible participant in daily work and decision-making.

Behind this transformation lie several families of generative models that have redefined how machines learn and produce content. Transformer architectures, introduced in 2017, revolutionized the processing of sequences such as text, audio, and images by enabling attention-based learning across long contexts [34]. This capability made language models particularly flexible and scalable, supporting a wide range of applications including text generation, summarization, translation, information extraction, and decision support across enterprise systems.

Conversational systems represent one prominent interface built on top of these models, which partly explains their rapid public adoption. Today, most widely deployed chatbots rely on *Large Language Models* (LLMs), although chat is only one of many ways in which such models can be operationalized. In many organizational settings, language models are embedded within background workflows rather than exposed through a conversational interface, for example, to analyze large document collections, generate structured summaries, reconcile information across sources, or support downstream decision-making processes.

A language model is a generative system trained to model the statistical structure of language by predicting the most likely continuation of a sequence given the context that precedes it. Internally, text is processed as a sequence of *tokens*, which are small units of text such as words, parts of words, or punctuation. Roughly 100 tokens correspond to 75 words in English, though this varies by language and content. Rather than producing entire sentences at once, the model generates output incrementally, selecting one token at a time based on the accumulated context. By training on large collections of text, language models acquire implicit representations of grammar, style, factual associations, and recurring patterns of expression.

LLMs extend this principle to an unprecedented scale. The term “large” refers both to the volume of data used for training and to the number of parameters within the model. This scale enables the capture of subtle regularities and long-range dependencies across diverse domains and tasks, allowing the same underlying generative mechanism to be adapted to a wide variety of organizational and technical contexts.

In parallel, other generative architectures enabled major advances in visual and creative domains. *Generative adversarial networks* (GANs) [35] introduced a competitive training paradigm in which two models are trained together. The generator produces synthetic data, such as images or video frames, while the discriminator evaluates whether the output resembles real data. Through this competitive process, the generator progressively improves its outputs in response to the discriminator’s feedback, leading to increasingly realistic synthetic content.

Autoencoders, and their successors, *Variational Autoencoders* (VAEs) [36], follow a different logic. Instead of competing, these models learn to represent data in a compact internal form that preserves its essential structure. This allows the system not only to reproduce inputs reliably, but also to generate new, plausible variations by slightly modifying this internal representation. Variational autoencoders formalize this process in a probabilistic way, enabling controlled generation rather than purely random outputs.

Together, these architectures illustrate complementary strategies for generative modeling: adversarial learning through competition, structured generation through controlled variation, and sequence-based generation through language models. Collectively, they form the technical backbone of modern generative AI systems across text, vision, and multimodal applications, i. e., that combine different types of inputs and outputs.

Differences in behavior and performance across Generative AI systems arise not from a single architectural choice, but from a combination of factors, including model design, training data, optimization strategies, and alignment techniques. As a result, models belonging to different families may appear similar at the interface level, yet exhibit systematically different strengths, limitations, and risk profiles.[7]

7 Throughout this book, model “families” refer to underlying Large Language Models developed by different companies and trained under distinct design choices and optimization objectives. For example, the GPT family denotes models developed by OpenAI; these models underpin ChatGPT, which is the end-user system combining the model with a user interface, safety layers, memory, and orchestration components. Similarly, the Gemini family refers to models developed by Google, while Llama models are developed by Meta. Although these systems may appear functionally similar from the user’s perspective, their underlying models differ significantly in architecture, training data, alignment strategies, and deployment constraints.

Beyond algorithmic innovation, several external factors enabled the rapid diffusion of Generative AI. Vast datasets, specialized hardware such as GPUs, and advances in parallel computing transformed previously prohibitive training processes into routine operations. At the same time, intuitive user interfaces, particularly conversational ones, lowered the barrier to adoption. For the first time, non-specialists could interact with complex AI systems using natural language alone.

For organizations, this wave is both exhilarating and disruptive. As illustrated in Figure 1.7, Generative AI extends automation into cognitive and creative domains, enabling tasks such as drafting reports, writing code, designing visuals, and simulating customer interactions. Productivity gains now span nearly every sector, from law and logistics to healthcare and entertainment. At the same time, this expansion raises fundamental questions about authorship, accountability, originality, and control. When a system generates content, who is responsible for it? What remains of human contribution, and how should it be recognized?

As a result, Generative AI has transformed what were once abstract philosophical debates into immediate governance challenges. Questions of trust, responsibility, and ownership are no longer theoretical. They are operational concerns for any organization deploying generative systems at scale.

The current boom also marks a shift in the relationship between technology and markets. Unlike earlier cycles of enthusiasm followed by disillusionment, the scale of investment, integration, and dependency makes a return to an "AI winter" increasingly unlikely.[8] Yet realism remains essential. The same accessibility that makes Generative AI powerful also amplifies risks, including bias, misinformation, over-reliance, and environmental cost.

Generative AI is therefore not merely another technological advance, but a new interface between humans and information. It reshapes how knowledge is produced, how creativity is expressed, and how companies compete. Understanding its mechanisms, opportunities, and limits is now a prerequisite for leadership and responsible governance.

This book is written to support decision-makers in navigating this transformation with clarity and context. Generative AI is neither a miracle nor a menace. Like any major innovation, it carries both promise and risk. Whether it empowers or destabilizes organizations depends on how deliberately it is understood, governed, and applied.

On terminology and focus. Before proceeding, a clarification of scope and terminology is necessary. While Generative AI encompasses a broad family of models operating over text, images, audio, and video, language-based systems currently represent the most widely adopted and most transversal form of Generative AI within organizations. Outside of domain-specific contexts that explicitly require visual, audio,

8 See Chapter 9 for details.

or video generation, language models underpin the majority of enterprise use cases, including document analysis, knowledge management, decision support, process automation, and customer interaction.

For this reason, the discussion throughout this book focuses primarily on language-based generative systems. Where no ambiguity arises, the terms *Generative AI* and *Large Language Models* may be used interchangeably, with the understanding that the underlying principles extend more broadly, while the concrete examples, architectural patterns, and managerial considerations center on language-driven applications.

For the sake of brevity, and unless otherwise specified, the term *AI* will occasionally be used in place of *Generative AI*. In such cases, it should be understood that the reference is to generative AI systems, and not to Artificial Intelligence in its broader historical or technical sense.

1.5.1 How Generative AI is priced

Unlike traditional enterprise software, which is typically licensed per user or per system, Generative AI is predominantly priced on a usage basis. Costs scale with how much a model is used rather than with how many users have access to it. This pricing logic applies across Generative AI modalities, including text, image, audio, and video generation, and reflects the fact that each interaction incurs a non-negligible computational cost at inference time.

Although pricing units differ across modalities, the underlying economic logic is consistent. Providers charge for the volume of computation performed, which increases with input size, task complexity, output volume, and output quality. Costs are variable, consumption-driven, and highly sensitive to user behavior and system design choices.

The specific unit of billing depends on the type of generative model. For language models, usage is measured in tokens processed. For image generation systems, pricing is typically based on the number of images generated, often adjusted by resolution or quality settings. Audio models are commonly billed per second or minute of audio processed or produced, while video generation systems scale with duration, resolution, and frame rate.

Despite these differences, the managerial implications are largely the same across modalities. Larger inputs, richer context, higher-fidelity outputs, and more ambitious tasks all translate into higher costs. Design decisions that appear innocuous at pilot stage, such as allowing unconstrained prompts or maximum-quality outputs by default, can lead to substantial cost escalation once systems are deployed at scale. Effective cost management therefore requires explicit constraints, monitoring mechanisms, and clear alignment between task requirements and model capabilities.

Before turning to how token costs work in practice, it is important to clarify that this discussion concerns model usage at scale, typically through APIs or internally deployed models, rather than consumer-facing interfaces. Many readers may be familiar with premium services such as ChatGPT, Gemini, or Claude, where access is provided through a fixed monthly subscription and cost is largely independent of usage. Enterprise deployments proceed differently: when models are accessed programmatically or embedded into workflows, costs scale directly with token consumption, closer to a utility like electricity than to packaged software. From an organizational perspective, Generative AI behaves economically more like infrastructure than like a licensed product, which is why prompt efficiency, context management, and output control become operational and economic concerns.

For text-based Generative AI systems, and in particular language models, costs are calculated using tokens as the basic unit of consumption. Every interaction consumes two categories of tokens: *input tokens*, which include the prompt, any retrieved context, and conversation history; and *output tokens*, which correspond to the text generated by the model. The total cost of an interaction is determined by summing the two and multiplying the result by the provider's per-token rate. For example, a prompt containing 100 tokens that produces a 200-token response results in 300 tokens of billable usage. Although output tokens are often priced slightly higher than input tokens, the overall pricing logic remains comparable across providers.

This structure means that communication style has a direct and measurable impact on cost. Long prompts, excessive context retrieval, or overly verbose outputs can significantly inflate token consumption. Managing cost therefore becomes an exercise in prompt efficiency and output control. In practice, techniques such as simplifying system prompts, retrieving only the most relevant passages, and imposing maximum output lengths can reduce usage substantially without degrading output quality.

1.5.2 Context window

The *context window* defines the maximum amount of text a language model can process in a single interaction, measured in tokens. It functions as the model's working memory, encompassing the user's prompt, any retrieved documents, conversation history, and the response being generated. This is not merely a technical specification but a fundamental constraint that shapes system design, operational costs, and performance characteristics.

A frequent source of misunderstanding is the impression that language models remember earlier parts of a conversation in the human sense. In reality, language models do not possess persistent memory across turns. They do not store past interactions, update internal state, or recall previous exchanges once an interaction has ended. The appearance of conversational continuity arises because earlier messages are implicitly appended to the latest prompt and re-submitted to the model at each turn. From the model's perspective, there is no evolving dialogue, but a single block of text processed anew each time.

Early models operated with context windows of 2,000 to 4,000 tokens, sufficient for brief interactions but inadequate for complex tasks. State-of-the-art models extend to hundreds of thousands or even millions of tokens. This expansion has enabled legal contract analysis across multiple documents, synthesis of extensive technical or scientific literature, and sustained analytical interactions that were previously infeasible at scale.

Larger context windows, however, introduce distinct trade-offs. Token costs scale with context length, making long-context interactions significantly more expensive. A system processing 100,000 tokens per request incurs costs an order of magnitude higher than one processing 10,000 tokens. This creates continuous cost pressure that distinguishes Generative AI from traditional software, where marginal usage costs approach zero once infrastructure is deployed. In Generative AI, every interaction consumes computational resources proportional to context length, making costs inherently variable. In Chapter 3, we discuss cost implications in more detail.

Performance also degrades with increasing context length. Models do not attend uniformly to all parts of long inputs: information at the beginning and end of the context tends to receive greater weight than material in the middle, a phenomenon often referred to as "lost in the middle". As a result, constraints or assumptions introduced earlier in a conversation may be partially ignored later on, even if they remain technically present in the context window. Mitigating this effect often requires additional engineering choices, such as summarization, context pruning, or careful placement of critical information.

1.5.3 Reasoning models

A recent development in Generative AI systems is the introduction of so-called *reasoning models*. These models are optimized not only to generate fluent outputs, but to internally perform multi-step reasoning, decomposition of complex problems, and structured deliberation before producing a final answer. From a user perspective, they often appear more reliable on tasks requiring logic, planning, mathematical reasoning, or the integration of multiple constraints.

It is important to clarify that reasoning models are not based on a fundamentally different pricing unit or computational primitive. Tokens are not intrinsically more expensive than in standard language models. What changes is the number of tokens processed. Reasoning models typically generate additional internal text representing intermediate steps, hypotheses, or partial solutions. Even when these intermediate steps are not fully exposed to the user, they still consume tokens and therefore computational resources.

In practical terms, the cost of a request to a reasoning model includes not only the tokens corresponding to the user prompt and the final answer, but also the tokens generated during the internal reasoning process. A task that could be answered in a few hundred tokens by a standard model may require several thousand tokens when explicit reasoning is performed. As a result, reasoning-intensive interactions can be significantly more expensive despite identical per-token pricing.

This cost structure has direct implications for system design. Reasoning models are most valuable in situations where correctness, consistency, and traceability outweigh raw throughput or latency constraints. Examples include legal interpretation, complex decision support, multi-criteria evaluation, or safety-critical analyses. Conversely, for high-volume or low-complexity tasks, such as summarization of short texts or template-based generation, the additional reasoning overhead may provide limited marginal value relative to its cost.

Reasoning models also interact strongly with context window. Longer contexts increase the space over which reasoning must operate, often amplifying the number of intermediate tokens generated. This compounds both cost and latency, reinforcing the need for careful prompt design, context curation, and selective use of reasoning capabilities. In practice, organizations increasingly adopt hybrid architectures, where lightweight models handle routine tasks and reasoning-optimized models are invoked selectively for complex or high-risk decisions.

Understanding reasoning models therefore requires shifting the focus away from token pricing in isolation and towards token dynamics: how many tokens are consumed, where they are generated, and whether the additional reasoning they enable produces proportional value for the task at hand.

1.5.4 Prompt engineering

Generative AI, for the broad public, is mostly accessed through textual inputs, via chat-like conversational interfaces. This democratizes access to the technology, enabling even people without a coding background to interact with powerful models. At the same time, this freedom must be governed by good practices to consistently produce the expected outputs. Users often report frustration when interacting with Generative AI systems, with the impression that the model "does not understand" what is being asked. In many cases, the issue lies not in the model's capabilities, but in how the request is formulated. A useful first question is whether the model can reasonably be expected to know the information being requested. In practice, this means asking whether a human, searching the internet or consulting internal documents, could plausibly answer the same question.

A second question follows: if the same request were given to a new employee who had just joined the company in this role, would they be able to proceed, or would they ask for clarification? If clarification is required, then the task has not yet been communicated effectively. In such cases, the prompt should be framed as one would brief a colleague: by specifying the task, the relevant context, and the expected outcome.

Prompt engineering is the practice of communicating effectively with generative models, particularly Large Language Models, in order to guide their behavior and outputs. Every response depends on how the request is formulated and the information made available to the model. A well-crafted prompt does more than request an answer;

it establishes the role the model should assume and the scope within which it should operate. In this sense, prompting is not a technical trick, but a form of managerial literacy.

The quality of prompting often determines whether a model behaves like an insightful assistant or a confused intern. Poorly specified requests tend to produce generic or unfocused outputs, while well-specified ones support more relevant and actionable responses. As an example, consider a simple managerial task: preparing a short briefing on the impact of generative AI for senior leadership.

Example 1: Poorly specified prompt

Explain how Generative AI affects businesses.

This prompt typically results in a high-level and generic response, reiterating well-known themes such as productivity, automation, and innovation, without addressing the specific decision-making needs of executives.

Example 2: Well-specified prompt for the same task

You are advising a European executive committee in a regulated industry. Write a one-page briefing explaining how Generative AI affects business strategy over the next two years. Focus on opportunities, operational risks, regulatory considerations, and investment priorities. Use a neutral, non-technical tone suitable for board-level discussion.

Here, the improvement does not come from the model itself, but from the clarity of intent, audience, scope, and constraints embedded in the prompt.

It is important to clarify the scope of this book. Its objective is not to teach prompt engineering as a technical skill. A wide ecosystem of tutorials, online courses, videos, and even dedicated books already cover this topic in depth. Rather than duplicating this material, we assume that readers of this book either already possess a basic familiarity with prompt engineering, will independently complement their skills as needed, or will delegate the operational aspects of prompting to specialized members of their teams.

This choice reflects the intended audience of the book. The focus here is on leadership, decision-making, and strategy in the age of Generative AI, not on operational mastery of individual techniques. Prompt engineering is therefore discussed as a capability to be understood, governed, and embedded into routine practices, rather than as a skill to be exhaustively taught step by step.

That said, we strongly encourage familiarity with prompting at all levels of seniority. Even for executives and senior leaders, hands-on exposure to prompting is valuable. It sharpens intuition about model behavior, clarifies limitations, and improves the quality of dialogue with technical teams. In this sense, prompt engineering is not merely an operational task, but a form of literacy that enhances leadership judgment, regardless of position or hierarchy.

Prompt engineering also has a direct financial dimension. Because most models are billed by tokens,[9] the length and clarity of prompts influence costs as much as accuracy. Reducing unnecessary background text, retrieving only the most relevant context, and setting limits on output length can cut expenses substantially without compromising quality. Good prompting is not only a matter of precision but of economy.

Beyond efficiency, prompt design should reflect a company's values and tone of voice. A legal department might emphasize caution and neutrality; a marketing team may seek creativity and engagement. Embedding these nuances in prompts ensures that the model behaves consistently across departments. As teams mature, they often develop prompt libraries, shared templates, and internal guidelines that standardize how the organization interacts with AI systems.

Prompt engineering also plays a vital role in risk management. Well-designed prompts can instruct a model to avoid speculation, to justify claims with sources, or to flag uncertainty when data are insufficient. These simple design choices can significantly reduce reputational and compliance risks.[10] The prompt becomes, in effect, the first layer of governance around the model's behavior.

Over time, effective prompting becomes less about clever tricks and more about developing a shared discipline of clarity. It teaches teams to formulate precise questions, to think carefully about context, and to define what a good answer looks like before seeking it. This reflective process often improves human reasoning as much as machine performance.

When mastered, prompt engineering transforms AI from a tool that merely reacts to inputs into a system that collaborates in thought. It lays the foundation for more advanced techniques such as fine-tuning and retrieval-augmented generation (RAG), and it cultivates a culture of deliberate communication between humans and intelligent systems. In organizations that invest in this skill, the quality of prompts becomes a quiet but decisive competitive advantage.

1.5.5 Fine-tuning

Public Large Language Models are the result of an initial *pre-training* phase. During pre-training, a model is exposed to extremely large and diverse collections of text in order to learn the general structure of language: grammar, common facts, patterns of reasoning, and widely shared modes of expression. This phase produces a *general-purpose* model that can operate across many domains, but that is not tailored to any specific need or task.

---

9 See Section 3.3.1 for details.

10 See Chapter 6 for details.

This generality is a strength, but for many specific use cases it is also a limitation. Pre-trained models do not naturally reflect a company's terminology, writing style, priorities, or decision logic. For this reason, organizations may choose to create a custom version of a pre-trained model through fine-tuning.

Fine-tuning is the process by which a pre-trained language model is adapted to specific context by exposing it to carefully selected examples of how it should behave [37]. In practice, this does not mean retraining the model from scratch. Instead, a team builds on the general linguistic competence already acquired during pre-training, and adjusts the model so that it consistently reproduces preferred language, tone, reasoning patterns, and conventions specific to the organization.

Concretely, fine-tuning involves a series of deliberate steps. First, tasks or domains that justify customization should be identified, such as customer support, policy drafting, legal analysis, or technical documentation. Second, relevant internal data are selected, cleaned, and reviewed to ensure they are accurate, representative, and legally usable. Third, curated examples are prepared that illustrate not only correct outputs, but also the expected style, level of detail, and framing. These examples are then used to adjust the pre-trained model so that this behavior becomes its default, rather than something imposed through repeated instructions. Fine-tuning is therefore not a single action, but a controlled engineering process typically carried out by trained professionals.

The appeal of fine-tuning lies in efficiency and consistency. A well-tuned model requires fewer instructions, produces more predictable outputs, and reduces the need for repeated prompt refinement. It can internalize organizational vocabulary, reflect internal procedures, and align with established communication norms. In contexts such as customer-facing communication, internal knowledge management, or regulatory documentation, this alignment can significantly reduce both time and cognitive effort.

However, fine-tuning also introduces new responsibilities. Because the model builds directly on organizational data, any errors, biases, or outdated assumptions present in that data risk being systematically reproduced. Poor data selection or insufficient validation can hard-code issues into the model's behavior. Fine-tuning also shifts costs: while usage may become more efficient, development, testing, monitoring, and retraining introduce fixed operational overhead. In this sense, the strategic question changes from "How do we use AI?" to "Are we prepared to maintain and govern it?"

From a governance and legal perspective, fine-tuning blurs the boundary between vendor and user. The customized model reflects the original provider's design choices alongside the organization's knowledge, values, and liabilities, and substantial modifications can reclassify the deploying organization as a provider in its own right under the AI Act, with the obligations that classification entails.[11] Fine-tuned models must therefore be treated as critical internal assets. Mature approaches involve an ongoing cycle: data

11 More on this in Chapter 7.

are refreshed, outputs are reviewed, and alignment with legal and ethical expectations is continuously verified.

Strategically, fine-tuning represents a step from dependency toward autonomy. A team that fine-tunes successfully develops a form of proprietary cognitive capital: a layer of machine-supported reasoning shaped by its own experience and expertise. Over time, this can become a differentiating capability in how the team communicates, decides, and operates. That said, restraint remains essential. Fine-tuning is most valuable in high-impact domains where precision, trust, and institutional memory matter more than rapid experimentation.

When applied with care, fine-tuning transforms generative AI from a generic capability into an organizational one. Rather than merely responding to instructions, the system begins to reflect how the organization itself thinks and communicates. Those that master this process will not only automate more effectively, but also act with greater coherence and consistency.

A further distinction matters at this point. Fine-tuning is often discussed as a way of adapting how a model behaves, but it can also be used to expose the model to new knowledge that was absent or underrepresented during pre-training. Specialized vocabulary, proprietary procedures, internal product catalogs, jurisprudence in a narrow legal area, or technical documentation that does not appear on the public web are typical examples. In these cases, the goal is not to refine expression but to extend what the model knows.

The two purposes look similar from the outside and are sometimes pursued in the same training run, but they impose different requirements. Behavioral fine-tuning typically needs a modest number of high-quality examples that demonstrate the desired pattern. Knowledge-oriented fine-tuning requires substantially more material and careful coverage of the relevant domain. It also raises a question that behavioral fine-tuning does not: when the underlying knowledge changes — a regulation is updated, a product is discontinued, a policy is revised — the model must be retrained, or it will confidently produce outdated answers. Knowledge baked into model weights is durable but inflexible, which is why teams managing volatile or rapidly expanding information often handle it outside the model rather than inside it, through the retrieval-based approaches discussed in the following section.

1.5.6 Retrieval-augmented generation (RAG)

Retrieval-augmented generation (RAG) [38] has become a practical bridge between the creativity of Generative AI and the reliability of factual information. In simple terms, RAG allows an AI system to generate text not only from what it has learned during training but also from external, verifiable sources of knowledge.

Recall that LLMs are trained on vast quantities of data, and they learn statistical associations between words and concepts. However, these models cannot access new or

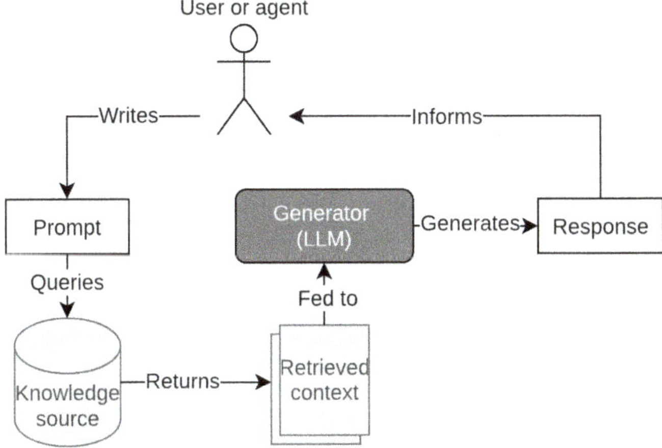

Figure 1.8: Overview of a RAG system.

proprietary information that was not part of their training set, and they can sometimes produce "hallucinations": answers that sound convincing but are factually wrong.[12] For companies, this limitation quickly becomes critical: managers need systems that are not only fluent but accurate, auditable, and aligned with their internal data and policies.

RAG addresses this challenge by combining two components, shown in Figure 1.8. The first is the retriever, which searches external databases or document collections to find relevant information in real time. The second is the generator, which takes that retrieved content and integrates it into a natural language answer. In other words, instead of inventing information, the system retrieves facts and uses them to construct a grounded, contextualized response.

For organizations, this architecture offers a powerful way to make generative AI knowledge-aware. It enables chatbots that can answer questions using a company's internal documentation, customer service platforms that rely on updated product manuals, or compliance assistants that quote specific legal articles and policies. Because RAG connects AI output directly to trusted data sources, it becomes possible to trace the origin of information, verify its correctness, and update the system without retraining the underlying model. Organizations can also decide exactly which databases the AI can access, ensuring that proprietary or confidential data remain protected for security and compliance.

However, managers should also recognize the dependencies and limitations. A RAG system is only as good as the data it retrieves and its standardization and systematization. Poorly organized, incomplete, or biased repositories will still produce unreliable answers. Building effective retrieval layers therefore requires investment in informa-

12 More on this in Chapter 6.

tion governance, metadata standards, and data quality. In addition, integrating RAG into workflows demands cross-functional collaboration between data engineers, domain experts, and compliance officers to ensure that what is retrieved and how it is presented remain trustworthy.

In strategic terms, RAG represents a shift from model-centric to data-centric AI. It reframes competitiveness not in terms of who has the largest model, but who has the most relevant, well-structured, and ethically managed data. For European companies, this is a significant opportunity. Europe may not host the largest LLMs, but it has strong traditions in data governance, domain expertise, and regulatory alignment. These strengths make it ideally positioned to lead in the adoption of RAG systems that are not only intelligent but also compliant, transparent, and explainable.

Finally, it is important to recognize that the goal of RAG partially overlaps with that of fine-tuning: both aim, in different ways, to extend the effective knowledge of the model beyond its original training. However, they do so through fundamentally different mechanisms and with very different implications. RAG extends knowledge at inference time by dynamically connecting the model to external sources, while fine-tuning embeds knowledge directly into the model itself. Choosing between RAG, fine-tuning, or a combination of both is therefore not a purely technical decision but a critical investment choice with long-term impact. This trade-off is examined in more detail in Chapter 3.

A more recent evolution, Graph RAG, extends the basic retrieval approach by representing knowledge not as isolated documents but as interconnected entities and relationships within a knowledge graph. Rather than retrieving passages based solely on semantic similarity to the query, Graph RAG traverses structured relationships between concepts – such as "Company X supplies Component Y to Product Z" or "Regulation A modifies Article B of Directive C." This enables more precise answers to complex queries that require reasoning across multiple connected facts. For organizations with rich relational data, such as supply chains, regulatory frameworks, or corporate hierarchies, Graph RAG can provide more contextually accurate responses than traditional document retrieval, particularly for questions requiring multi-hop reasoning. However, it introduces additional complexity: knowledge graphs must be constructed, maintained, and kept synchronized with underlying data sources, adding another layer to the operational burden described earlier. The choice between document-based RAG and Graph RAG therefore depends on whether the incremental accuracy gains justify the additional engineering and curation costs.

Now let us consider a compliance officer in a Luxembourgish financial institution who asks an internal AI assistant: "Under which conditions can we reuse customer data collected for onboarding in a new credit risk model?" Without RAG, a generative model would answer based on generic training data, potentially mixing jurisdictions, outdated interpretations, or best practices that do not apply to the organization. The response might sound confident but would be difficult to verify and risky to rely on.

With RAG, the system first retrieves relevant passages from the institution's internal data governance policy, the applicable articles of the GDPR, and recent internal legal memos stored in the document repository. These documents are selected because they are semantically related to data reuse, purpose limitation, and model development. The generative component then synthesizes an answer that explicitly reflects those sources, for example by stating the conditions under which reuse is permitted, the safeguards required, and the internal approval process to follow.

Crucially, the system can also indicate where each element of the answer comes from, allowing the officer to trace the response back to specific policy sections or legal provisions. If the policy is updated, the next answer automatically reflects the change without retraining the model. In this way, the AI assistant does not replace legal judgment, but accelerates access to relevant, authoritative information while preserving accountability.

1.6 AI agents

As Generative AI builds upon earlier AI methods, it enables the emergence of more sophisticated systems. In practical applications, this evolution is most visible in the rise of AI agents, marking a shift from systems that primarily respond to queries to systems that can take actions in pursuit of defined objectives.

The term AI agent predates Large Language Models by several decades. In classical Artificial Intelligence, agents referred to systems capable of perceiving an environment and acting according to predefined rules, optimization objectives, or learned policies. Such agents were already used in domains including robotics, control systems, game playing, and decision automation. This long history partly explains why the term is now surrounded by ambiguity and inconsistent usage.

In this book, the term AI agent is used in a specific and contemporary sense. We refer to agentic systems in which an LLM acts as the central reasoning component, with access to external tools and a defined degree of autonomy to pursue objectives. While these systems build on earlier agent concepts, their capabilities and risk profiles differ substantially due to the generative and general-purpose nature of LLMs.

In short, an agent is an AI system that does not merely respond, but also decides. While a generative model may write a report or summarize a document only when explicitly prompted, an agent can determine when such actions are required, which information must be gathered, and which sequence of steps should be executed to achieve a desired outcome. To do so, it interacts with external resources, such as databases, APIs,[13] calculators, or services, within predefined constraints. By chaining model outputs with tool use, the agent decomposes complex objectives into intermediate steps and executes them iteratively, closing the loop between perception, reasoning, and execution (see Figure 1.9).

13 An API (Application Programming Interface) is a standardized way for software systems to exchange information or trigger actions.

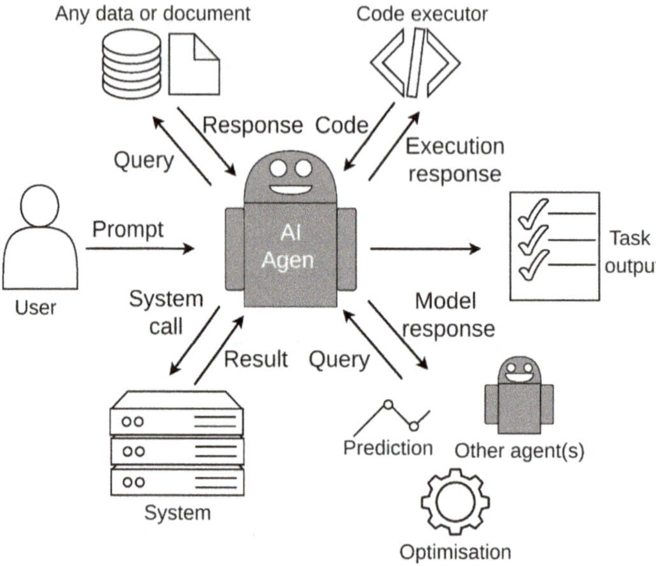

Figure 1.9: Overview of AI agents capabilities.

From an architectural perspective, agent-based systems consist of multiple coordinated components. A central reasoning module, implemented using an LLM, interprets goals and context. This is coupled with mechanisms for perception, planning, and action execution, enabling the system to interact with software systems and operational processes. Some agents also incorporate feedback mechanisms that allow behavior to adapt over time. What defines an agent is not any single module, but the integrated architecture that enables autonomous, goal-directed behavior rather than isolated responses.

This structure combines elements from reinforcement learning, which emphasizes goal-oriented behavior and feedback, with symbolic and programmatic reasoning, which enables interaction with structured tools and data. What distinguishes agents from earlier AI systems is their autonomy and persistence. They are not passive tools invoked on demand, but active systems operating continuously within defined environments, objectives, and constraints.

In practice, AI agents already operate across multiple domains. Personal and productivity agents manage calendars, coordinate tasks, and draft communications. Customer service agents resolve multi-step requests, escalating only when necessary. Operational agents in logistics, finance, or manufacturing monitor systems, detect anomalies, and initiate corrective actions. Emerging strategic agents assist managers by aggregating information, simulating scenarios, and proposing courses of action aligned with organizational objectives.

An increasingly important aspect of agent-based systems concerns how humans interact with them during development and operation. In software engineering, this has led to practices sometimes described as *vibe coding*, where developers collaborate with an AI agent by expressing high-level intent, constraints, and feedback in natural language, while the agent generates and iteratively refines code. Rather than replacing engineering discipline, this approach shifts effort toward supervision, validation, and correction. Developers increasingly act as directors and reviewers of agent behavior, rather than sole authors of implementation details.

For managers, this evolution has significant implications. Agent-based development can substantially increase productivity, but it also introduces new challenges, including hidden dependencies, opaque logic, and reduced shared understanding of systems. As a result, organizations must adapt development practices, code review processes, and accountability structures to reflect a model in which humans increasingly supervise autonomous systems rather than execute every step themselves.

A related question, and arguably the more consequential one for managers outside software engineering, concerns the appropriate degree of autonomy for a given deployment. Autonomy is not binary. Agents can be configured along a spectrum: from purely advisory systems that propose actions for human approval, through systems that execute reversible actions within tightly scoped boundaries, to systems that operate with minimal supervision over extended time horizons. Each step along this spectrum trades human oversight for speed and scalability, and each carries different risk and liability implications. The widespread enthusiasm for autonomous agents in trade press often obscures a simpler operational truth: in most regulated and high-stakes environments, the appropriate design is not the most autonomous one possible, but the least autonomous one compatible with the desired outcome. Bounded autonomy, i. e. where the agent acts independently within a narrow operational envelope and escalates anything outside it, typically delivers most of the productivity benefit at a fraction of the governance cost.

A critical and still evolving challenge concerns the reliability of AI agents and their orchestrators. Unlike single-response systems, agents must be evaluated not only on output quality, but on their ability to complete tasks, use tools correctly, interpret intent, and behave consistently over time. This has motivated the development of evaluation frameworks that assess agent performance along multiple dimensions, such as task success, tool-use accuracy, and intent resolution. These dimensions can be combined, with use-case-specific weighting, into reliability indicators tailored to specific and strategic needs. Such evaluation is a prerequisite for deploying agents in high-impact or safety-critical processes.

To support deployment at scale, frameworks are emerging that constrain how agents access tools, data, and external systems. These frameworks specify what an agent can see, what it can do, and how it may interact with its environment, enabling integration into operational workflows while limiting exposure to data leakage, loss of control, or regulatory non-compliance.

Taken together, these considerations point to a broader shift in how organizations approach AI adoption. The focus is moving from isolated automation to the design, governance, and evaluation of autonomous systems that can operate across multiple steps and contexts. The next phase of AI adoption will therefore center not on more sophisticated chat interfaces, but on managing intelligent agents whose autonomy must remain aligned with organizational objectives and European principles of transparency, trust, and human-centric design.

1.7 From learning paradigms to business impact

Several business use cases can be associated with the main learning paradigms discussed above. Table 1.1 summarizes these associations for the paradigms considered, with the aim of illustrating how different approaches typically translate into practical outcomes, industry relevance, and strategic choices.

Table 1.1: Applications of each AI paradigm for organizations.

Paradigm	Core principle	Typical business applications	Business implications
Supervised learning	Learning from labeled data to predict outcomes or classify observations.	Demand forecasting, risk scoring, process optimization, quality control.	Supports operational excellence and decision automation. Enables measurable performance improvement but depends on historical data availability and accuracy.
Unsupervised learning	Identifying hidden patterns and structures in unlabeled data.	Market segmentation, anomaly detection, customer clustering, fraud monitoring.	Enhances strategic understanding of markets and users. Encourages data-driven exploration and innovation but requires interpretative skills to act on insights.
Deep learning	Hierarchical representation learning enabling perception from unstructured data (text, images, audio).	Image recognition, speech processing, natural language understanding, predictive maintenance.	Extends automation into perception and cognition. Increases dependence on computational resources and data governance. Demands specialized talent and ethical controls.
Generative AI	Learning to generate new content or simulate complex distributions.	Content creation, design assistance, code generation, personalized marketing, simulation.	Shifts focus from efficiency to creativity and augmentation. Raises issues of originality, trust, and compliance. Requires strong oversight, transparency, and a responsible innovation culture.

These associations should be read as indicative rather than exhaustive or exclusive. In practice, real-world systems often combine multiple learning paradigms, and the same business use case may rely on different techniques depending on data availability, maturity, and organizational constraints. The table therefore provides a simplified mapping intended to support high-level understanding and comparison, rather than a strict technical classification. The next chapter builds on this overview by presenting concrete use cases and implementation examples drawn from practice.

For leaders, the table provides a trajectory to maturity. As organizations progress from supervised learning to generative AI, the nature of value creation changes. The focus shifts from prediction to augmentation, from efficiency to innovation. The table also underlines an important insight: no single method is universally superior. Each serves a different strategic purpose, and their impact depends on the organization's context, data readiness, and human capabilities.

2 Value creation with generative AI

Managers and executives do not need yet another abstract promise that “AI will transform the company”. What is required are practical results that are credible, repeatable, and capable of scaling across teams, while fitting Europe’s reality of multilingual markets, stringent regulation, and diverse company sizes. Generative AI is compelling precisely because it delivers this combination. It operates where work actually takes place: in handling documents, developing conversations, managing meetings, and supporting decision-making. It shortens the path from idea to outcome, not by replacing judgement, but by removing the friction that slows experts down. Figure 2.1 illustrates several use-cases, many of which are discussed in this chapter to provide examples of genAI capabilities and areas of application.

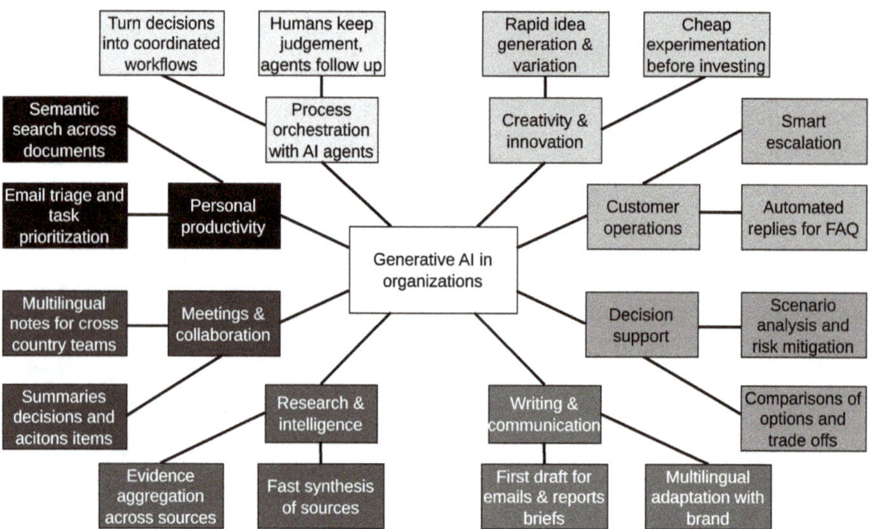

Figure 2.1: Several use-case capabilities of generative AI.

2.1 Writing and communication

One of the most immediate use cases, already implemented even in widely used consumer applications such as smartphone apps, is the compression of writing time. LLMs can produce effective first drafts for emails, briefs, reports, and policy notes within minutes, allowing teams to start from a coherent structure rather than from a blank page. A procurement manager no longer spends two hours crafting a supplier negotiation email: the AI produces a structured first version in under two minutes, preserving strategic points while handling tone, format, and supporting details. Domain expertise is then invested in refining the message, rather than in constructing sentences.

https://doi.org/10.1515/9783112254103-002

The technology underpinning this capability is relatively straightforward. An AI system can learn an organization's preferred style from a small number of approved examples through prompt engineering (see Section 1.5.4), without requiring custom model development or specialized expertise. After providing a handful of representative supplier emails as templates, the system infers tone, structure, and recurring formulations, and applies these patterns to new contexts. Granting access to internal knowledge bases through RAG (see Section 1.5.6) – such as previous negotiations, product specifications, or pricing histories – allows drafts to become not only well written but also contextually grounded. In many companies, production-level quality is reached after limited experimentation and a short feedback cycle. The technical barrier is significantly lower than executives often assume, which partly explains the rapid adoption of this application across European companies of varying size and maturity.

Observable effects include increased throughput and reduced cycle time. Marketing teams that previously required several days to create a product launch brief can often deliver within two days, as the AI handles research synthesis, competitive framing, and initial messaging structures. Quality frequently improves as well, due to consistent application of structure and tone. An insurer based in Amsterdam can report a 15 % increase in client-confirmed quality scores after introducing AI-assisted drafting, largely because reports follow a clear narrative logic and highlight exceptions systematically rather than obscuring them in dense prose.

The effect is amplified in multilingual contexts. Translation is another area in which LLMs perform particularly well.[1] Modern systems do not translate word by word; instead, they reconstruct meaning in the target language, adapting idioms, sentence structure, and levels of formality to local expectations. A sustainability report drafted in English can be adapted into French, German, Spanish, and Polish within hours,[2] rather than weeks. Crucially, these versions read as if they were originally authored in the target language. Technical terminology is preserved through managed glossaries, while stylistic flexibility is applied elsewhere. Brand voice remains consistent because the system learns from approved materials in each language, rather than relying solely on source-language transfer.

This capability is particularly relevant when, e. g., a Milan-based fashion house must communicate supply chain changes to partners across several countries before a product launch, or when a Brussels consultancy needs to brief clients throughout Europe on new regulatory requirements. The strategic implication is that communication and marketing functions can operate at the pace of product and policy development, rather than

---

1 Fun fact: the transformer architecture was first developed for machine translation. Its attention-based approach became the seed for modern large language models only later on, as explained in Section 1.4.

2 Why hours rather than seconds? While LLMs perform well at translation, localization remains imperfect. Producing text that reads entirely naturally to a native speaker still benefits from human review. Short, idiomatic texts can be more challenging than long and standardized documents. Nonetheless, reviewing and correcting generated text is significantly more efficient than drafting from scratch.

trailing behind them. Multilingual capability, historically treated by European companies as a structural cost, can instead become a source of speed and differentiation, provided that appropriate infrastructure and human oversight are in place.

2.2 Research and intelligence

Research activity can accelerate significantly when professionals are able to formulate targeted questions and receive compact overviews that promote further inquiry. For example, a compliance officer preparing for an audit may query the main GDPR considerations for cross-border customer data flows between Croatia and Portugal, and obtain a structured synthesis pointing to relevant regulatory provisions, enforcement patterns, and operational checkpoints. Rather than replacing analysis, such outputs organize the search space, allowing attention to be directed quickly towards the most relevant issues.

The underlying mechanism goes beyond simple keyword matching. Instead of relying solely on the lexical overlap between queries and documents, the AI system captures conceptual relationships, enabling relevant material to be retrieved even when different terminology is used across sources. It can also combine signals from multiple documents, supporting synthesis across regulatory texts, guidance, and enforcement practice. When supported by appropriate retrieval and citation mechanisms, this approach allows experts to navigate large and heterogeneous information landscapes more efficiently.

In operational terms, the value lies in acceleration, rather than automation of judgement. References and excerpts provide a traceable basis for verification, enabling professionals to confirm interpretations and identify gaps as part of their normal workflow. As discussed in Chapter 3, this architecture reduces the cost of exploration and comparison while preserving expert oversight and accountability.

Intelligence thus becomes embedded within routine operations rather than being treated as a periodic and manual activity. Instead of producing isolated reports, analytical pipelines can support continuous monitoring, with automated summarization highlighting emerging trends and anomalies. Strategy and research functions can track competitor behavior, regulatory developments, and market signals on a recurring basis, providing concise updates to decision-makers without expanding headcount.

As an illustration, a mid-sized logistics company in Bucharest can shorten its competitive intelligence cycle from quarterly reports to weekly internal briefings. This enables management to respond more rapidly to pricing adjustments and route innovations. The research function does not shrink; rather, effort shifts away from manual data collection towards interpretation, validation, and strategic assessment. In practice, cognitive work moves from locating information to evaluating relevance and implications.

Design choices play a decisive role, and European companies are adopting different configurations. Some develop centralized intelligence platforms that serve multiple departments from a shared knowledge base. Others deploy function-specific instances with tailored data access and output formats. Centralization offers economies of scale and consistency, but risks producing outputs that are insufficiently adapted to specific workflows. Distributed approaches integrate more naturally into existing processes, yet require coordination to avoid fragmentation and duplication. A recurring pattern among successful implementations combines lightweight centralization of infrastructure, security, and model management with workflow-level customization of prompts, data sources, and interfaces. This mirrors the "platform with products" model familiar from cloud transformations, balancing standardization with flexibility.

In legal and regulatory work, the impact is particularly pronounced. Contract reviewing, that previously required several hours per document, can be reduced to under an hour, as systems flag standard clauses, highlight deviations, and surface risk-related language automatically. A construction firm in Lyon can review 180 subcontractor agreements within a single week rather than over a month, allowing procurement teams to negotiate more effectively before project timelines tighten. Legal expertise is redirected towards negotiation strategy and relationship management, rather than exhaustive clause-by-clause review.

The greatest leverage emerges when systems incorporate feedback from domain experts over time. As legal professionals review flagged clauses, false positives and overlooked risks are corrected as part of routine work. These adjustments progressively improve system calibration without requiring technical redevelopment. Within a few months, the Lyon firm's system can align with the organization's specific risk appetite, flagging aggressive liability caps while disregarding minor warranty deviations that have historically been accepted. The result is not only faster processing, but closer alignment with business judgement. This feedback-driven dynamic helps explain why adoption often accelerates after an initial period rather than plateauing.

No specific company or product is endorsed here. Nonetheless, a broad ecosystem of mature tools is already available across the European market, supporting activities such as research, tailored information monitoring, and legal drafting. Organizations are therefore encouraged to explore existing solutions and undertake structured experimentation to assess their practical value within their own operational context.

2.3 Meetings and collaboration

Meetings benefit from automated knowledge capture that goes far beyond simple transcription. A product development meeting in Stockholm can generate a summary with key decisions, open questions, assigned owners, and deadlines – all distributed within 15 minutes of the meeting's end. Responsibilities are listed, deadlines are explicit, and follow-up happens without heroics or memory lapses.

The technical sophistication here is easy to underestimate. Early transcription systems required clean audio and struggled with accents. Modern systems handle overlapping speech, background noise, and the broad range of European accents with very high accuracy. They distinguish speakers automatically and identify when discussion loops back to earlier points. The AI layer then performs what linguists call "discourse analysis": identifying decision points, extracting action items, and distinguishing firm commitments from tentative suggestions. The result is not a transcript but a structured knowledge asset. We will examine the mechanisms later, but the operational impact is immediate: information that would have been lost or misremembered now becomes retrievable and actionable.

For cross-border teams, multilingual capabilities remove another layer of friction. A weekly leadership call with participants from Hungary, Denmark, and Poland can be transcribed and summarized in each language, so everyone reviews decisions in their native tongue without waiting for manual translation. Technical terms remain consistent across languages through managed glossaries. This matters in Europe and beyond, where cross-border projects routinely span multiple legal systems, languages, and contracting traditions, and where trust and nuance often determine whether complex partnerships hold. In this context, getting a deadline or a deliverable properly can save a €10 million project from derailing, before any formal dispute arises.

The cumulative effect on project velocity is substantial. Teams report 20–30 % faster project cycles simply because less time is lost to "What did we decide?" and "Who was supposed to handle that?" [39]. Information becomes retrievable and actionable rather than scattered across email threads and personal notes. There is also a subtler benefit that surprised many early adopters: meeting culture improves. When participants know that decisions and actions will be captured reliably, discussions become more focused and commitments more explicit. People prepare more thoroughly because they know vague statements do not provide cover later. The AI does not just record meetings: it changes the incentives around how people prepare for and conduct them.

An implementation pattern that works is: start with high-stakes, recurring meetings where decisions have cross-functional impact. Then, learn what summary format serves the audience: some teams want exhaustive detail, others want only decisions and actions. Expand to similar meeting types once you've calibrated quality standards. Avoid the temptation to record everything – not all meetings merit structured capture, and recording fatigue is real. The goal is to make critical decisions traceable and actionable, not to create a surveillance theater that makes people uncomfortable to speak candidly.

2.4 Customer operations

Customer operations often experience the effects of AI adoption at an early stage [40], particularly in the handling of high-volume and predictable requests. AI assistants can address routine issues such as password resets, order tracking, return policies, or basic troubleshooting, while redirecting less structured or higher-risk cases to human agents. In practice, this allows organizations to absorb temporary demand spikes without proportional increases in staffing. For example, during a network upgrade, a telecom operator in Madrid can manage a surge in customer enquiries by resolving the majority of standard requests automatically and prioritizing the remaining cases according to urgency and complexity.

At a high level, the technical architecture is conceptually simple. An AI layer mediates between the customer interface and existing knowledge bases, interpreting requests, retrieving relevant information, and generating responses. When uncertainty is detected or signals of customer dissatisfaction emerge, the interaction is escalated to a human agent. Importantly, escalation does not restart the process: the agent receives the full conversation history, relevant customer context, and candidate solutions, enabling continuity and efficiency. While technical implementation involves important design choices, the operational effect is primarily a reduction in repetitive handling and shorter resolution times for standard cases.

From the customer perspective, response times tend to decrease for straightforward requests, while more complex cases receive focused attention from experienced agents. From the company perspective, the personnel spends less time on repetitive interactions and more time on cases requiring judgement, empathy, or negotiation. In several deployments, employees' feedback suggests that work shifts towards problem-solving rather than scripted responses, with implications for perceived job quality.

Beyond external interactions, similar mechanisms can support internal processes such as onboarding and training. New employees can query internal systems in natural language and receive responses grounded in current procedures, with direct references to source documents. This reduces reliance on informal knowledge transfer and helps standardize answers to recurring operational questions.

Over time, customer interactions also become a source of structured operational signals. Aggregated patterns, such as sudden increases in queries related to billing or delivery timelines, can reveal process weaknesses or communication gaps. When monitored systematically, these signals allow teams to intervene before issues escalate into formal complaints or reputational concerns. In this sense, customer operations contribute to organizational learning in addition to their traditional service function.

Experience from deployments points to the importance of a cautious implementation strategy. Most companies begin with high-volume, low-complexity interactions where the consequences of error are limited. Scope is expanded gradually as confidence develops among both customers and staff. Attempts to automate complex or sensitive cases too early tend to undermine trust and increase escalation costs. In practice, effectiveness depends less on maximizing automation rates than on clearly defining escalation milestones and preserving human judgment where it is most valuable.

2.5 Personal productivity

Daily personal productivity improves in quieter but equally meaningful ways. LLMs can help triage emails and tasks, suggesting what is urgent and why, so managers spend less time juggling and more time deciding. An employee typically spends 2.6 hours on emails per day [41]. The AI can surface the five emails that require immediate attention, draft responses to routine requests, and flag the three that need strategic thought. Two hours per day are reclaimed from inbox management.

The system learns what kinds of messages historically prompted immediate action versus those safely deferred. It considers sender, subject matter, timing, and content to predict urgency. Unlike simple rules ("mark anything from the CEO as urgent"), it understands nuance; for instance, a CEO's casual question about office catering is not urgent, but a terse "We need to talk about the Q3 forecast" demands immediate attention. The system improves through implicit feedback: which suggested priorities did you actually act on? Over time, it calibrates to your specific judgment patterns. The technical mechanisms are subtle, but the user experience is simple: your inbox becomes manageable again.

Semantic search reduces document hunting. People describe what they need in ordinary language: "Find the customer satisfaction analysis from Q3 with the regional breakdown", and then retrieve relevant passages, even if the document used different wording or was titled "Market Performance Review Autumn 2024." A product manager no longer wastes 20 and more minutes searching SharePoint folders or Slack threads; they get the answer in a few seconds and move to analysis.

The effect is cumulative. Minutes saved per query across thousands of queries become weeks of regained focus. Let us image a management consultancy in Frankfurt, which calculates that intelligent search and AI-assisted email management returned 8 working days per consultant per year: this time can be reinvested in client strategy, business development, and professional learning. For 200 consultants, that amounts to 1,600 days of billable capacity without hiring extra persons. When accounting for the opportunity cost at €800–1200 per day for consultant time, the ROI becomes compelling even before considering the more difficult-to-quantify benefits.

Moreover, the deeper value is cognitive: reducing context switching and information foraging preserves mental energy for high-value work. Knowledge workers report not just time savings but reduced cognitive fatigue and improved end-of-day clarity. The AI handles the "where is that document?" and "what needs responding to?" overhead, allowing sustained focus on analysis, design, and strategy. This qualitative benefit is harder to measure but shows up in engagement scores, retention rates, and the subjective experience of "I actually finished what I set out to do today" rather than "I spent all day reacting to interruptions."

2.6 Decision support

At the decision stage, AI can support managers by organizing and comparing complex information in a more structured way. For example, when a CFO evaluates multiple ERP vendors, an AI-assisted analysis can aggregate inputs from Request for Proposal responses, analyst reports, and reference checks into a single comparative view. Typical dimensions include licensing models, estimated implementation effort, integration constraints, and vendors' track records. Rather than producing a recommendation, the system highlights areas of convergence and divergence across sources, as well as gaps where information is incomplete or uncertain. The final decision remains with the CFO, but the underlying evidence and assumptions are easier to inspect.

The underlying capability is multi-document synthesis with structured outputs. Within predefined evaluation frameworks, AI systems can help organize information according to agreed criteria, such as total cost of ownership, implementation risk, or alignment with an existing digital roadmap. Weightings can be made explicit and adjusted, allowing decision-makers to see how conclusions change under different priorities. In this role, AI does not replace analysis, but reduces the effort required to assemble and maintain consistency across inputs that would otherwise be handled manually.

Similar support applies to scenario exploration in strategic planning. When organizations consider expansion into new markets, AI-assisted analysis can help consolidate information on demand indicators, cost structures, regulatory constraints, and competitive conditions. Assumptions can be documented, sensitivities explored, and alternative scenarios compared more systematically. While such tools do not eliminate uncertainty, they can make it easier for teams to examine a broader set of plausible futures and to communicate the implications of key assumptions to senior management or boards.

One methodological benefit is the ability to explore more variations than what is typically be feasible under time constraints. Strategy teams often limit analysis to a small number of scenarios because of the effort involved in building and maintaining models. AI-supported workflows can extend this range by automating parts of the comparison and sensitivity analysis, helping teams identify which variables have the greatest influence on outcomes and which are less critical. This shifts emphasis from identifying a single "best" forecast to understanding robustness across different conditions.

In due diligence and risk assessment, similar techniques can assist with document-intensive reviews. AI tools can help scan large volumes of contracts, reports and files, so as to surface inconsistencies, unusual clauses, or deviations from standard terms. This does not remove the need for expert judgment, but it can reduce reliance on sampling driven purely by time and cost constraints. Experts remain responsible for assessing materiality and implications, but they do so with broader visibility over the available information.

Across these use cases, effective implementation follows a cautious pattern. Organizations tend to begin with recurring decisions that already have explicit criteria and established processes. Templates and review structures are defined in advance, and outputs are compared against past decisions to assess reliability and identify systematic gaps. A common principle is to avoid automating the decision itself – which is also a main requirement under the EU AI Act for high-risk systems, as explained in Chapter 7. AI is here used to structure information, expose trade-offs, and support reasoning, while accountability for judgment remains clearly human. For this reason, organizations that clearly separate analytical support from decision authority tend to achieve more reliable outcomes. The governance implications of this separation are discussed in Chapter 4.

2.7 Creativity and innovation

Creativity accelerates through rapid ideation across more options than traditional processes usually explore. A consumer goods company can generate 50 tagline options for a sustainability campaign in under an hour, then tests the top 10 with focus groups. Ideas arrive faster, iteration cycles shorten, and more options are tested before committing budget. The creative process has not been replaced: it has been restructured.

The creative process benefits from volume and variety. AI can generate hundreds of options, exploring stylistic dimensions that human teams might not consider spontaneously [42]. The real value then comes from the interaction cycle: humans provide direction and constraints, e. g. “make it aspirational but not preachy, reference Nordic heritage subtly”, AI generates options, humans select and refine promising directions, AI elaborates on those directions with variations. This back-and-forth process mirrors how experienced creative teams work internally, but it is compressed from days to hours.

Product innovation benefits as well. Engineers can describe a design challenge, e. g. “We need a lightweight mounting bracket for solar panels that withstands 120 km/h winds and costs under €8”, and receive initial design concepts, material suggestions, and comparable solutions from adjacent industries. A solution from aerospace might inform renewable energy; a material from consumer electronics might work in industrial equipment. The AI does not replace engineering judgment, but it compresses the “What if we tried...?” exploratory phase from weeks to days. A German industrial manufacturer can reduce prototype cycle time by 25 %, allowing them to test three design variants where they previously tested one. More experiments before commitment means better final designs and fewer expensive pivots during production.

Content production can scale without being diluted. A publisher in Paris can generate outlines of podcast episodes, social media teasers, and newsletter summaries from long-form interviews, reducing production time. Quality remains high because human editors curate tone, select highlights, and ensure narrative coherence. The team publishes twice as often without expanding headcount, building audience and revenue faster than competitors still locked in manual workflows. The economics shift: marginal cost of content production drops dramatically, allowing experiments that would not have been viable before.

Prototyping also receives a dramatic boost. Developing an app prototype (its version 0.1.0) now takes only hours to a few days: from the ideation to the design of must-have functionalities, to having a working product to show to colleagues or investors, it is now a matter of clear vision and prompting, rather than coding skills and tedious debugging. A pair of math PhD students we know prototyped a split-bill app in an evening, without having coded once in their life. Refinement, safe coding, design, validation, and v1.0.0 release still require the involvement of skilled app developers, but the step from ideation to minimal live products is now easily bridged.

The strategic insight is that AI changes the economics of experimentation. Traditional creative development invests heavily in a few concepts because iteration is expensive. AI makes iteration cheaper, allowing more exploration before committing resources. Marketing teams can test 20 campaign angles with AI-generated mock-ups, then invest production budget only in the 3–4 concepts that test well with audiences. Product teams can explore 15 feature variations quickly through simulated user scenarios, then build prototypes for the most promising 4. This shifts risk management from upfront judgment ("which idea will work?") to rapid empirical testing ("let us find out quickly and cheaply").

Often, creative teams may initially resist AI assistance, viewing it as threatening to craft and authorship. On the contrary, a framing that works is: AI handles divergent generation (producing many options quickly), humans handle convergent selection and refinement (choosing what is excellent and making it great). AI compresses the "blank page" phase and the "let us try this angle too" exploration, while humans own the "is this actually good?" judgment. Creative directors report that AI does not reduce the need for taste and judgment, but it increases it, because there are more options to evaluate and the bar for excellence can become higher. As AI is never 100 % creative but synthesises existing results, human creativity is even more important, so as to recognize the most promising options and build upon them with originality. The skillset shifts from "generate ideas under time pressure" to "recognize good ideas and refine them to perfection": a shift some find uncomfortable but most find energizing once they experience it.

2.8 Process orchestration with AI agents

A growing transversal capability is the use of AI agents to support the coordination of workflows across tools and teams. Unlike assistant functions focused primarily on writing, analysis, or research, these agents are designed to connect analytical outputs to subsequent operational steps. Their role is not to replace decision-making, but to reduce friction between deliberation and execution, which is often a source of delay in complex companies.

In practice, the potential benefits emerge when tasks span multiple systems, formats, or stakeholders. For example, after reviewing a negotiation summary, a commercial manager in Tallinn may rely on an agent to prepare follow-up actions such as drafting a customer communication, updating the CRM, or scheduling an internal handover. The manager remains responsible for content and intent, while the agent supports the procedural aspects that would otherwise require manual coordination across tools.

This capability is particularly relevant in the European contexts, where processes are often shaped by documentation requirements, cross-border coordination, and internal control frameworks. In a procurement review in Salzburg, for instance, an agent may assist staff by assembling supporting documentation, applying standard templates, checking eligibility criteria, and logging actions for audit purposes. Human judgment remains central, but execution can become more structured and traceable.

Similar patterns apply across organizational boundaries. A customer complaint initiated in Luxembourg City may trigger a sequence of actions across CRM, ticketing, and communication systems used by teams in Ljubljana or Athens. Rather than relying on *ad hoc* email exchanges, the workflow can be coordinated more systematically, with clearer handovers and status visibility.

The effects are therefore not limited to speed. When routine follow-up actions are supported consistently, teams may be able to focus more attention on decision-making and exception handling. Managers gain clearer visibility into task status and dependencies, while compliance-related steps are less likely to be omitted unintentionally.

At the same time, it is important to recognize that this approach introduces new dependencies and risks. Issues such as inappropriate automation, unclear accountability, propagation of errors across systems, or excessive reliance on agent-generated actions can undermine effectiveness and trust if not properly managed. These risks, along with mitigation strategies, are discussed in detail in Section 6.

Experience suggests that adoption is most effective when it is gradual. Organizations typically begin by using agents to prepare actions for human review, then allow limited execution of low-risk steps once confidence is established, and only later expand scope. This progression helps avoid both premature automation and under-utilization, while giving governance structures time to adapt. Importantly, human involvement should not be reduced to mechanical checking of agents' outputs. Instead, human oversight should focus on judgment, prioritization, and exception handling, supported by appropriate governance and technical safeguards.

Overall, AI-supported process orchestration can help make workflows more coherent in environments characterized by high complexity. Its value lies less in automation for its own sake than in improving coordination and transparency. For European organizations operating across jurisdictions, languages and legacy systems, this capability can be useful when introduced cautiously and governed carefully, complementing rather than displacing human responsibility.

2.9 The emergence of a new cognitive infrastructure and the case of Shadow AI

As organizations explore the expanding range of generative AI use cases, it quickly becomes clear that adoption rarely follows a purely top-down trajectory. In many cases, a significant share of AI usage already occurs informally, outside officially approved tools, processes, or governance structures. This phenomenon is commonly referred to as *Shadow AI* [43].

Shadow AI denotes the use of AI tools, models, or services that employees or teams adopt independently of guidelines, without explicit authorization or oversight. The pattern echoes earlier phases of digital transformation, such as shadow IT, in which departments adopted technologies faster than central functions could formalize them. What distinguishes the current wave is the power, accessibility, and general-purpose nature of generative AI. Through simple web interfaces, browser extensions, or APIs, employees can draft documents, summarize reports, analyse data, generate code, or prototype ideas with minimal technical effort.

From a leadership perspective, Shadow AI should not be interpreted solely as a governance failure or compliance risk. It is also a strong signal, as it reveals where employees perceive immediate value, which tasks are bottlenecks, and where official tooling or processes lag behind operational reality. A marketing team drafting content with generative AI, a consultant summarizing internal reports using external tools, or a developer experimenting with an open-weight model[3] typically reflects unmet needs rather than malicious intent [43–45].

At the same time, unmanaged Shadow AI creates exposure. Informal use can lead to unintended data sharing, regulatory blind spots, reputational risks, and fragmentation of knowledge. These risks are discussed in detail later in the book (see Chapter 6). At this early stage, however, the key insight for leaders is more strategic than defensive: Shadow AI highlights a tension between agility and control that must be actively managed rather than ignored.

Stepping back, what ties Shadow AI and formal AI initiatives together is the emergence of a new layer of *cognitive infrastructure* across the organization. Generative AI does not correspond to a single application or function. Instead, it reshapes how communication, knowledge, and coordination operate across roles and departments. It reduces the cost of drafting, searching, translating, and synthesizing information, allowing people to shift effort from retrieval and formatting toward analysis, judgment, and design.

These features resemble those of an infrastructure rather than of an application software. Like email or document management systems, generative AI becomes foundational to how work happens across functions. Unlike previous infrastructure layers, however, it adapts to work patterns rather than forcing work to adapt to rigid systems. Interaction occurs through natural language, and intent is inferred rather than explicitly encoded. These broad and low-friction properties explain why adoption often outpaces formal rollout plans and training programs.

The effects compound across functions and geographies. Improvements in documentation quality, explanation clarity, or decision framing in one team propagate downstream to others that consume the same information. Effective prompt patterns, once discovered, spread across the organization. Learning accumulates collectively rather

3 See Chapter 3.

than remaining siloed. As a result, gains are often nonlinear: productivity, consistency, and quality improve faster than would be expected from isolated projects.

For European organizations in particular, this dynamic can turn traditional constraints into advantages. Multilingual capability, documentation discipline, and mature compliance cultures can be amplified rather than slowed by generative AI. Instead of competing primarily on cost, companies can extend quality, rigor, and transparency across markets and use cases at scale. The competitive question shifts from whether quality can be maintained to whether competitors can match that quality at comparable speed.

The governance implication follows directly. Because genAI functions as an infrastructure, it requires platform thinking rather than project thinking. Some elements benefit from centralization, including security, model access, monitoring, and compliance oversight. Others require decentralization, such as domain-specific use cases, prompt development, and workflow integration. Organizations that succeed typically establish lightweight central capabilities and guardrails, while allowing business teams to drive value realization. Shared libraries, communities of practice, and outcome-oriented measurement help ensure that experimentation becomes cumulative rather than fragmented.

In this sense, Shadow AI is neither a problem to suppress nor a phase to endure. It is an early indicator that a new cognitive infrastructure is already taking shape. The leadership challenge is whether this infrastructure will remain invisible and unmanaged, or whether it will be shaped deliberately into a transparent, responsible, and scalable foundation for performance and growth.

2.10 Looking ahead

Concrete examples of transversal opportunities created by generative AI are already visible across organizations, not as future projections but as present realities. On top of those surveyed here, others are emerging as we write [46]. These outcomes are neither speculative nor confined to pilot initiatives. Companies across Europe and beyond are realizing them today, from family-owned Mittelstand firms to publicly listed multinationals, and across sectors ranging from financial services to manufacturing and retail. Technical barriers are lower than commonly assumed, while economic returns tend to materialize more quickly than with typical enterprise technology investments. The strategic implications therefore extend beyond incremental efficiency gains, reaching into questions of competitive positioning, capability, and long-term differentiation.

To provide figures on top of the examples above,[4] studies have showed that genAI may improve average performance up to 66 % in real-world business scenarios, such

4 Of course, the examples in this Chapter pertain to European as well as worldwide markets: most benefits are global, with several specific cases that are particularly relevant for the EU zone, such as multilin-

as programming, troubleshooting, and critical thinking, where time reductions exceed 70 % [47, 48], including drops in writing or programming time, handling more inquiries per hour, or producing documents and reports. AI also narrows skill gaps, delivering the largest gains for less-experienced workers by providing rapid access to information and support [49]. In general, the European Central Bank [50] estimates that AI could boost euro area productivity by 0.35 percentage points annually, with cumulative gains of 3.5 percentage points over ten years under widespread adoption. Such adoption still has impressive room for growth, as a recent report [46] suggests that not even 10 % of the AI capabilities in various domains have been reached yet.

Hence, the question facing organizations is no longer whether to engage with generative AI, but how to adopt it in a manner that aligns with existing culture, capabilities, and operational constraints. Experience to date suggests that effective adoption often begins with use cases that combine clear value with limited risk, where AI supports rather than substitutes human judgment. Chapter 4 examines criteria for selecting such initial use cases in more detail.

Early efforts typically focus on demonstrating practical benefits within a relatively short time frame, helping to build familiarity and trust. As adoption progresses, responsibilities and accountability mechanisms need to evolve alongside usage, ensuring that increased confidence does not translate into unexamined reliance. Over time, organizations can extend successful patterns to adjacent functions and workflows, adapting based on feedback and observed outcomes. Sustained value depends not only on individual applications, but also on investment in governance, infrastructure, and measurement practices that support experimentation while maintaining control and coherence.

Mind that realizing these opportunities requires understanding what is possible, as well as how it works and what can go wrong. In Chapter 6, we will explore the risks that require managerial attention: from hallucinations and bias to data security and dependency dynamics. In Chapters 8 to 10, we will consider the bigger strategic picture in Europe: regulatory evolution, competitive dynamics, talent implications, and positioning choices that will shape who wins and who falls behind.

The goal should thus not be to chase every capability or implement every use case. It should be to identify the two or three leverage points that unlock the most value for the specific business, given their starting position and strategic direction. Then, selecting the appropriate speed is crucial: fast enough to capture advantage, careful enough to build trust and manage risk. The window for differentiation is open now. It will not remain open indefinitely as these capabilities become commoditized and expected rather than distinctive. Organizations that master this infrastructure early are more likely to shape market dynamics, while those that delay in search of perfect clarity might find themselves responding to shifts initiated by others.

---

gual integration, support for compliance, or assistance to decision-making in culturally-aware scenarios; we will dig deeper into these scenarios later in the book.

3 Aligning AI capabilities with organization needs

There are several reasons why a company may decide to adopt AI. In some cases, adoption is driven by hype or fear of missing out. In others, it is motivated by competitive pressure, i. e., feeling compelled to match what peers or competitors are already doing. More substantively, AI may be introduced to optimize or improve existing processes, or to address problems that could not previously be solved with traditional tools.

These motivations are not equivalent. Hype-driven adoption is fragile and often results in unnecessary costs and organizational friction. Competitive pressure can be legitimate, but only when there exist foundational capabilities required to absorb innovation effectively. Process optimization reflects an engineering mindset, focused on improving measurable outcomes within existing structures. Addressing previously unsolved problems, by contrast, requires a more exploratory and risk-tolerant approach, with the potential for qualitative leaps in capability and value creation.

This distinction matters because different motivations naturally lead to different forms of AI adoption. Optimizing a well-defined process may only require narrowly scoped models with limited autonomy. Tackling open-ended or evolving problems, instead, often pushes organizations toward more general, adaptive, and autonomous systems. Understanding this progression is essential for making informed strategic and governance choices.

This chapter therefore provides guidance on how to navigate AI adoption across increasing levels of complexity, from decisions about why to introduce AI, to how different technical paradigms shape control, risk, and impact.

3.1 From Machine Learning to agentic AI: complexity and controls

Let us place the AI technologies into perspective. The landscape of AI is not homogeneous; it consists of a spectrum of architectures, levels of autonomy, and degrees of complexity. Each point along this spectrum represents not only a technical capability but also a managerial choice about control, coordination, and accountability. At one end are single-specialized applications such as Machine Learning, Deep Learning, Large Language Models, and Retrieval Augmented Generation systems, each designed to perform specific and well-defined tasks.[1] At the other end are agentic AI and full AI ecosystems, where multiple intelligent components interact dynamically with each other and, in many cases, with humans in the loop. Figures 3.1 and 3.2 provide a scheme of such spectrum, focusing first on generalizability vs control, and then on opportunities, costs, and compliance.

1 See Chapter 1.

https://doi.org/10.1515/9783112254103-003

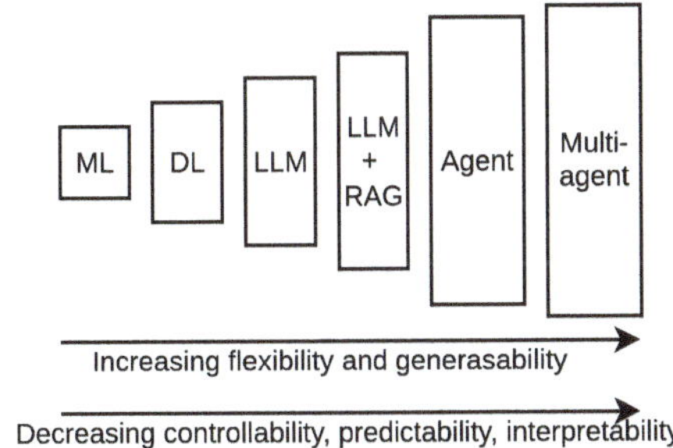

Figure 3.1: Evolution of generalizability vs. control from Machine Learning to agents.

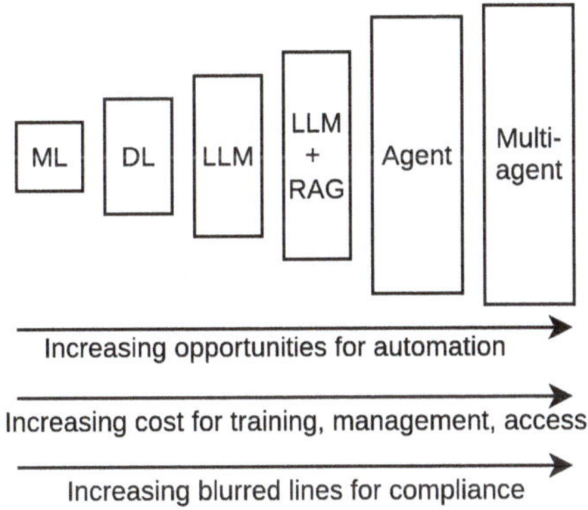

Figure 3.2: Evolution of opportunities, costs and compliance from Machine Learning to agents.

Single AI applications are narrow by design. They rely on one model executing a limited set of operations, such as classifying an image, forecasting demand, or generating text. Their architecture is relatively static, their inputs and outputs well-defined. Such systems typically operate through statistical inference, sometimes complemented by symbolic reasoning or information retrieval. Their value lies in precision, speed, and scalability. Yet, as repeatedly observed by firms and consulting agencies, even these narrowly focused systems can generate significant business impact when embedded in redesigned processes that combine human expertise and algorithmic decision capabilities [51].

In contrast, multi-agent and ecosystem-based systems mark a qualitative leap. They bring together several specialized models that coordinate, negotiate, or cooperate to achieve broader objectives. A recommendation system, for example, might integrate a user-profiling agent, a content-ranking agent, and a conversational interface. In more complex settings, such as supply-chain optimization or autonomous logistics, agents may act semi-independently, dividing labor, learning from one another, and making local decisions that contribute to global goals. This evolution reflects a shift from predictive tools to reasoning entities capable of understanding context, planning actions, and executing them across connected environments [52].

With a vague metaphor, we may think of specialized and single AI models as executors, such as very junior profiles: they perform a task, given that they are each time probed with a request. On the other hand, the *multi-agent* AI systems are closer to planners (from lower to middle managers, in a way), in the sense that, once given a scope, they are able to plan the tasks and then execute them. This transition turns AI from a passive analytical tool into an active strategic partner. However, as the abilities increase, so must the reliability of the performer.

With increasing complexity comes greater flexibility and generalization. Moving from simple Machine Learning algorithms to multi-agent ecosystems enables systems to handle a broader range of tasks, adapt to novel situations, and respond intelligently to changing environments. This flexibility explains why companies are exploring agentic architectures for adaptive customer service, dynamic pricing, or autonomous process orchestration. Yet this flexibility comes at a cost: as complexity increases, controllability, predictability and interpretability usually decrease.

Controllability refers to ensuring that a system behaves as expected under defined conditions. Predictability concerns the capacity (or, at least, the possibility) to anticipate the system's output for a given input. Interpretability relates to the human ability to understand *why* a particular output was produced. These three qualities are the pillars of trustworthy automation. In traditional engineering disciplines, such as aviation or industrial control, they are achieved through deterministic design: systems follow explicit rules, and outcomes are bounded within known parameters. AI systems, by contrast, operate on probabilistic inference. They rely on statistical regularities in data rather than fixed logical rules. Consequently, they can perform exceptionally well in many scenarios but lack guarantees. A single anomalous input, an unexpected event, or an ambiguous request may trigger behavior outside anticipated norms[2] [54].

This inherent uncertainty reshapes the nature of responsibility. In deterministic systems, behavior can be specified exhaustively and traced back to discrete design or operational choices. In probabilistic systems, performance instead reflects evolving data distributions, contextual variation, and interactions across components. These systems increasingly extend beyond prediction or conversation into the orchestration of actions, introducing a broader set of interdependencies that must be actively managed [55]. As a result, effective oversight requires a shift in managerial stance. Rather than treating AI as a static system to be controlled once deployed, organizations benefit from approaching it as a capability to be steered over time. This involves defining clear objectives,

2 As an example, Tesla autopilots may stop in front of trucks hauling traffic lights [53], since that situation was never seen and is mapped to a "normal traffic light" scenario. Beyond causing operational errors, such blind spots also increase the system's attack surface: adversaries can deliberately exploit rare or ambiguous configurations to trigger unintended behavior, highlighting how distributional gaps can translate not only into safety risks but also into security vulnerabilities.

monitoring outcomes continuously, and adjusting configurations, thresholds, or operating conditions as evidence accumulates. In this model, management focuses less on eliminating uncertainty and more on maintaining alignment between system behavior, internal goals, and evolving operational contexts.

The higher the complexity of an AI system, the harder it becomes to predict outcomes, explain reasoning, and assign responsibility. Yet the temptation to pursue increasingly sophisticated architectures is strong because complexity expands the frontier of automation. Research on AI value creation shows that firms capturing the greatest returns are those that integrate advanced models into their operating core, but only when accompanied by strong governance, process redesign, and human oversight [51]. Complexity without governance yields fragility; governance without ambition yields stagnation.

This tension between capability and control defines the managerial challenge of agentic AI. Multi-agent systems promise efficiency, adaptability, and strategic insight, yet they require investment in supervision, compliance, and risk management. In recent executive analyses, many leaders acknowledge that the biggest obstacle to scaling AI is not technical but organizational, due to unclear accountability and fragmented governance frameworks [56]. When an autonomous agent triggers a financial error or compliance breach, determining responsibility becomes ambiguous: is it the data scientist who designed the model, the engineer who deployed it, the business unit that relied on it, or the leadership that approved its use?

The managerial implications are profound. Whereas traditional AI functioned as a tool, agents operate as collaborators that share responsibility for outcomes. They blur the boundary between automation and delegation. On one hand, this offers unprecedented opportunities, as surveyed before. On the other, this creates new forms of dependency and ethical complexity. The moving consensus around the topic is that the future of organizational intelligence lies not in replacing human decision-makers, but in orchestrating hybrid teams of humans and machines, each contributing complementary strengths [55].

Strategically, the rise of agents signals a movement from process automation to decision automation. This evolution forces companies to rethink governance structures, not just technical architectures. Clear rules of engagement must define when agents may act autonomously, when human validation is required, and how transparency is maintained. Companies and institutions embedding AI governance into their corporate frameworks, establishing review boards, audit mechanisms, and escalation protocols, achieve more sustainable returns and lower reputational risk [51]. Analyst firms emphasize that the success of AI initiatives depends less on technical sophistication than on the organization's ability to align system autonomy with appropriate governance maturity [57].

Rather than treating autonomy as an end goal, this section examines it as a capability that must be deliberately bounded, governed, and aligned with one's own objectives.

As AI systems move from isolated tools toward agentic architectures, the central question for executives is no longer whether greater autonomy is technically possible, but under what conditions it should be exercised, supervised, and constrained.

3.2 Choosing the right tool for the right problem

The discussion of complexity and autonomy leads to a less obvious but critical consequence for decision-making: in the context of AI, selecting a more powerful or autonomous system is not merely a question of performance, but one of governance, risk, and long-term commitment. While the range of generative AI opportunities is broad, effective adoption depends on aligning technical sophistication with the structure of the problem, the tolerance for error, and the degree of control required. In this domain, excess capability often introduces fragility rather than advantage.

Innovation still begins with problem definition rather than tool selection, but AI complicates this familiar managerial principle. Unlike many earlier technologies, AI systems differ not only in efficiency or scale, but in opacity, adaptability, and downstream implications for accountability. When technology selection precedes a clear articulation of the problem, hidden costs may frequently arise, related to explainability, monitoring, and compliance that only become visible after deployment. In AI-driven systems, this understanding determines not only feasibility, but sustainability [58].

This challenge persists even in mature organizations with strong technological capabilities. AI systems span a wide spectrum, from narrowly scoped statistical models to large, general-purpose architectures. The availability of highly capable models creates a bias towards over-engineering, particularly when those models are easy to access and promise broad applicability. Yet for well-defined tasks, additional model complexity does not necessarily translate into better outcomes. Instead, it often reduces predictability, increases operational overhead, and complicates governance [59].

A concrete illustration helps clarify the trade-off. Consider a document classification or semantic search task in a regulated setting such as healthcare. Both a model such as BERT [60] and an LLM such as Gemini [61] are built on the same transformer principles (and are from the same company too, i. e., Google). The difference lies not in the underlying idea, but in scale, cost, and how their outputs are produced and controlled.

Gemini can analyze documents directly and generate fluent summaries or explanations. This offers flexibility and expressive power, but it also comes with higher operational costs and less stable behavior. The same document may be phrased or interpreted slightly differently across runs, because the system is designed to generate language rather than to apply fixed decision logic. In regulated environments, this variability complicates auditability: explaining why similar documents received diverse outcomes becomes more difficult when the system's reasoning is not fully repeatable.

In contrast, a smaller model such as BERT can be used in a constrained role, focused on understanding and comparing documents rather than generating text. In this setup, documents are analyzed once and then handled through simple, explicit rules for ranking or classification. The behavior of the system remains stable across repeated runs, costs are significantly lower, and the logic used to reach a decision can be inspected and documented. Semantic understanding is provided by the model, while decision-making remains transparent and controllable. The practical question is therefore not which technology is more advanced, but which operational profile best fits the constraints, risk tolerance, and accountability requirements of the deployment context.

For tasks such as clustering, similarity search,[3] or relevance ranking,[4] this approach often delivers comparable performance while providing managers with clearer levers of control. Embedding-based systems[5] can be evaluated through stable benchmarks, decision thresholds can be defined and adjusted explicitly, and system behavior can be monitored in a transparent and repeatable manner. This supports predictable operation and straightforward oversight.

This does not imply that more advanced models lack value. Generative systems are appropriate when tasks involve open-ended reasoning, synthesis across heterogeneous sources, or interaction in natural language. The strategic error arises when architectural complexity is treated as a default rather than a deliberate choice. In AI systems, additional capability almost always comes with additional uncertainty, and the relationship between power and reliability is not linear.

Strategic choices therefore involve treating AI not as a monolithic technology, but as a portfolio of distinct capabilities, each with specific strengths, limitations, and governance implications. The relevant question is not whether AI can be applied, but which class of AI, if any, is appropriate given the decision context. AI offers an unprecedented expansion of organizational capability, but its impact depends on calibration rather than ambition alone. When technological choices follow clearly defined problems, AI functions as an enabler of strategy. When technology leads and problems are forced to adapt, complexity tends to grow faster than value.

In the next sections, we will survey the main dimensions to consider when deciding upon which AI system to employ, providing a checklist of the priority variables to take into account.

---

3 Retrieving items that are most similar to a given query according to a numerical distance or similarity measure, typically used in search, retrieval, and recommendation systems.

4 Ordering items according to how well they match a query or objective, such as ranking documents by relevance to a user question.

5 Systems that represent text, images, or other data as numerical vectors (embeddings), enabling similarity, clustering, and ranking through well-defined mathematical operations.

3.2.1 Proprietary vs. open and open-weight models

The economics of AI differ markedly depending on whether an organization adopts proprietary models or models that are openly available for self-deployment. Table 3.1 summarizes the key distinctions, but understanding how these models translate into actual costs requires going one layer deeper, into how usage is measured, deployed, and billed (cf. Section 1.5.1).

Table 3.1: Comparison of proprietary and open or open-weight AI models from a managerial perspective.

	Proprietary AI	Open / open-weight AI
Cost model	Licensing fees, subscriptions, or usage-based pricing (e. g., tokens). Costs are easy to start with but can increase rapidly as usage scales.	No license fees. Costs arise mainly from infrastructure (compute, storage) and internal expertise required to operate, secure, and maintain the system.
Dependency on suppliers	High dependency on a single provider's ecosystem, pricing, roadmap, and contractual terms. Switching providers can be costly and operationally disruptive.	Lower dependency on external vendors. Organizations retain technical autonomy over the system, but responsibility shifts to internal teams and long-term skill availability.
Evolution and upgrades	Upgrade cycles are driven by the vendor. New releases may require revalidation, re-integration, or reconfiguration of existing workflows.	Organizations control when and how to adopt new versions. This offers flexibility, but requires internal resources for testing, migration, and maintenance.

Throughout this section, the term "open" is used in a broad, operational sense, encompassing both fully *open-source* models released under permissive licenses and so-called *open-weight* models, whose parameters are publicly available even if training data and pipelines remain proprietary. While these categories differ in legal and licensing terms, the distinction is not primarily legal. From a deployment and governance perspective, both exhibit similar economic, technical, and governance characteristics: they can be self-hosted, integrated into existing infrastructure, audited at the model level, and operated with a high degree of control over cost, latency, and data flows. It is these shared operational properties, rather than formal licensing conditions alone, that motivate their joint treatment in this discussion.

Proprietary AI services such as ChatGPT (OpenAI), Claude (Anthropic), Gemini (Google DeepMind), or Grok (xAI) [62, 63, 61, 64] are typically consumed through cloud-based platforms operating under a software-as-a-service model. Users pay via subscriptions or usage-based billing, where costs scale with the volume and complexity of requests. Open and open-weight systems such as Mistral, LLaMA, BLOOM, or DeepSeek, by contrast, can be downloaded freely and deployed on internal infrastructure, whether on-premises, in private clouds, or in public cloud environments under the organization's control [65–68]. While this eliminates licensing fees, costs shift to infrastructure provisioning and to the internal expertise required to operate and secure these systems [69–72].

In most cases, the real difference lies not in absolute expenditure but in the structure of spending and control. Proprietary AI tends to generate variable costs: it is quick to adopt, predictable at small scale, but can grow rapidly as usage expands. Open and open-weight AI introduce higher fixed costs: upfront investment in infrastructure and skills, offset by more stable and often lower marginal costs at scale. Proprietary systems trade money for speed, convenience, and access to cutting-edge capabilities; open systems trade convenience for autonomy, privacy, and strategic independence.

Deployment choices, particularly the use of cloud infrastructure, cut across both model families and materially affect their economics. For most companies, the cloud has become the default environment for developing and deploying AI systems, driven by practical considerations such as capital expenditure, time-to-market, and operational flexibility. Cloud platforms provide elastic access to compute, storage, and managed AI services, lowering barriers to experimentation and reducing procurement friction. They also offer security controls, logging, and certifications aligned with standards such as ISO and regulatory frameworks such as the GDPR, shifting part of the compliance burden from infrastructure management to contractual and procedural oversight.

At the same time, cloud deployment introduces structural dependencies that amplify existing trade-offs between proprietary and open approaches. Data governance and sovereignty concerns emerge when data are processed outside the European Union, even when legal safeguards are in place. These risks apply whether the choice falls onto proprietary models via APIs or onto open or open-weight models on third-party cloud infrastructure.

As a result, mature organizations rarely adopt a single model or deployment strategy in isolation (see Chapter 4). Instead, they develop hybrid architectures: proprietary APIs may be used for high-value reasoning or customer-facing applications, while open or open-weight models are deployed for internal automation, multilingual search, or analytics in controlled environments. Public cloud resources are combined with private or on-premises infrastructure to balance elasticity with control, while sensitive data and critical workloads remain under direct governance. European initiatives such as Gaia-X further aim to support this hybrid approach by promoting interoperability, transparency, and portability across providers, rather than prescribing a single technological solution [73].

What ultimately distinguishes successful adopters is not whether they choose proprietary or open models, nor whether they deploy them in the cloud or on-premises, but how clearly they understand their cost of control. Proprietary systems externalize complexity at the price of dependency; open and open-weight systems internalize complexity in exchange for sovereignty. As AI becomes embedded in core business processes, these choices increasingly reflect long-term strategic priorities rather than short-term technical preferences. The central question is no longer how much intelligence costs, but how much control an organization is willing and able to assume over the systems shaping its decisions.

3.2.2 Choosing the right model

Selecting an LLM involves trade-offs that extend beyond purely technical performance. In addition to output quality, teams must consider cost, energy consumption, operational complexity, and dependency on external providers. The objective is therefore to identify a model that meets defined performance requirements while minimizing these associated constraints. In practice, this is best approached through a controlled, stepwise evaluation process that begins in a safe testing environment and progressively narrows the available options. Figure 3.3 illustrates an example of how such a decision process can be structured [74]. While budget limits, hardware availability, regulatory requirements, and performance thresholds vary across organizations, the underlying logic provides a robust starting point.

The process should begin in a sandboxed (or at least, controlled) environment where experimentation is possible without exposing sensitive data. Synthetic or anonymized datasets allow teams to test feasibility while avoiding compliance and security risks. At this stage, the goal is not optimization but validation: determining whether the task can be meaningfully addressed and establishing a baseline under controlled conditions [75].

A pragmatic way to set this baseline is to start from the top. Many organizations benchmark a strong proprietary model via API on the safe dataset to approximate an upper bound on achievable quality. If even this benchmark does not meet minimum expectations, the implication is rarely that another model will fix the issue. More often, the task framing, data inputs, workflow design, or the degree of required human involvement must be revisited. This initial benchmark therefore helps anchor what "acceptable performance" means for the use case and context [76].

Once feasibility is established, the process moves in the opposite direction. Smaller, lighter, and potentially open/open-weight models are tested on the same data, stepping down in size until performance falls below the threshold. The objective is to stop at the smallest model that still delivers sufficient quality, following a principle of minimum sufficient capability. This supports cost control, energy efficiency, and operational sustainability while reducing unnecessary complexity.

At this point, organizational constraints become decisive. Where data protection, confidentiality, or sovereignty requirements restrict the use of external services, attention shifts toward models that can be deployed within controlled environments, which often includes open/open-weight options. Where such constraints are less binding, proprietary and open/open-weight models can be evaluated on comparable terms. Importantly, testing open/open-weight models does not require early infrastructure commit-

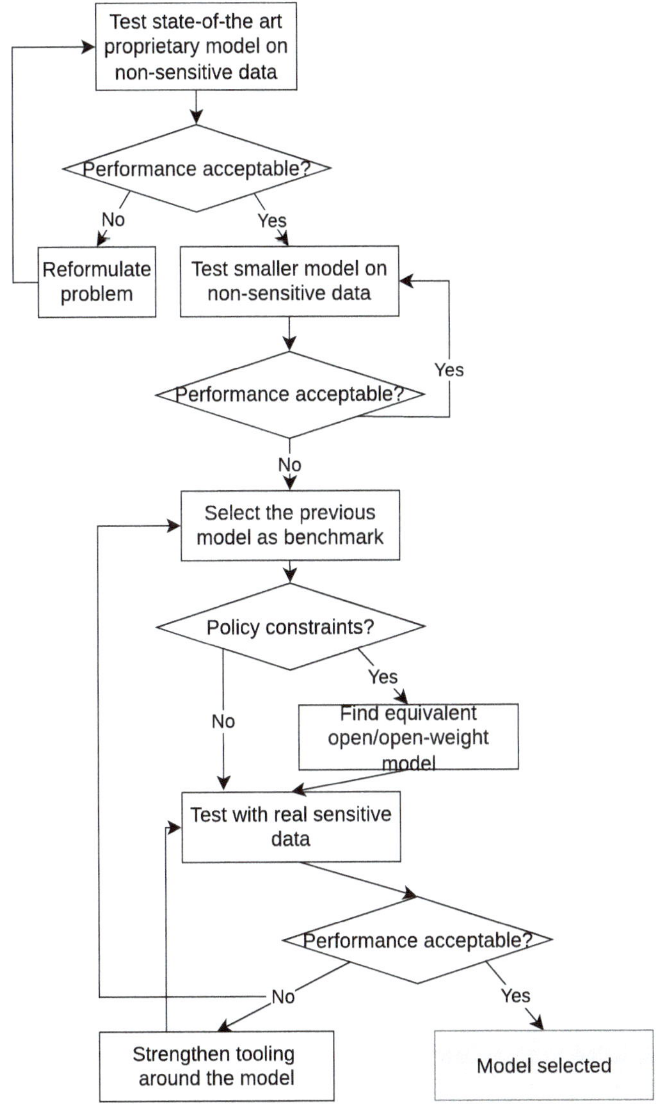

Figure 3.3: Example of how organizations can structure model selection, from safe benchmarking to deployment validation.

ment: many are available through managed services that expose them via APIs, allowing teams to benchmark and iterate in the same way as with proprietary systems, without first deploying or maintaining their own infrastructure.

A non-negotiable validation step follows when the shortlisted model is tested on real data under appropriate safeguards. Performance on synthetic data does not always transfer cleanly to production settings, where edge cases and domain-specific characteristics appear. If results fall short, it is possible to refine prompts, strengthen surrounding controls, test a slightly stronger model, or explore fine-tuning before reassessing suitability.

Model size has direct financial and operational implications. Larger models typically increase variable costs when used via APIs and raise compute requirements when deployed internally, which affects operating expenses, energy use, latency, and hardware capacity planning. Downsizing is therefore not only an economic consideration but also an engineering one, enabling smoother deployment and more predictable system behavior. In practice, mixed strategies can be adopted, using multiple models for different tasks. Routine workflows rely on lightweight systems, while more complex or sensitive analyses invoke stronger models selectively. In more mature setups, dynamic routing can be introduced based on task complexity, sensitivity, or resource availability. This reflects a shift toward adaptive enterprise architectures rather than a single-model approach.

As a general rule, most effort should be concentrated on the feasibility benchmark and the final validation on real data. The intermediate phase should be disciplined, focusing on systematic comparison and prompt refinement rather than broad experimentation. When the final candidate is a proprietary system, benchmarking an open/open-weight alternative is often prudent to clarify trade-offs in cost, dependency, and governance. Ultimately, model selection is an exercise in proportion. The right model is not the most powerful one available, but the one that fits the organization's objectives, constraints, and governance requirements while remaining economically and operationally sustainable over time.

3.2.3 Fine-tuning vs. prompt engineering vs. RAG

Once a company understands the cost mechanics of generative models, the next question is how to make them genuinely useful for its specific needs. Most managers quickly discover that out-of-the-box models perform impressively on generic tasks but struggle with domain-specific knowledge, tone, or contextual sensitivity. The challenge is knowing when and how to intervene.

Figure 3.4 illustrates a practical decision flow for this evaluation. Rather than presenting fine-tuning, prompt engineering, and RAG as equivalent alternatives, the framework guides managers through a sequence of increasingly intensive interventions, each addressing a specific type of performance gap.

The first question is whether intervention is needed at all. Many companies rush to customize models without first testing whether the base model already meets requirements. If performance is acceptable for the intended task, the most efficient strategy is to use the model as-is. This baseline assessment prevents premature investment in adaptation and establishes a clear performance benchmark against which to measure the value of subsequent interventions.

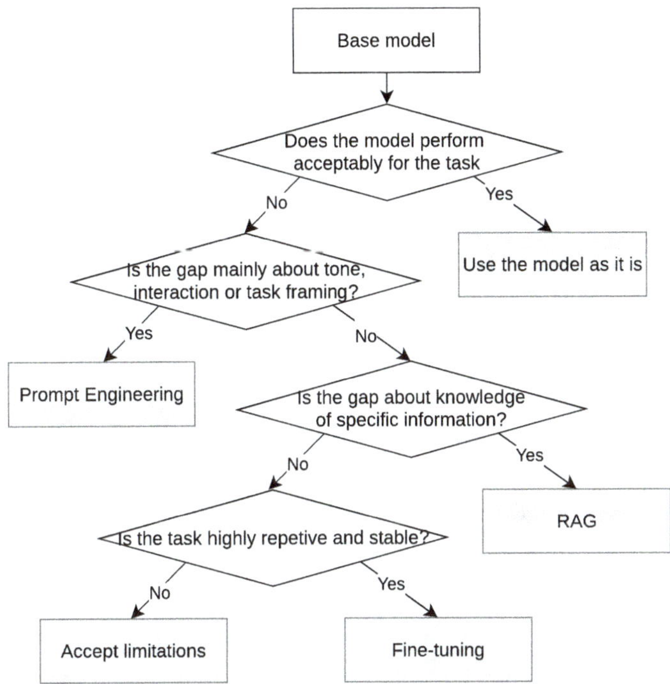

Figure 3.4: Illustrative decision flow for adapting generative AI systems to organizational needs. The figure shows how prompt engineering, RAG, and fine-tuning can be combined progressively, starting from the least irreversible interventions and escalating only when necessary.

If the base model falls short, the next question is diagnostic: what type of gap exists? Not all performance problems require the same solution. The nature of the shortfall determines the most appropriate response.

When the gap concerns tone, interaction style, or task framing, prompt engineering is the natural starting point. A model that performs well technically but responds too formally for customer service, or cannot follow a specific report structure, can often be redirected through carefully designed prompts. Prompt engineering is fast to deploy, inexpensive, and highly flexible. When embedded into structured workflows, well-designed prompts can make a general-purpose model behave in ways that feel tailored to organizational needs.

At the same time, prompt engineering has structural limits. Prompts are inherently context-dependent, and what works well in one scenario may degrade in another. Without explicit structure, versioning, and documentation, organizations risk accumulating fragmented prompt collections that are difficult to maintain, reuse, or audit. From a managerial perspective, prompt engineering should therefore be seen as an accelerator rather than a complete solution: necessary in most deployments, but rarely sufficient on its own to guarantee robustness, traceability, or long-term scalability. When treated as managed artifacts rather than improvised inputs, however, prompts gain strategic value. Prompt bases/libraries and associated tooling can survive model upgrades, preserving knowledge even as underlying models evolve.

When the performance gap stems from lack of specific information, RAG becomes the appropriate intervention. If the model lacks access to proprietary data, internal policies, technical documentation, or domain-specific knowledge, no amount of prompt refinement will close the gap. RAG reshapes the information pipeline around the model by dynamically retrieving relevant content from external knowledge sources such as internal reports, policies, manuals, or research documents. This grounds model outputs in controlled, up-to-date information, improving factual accuracy and contextual relevance without retraining the model.

From a managerial standpoint, this decoupling of knowledge from model capability is critical. Updating documents or policies immediately affects system behavior without requiring model updates. This makes RAG particularly attractive in regulated environments, where traceability, explainability, and control over information sources are essential. The primary cost of RAG lies upstream: documents must be curated, cleaned, segmented, embedded, and continuously maintained. Weak document quality or poorly designed retrieval pipelines directly undermine performance, regardless of model strength. However, once established, RAG infrastructures tend to be reusable across use cases and resist model evolution, reducing the risk of obsolescence when base models change [77].

If the task is highly repetitive and stable, and neither prompt engineering nor RAG delivers acceptable performance, fine-tuning becomes viable. Fine-tuning represents the most direct form of adaptation, as it alters the model itself. By retraining on proprietary data, organizations can align outputs with internal terminology, style, or procedures. Fine-tuned models are particularly effective for tasks like document classification, standardized report drafting, or summarization of technical standards. Because the model learns from examples rather than relying on prompts, results tend to be more consistent and predictable.

However, fine-tuning introduces significant maintenance and governance implications. Teams may become responsible for the learned behavior of the model, raising compliance and accountability questions under the EU AI Act, as discussed in Chapter 7. Moreover, fine-tuning tightly couples the solution to a specific base model. When a new and more capable base model becomes available, prior fine-tuning efforts may need to be repeated, effectively turning earlier investments into sunk costs [77, 78]. Fine-tuning therefore offers precision at the expense of flexibility and should be reserved for high-value, stable workflows where the investment can be justified.

Finally, if none of these interventions are appropriate, the organization may need to accept the model's limitations. Not every task is well-suited to current generative AI capabilities, and forcing a technical solution where none fits can waste resources and create unrealistic expectations. Recognizing when a task lies outside the productive range of available models is as important as knowing how to adapt them.

In practice, one rarely relies on a single technique in isolation. Mature deployments typically combine these approaches: prompts structure the interaction, RAG supplies authoritative context, and fine-tuning refines performance for specific high-value workflows. The decision flow in Figure 3.4 should therefore be understood as a diagnostic tool rather than a rigid sequence. It establishes priorities and helps managers avoid premature complexity, but does not preclude combining techniques as needs evolve.

The managerial objective is clarity about when each intervention adds value. Avoiding the illusion that prompt tricks alone can replace structure is as important as resisting the temptation to fine-tune indiscriminately at high cost and risk. Effective use of generative AI depends on aligning techniques with context and constraints, ensuring that technology adapts to the organization rather than forcing the organization to adapt to the technology.

3.2.4 When to turn to AI agents

As tasks move beyond single-inference use cases, a clear opportunity emerges: deploying generative AI not merely as a tool producing isolated outputs, but as an autonomous agent capable of executing multi-step workflows. When applied appropriately, agents enable a qualitative shift in automation. Rather than assisting individual tasks, they can coordinate entire processes including planning, execution, verification, and iteration. Early deployments already show tangible efficiency gains across domains such as customer support, data analysis, procurement, and internal operations, where agents reduce coordination overhead, standardize execution, and accelerate turnaround times in ways that are difficult to achieve through human labor alone [79, 80].

These gains, however, are not uniform across tasks. Figure 3.5 summarizes a high-level decision guide for distinguishing contexts where agentic approaches are likely to add value from those where they are not. A first consideration is temporal and structural complexity. Agents are most effective when work unfolds over multiple dependent steps executed over time, rather than as a single, self-contained interaction. In such workflows, agents can maintain context across steps, manage hand-offs between systems, and ensure consistent execution, reducing the coordination overhead that typically dominates human-driven processes.

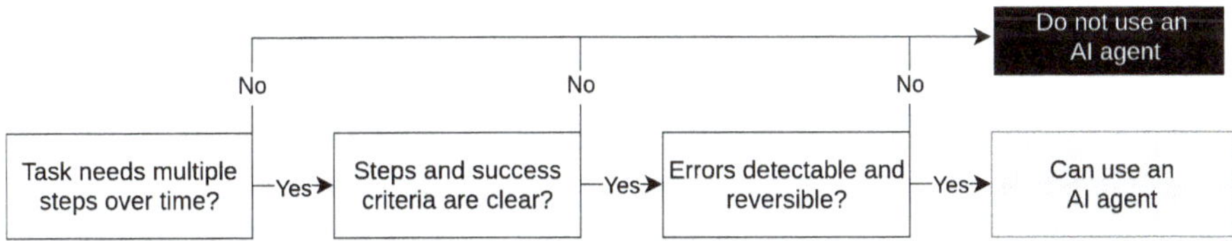

Figure 3.5: A simple decision framework to assess whether a task should be handled by an AI agent.

A second consideration is the clarity of success criteria. Agentic systems perform best when outputs can be evaluated against clearly defined acceptance criteria, even when those criteria rely on approximate targets or probabilistic thresholds. Clear success conditions enable validation, monitoring, and escalation, allowing teams to detect deviations early and intervene when necessary. Where success is highly subjective, context-dependent, or only recognizable in hindsight, increased autonomy becomes harder to justify and more difficult to govern.

A third and often decisive factor concerns error characteristics, in particular whether errors are detectable and reversible. In workflows where mistakes can be surfaced through checks, comparisons, or downstream signals and corrected at limited cost, agentic automation is more viable. Conversely, in domains where errors propagate silently, are difficult to detect, or carry severe legal, safety, or reputational consequences, agents should be tightly constrained or avoided altogether.

It is important to emphasize that the decision guide in Figure 3.5 intentionally abstracts away from many real-world complexities and should be understood as a high-level framing device rather than a comprehensive assessment methodology. In practice, agent suitability is shaped by a combination of technical design, organizational maturity, and governance arrangements, and rarely maps cleanly onto a small set of binary criteria. Tasks may mix automated and human-driven steps, evolve over time, and exhibit different risk profiles across stages. Error tolerance itself depends on architectural choices, monitoring mechanisms, and escalation paths. The figure is therefore best used to frame early discussions and rule out clearly unsuitable use cases, not to replace detailed design and risk analysis.

From a managerial perspective, this framing clarifies why agents should not be adopted indiscriminately. In domains where human performance is already highly reliable, where judgment is deeply contextual, or where the cost of failure is unacceptable, decision-support tools or narrowly scoped automation may deliver most of the value without introducing additional complexity. Agentic approaches are most compelling precisely where coordination overhead, inconsistency, or fragmentation, rather than task difficulty, is the dominant constraint.

In practice, successful deployments rarely involve full delegation. Instead, companies and institutions adopt selective and staged autonomy, assigning agents responsibility for bounded components of a workflow under defined oversight. Agents may conduct research, prepare analyses, classify requests, or draft outputs, while humans retain approval authority for consequential decisions. This mirrors existing accountability structures and is often easier to audit, as agentic systems can produce systematic logs of actions, confidence levels, and decision traces.

Selective autonomy is sustainable only when its outcomes are visible. Unlike single-shot generative AI, where a flawed output is immediately seen by the user, an agent operating over multiple steps can fail silently for extended periods: a misclassification propagates through downstream actions, a tool call returns the wrong record, an intermediate decision drifts from the intended policy. Production deployments therefore require deliberate observability: structured logs of each step the agent takes, recorded confidence levels and tool-use outcomes, explicit thresholds that trigger escalation to a human reviewer, and periodic audits comparing agent behavior against expected patterns. Monitoring drift over time is equally important, since the same prompt and the same agent configuration can produce different behavior as underlying models are updated. Organizations that treat observability as an afterthought typically discover problems only when they have already caused operational, financial, or reputational damage.

Finally, the use of agents does not relax foundational requirements around model choice, data governance, or infrastructure design. Because agentic systems rely on a generative AI backbone, all considerations discussed earlier regarding proprietary versus open models, data handling, cost structures, and compliance remain fully applicable.

3.2.5 Case study: adapting a generative AI system for internal knowledge work

A Germany-based industrial engineering group introduces a generative AI assistant to support project documentation across its energy and infrastructure divisions.

The team begins in a sandboxed environment using synthetic project scenarios based on public grid standards, avoiding exposure of sensitive infrastructure specifications. To establish an upper bound on achievable quality, they benchmark a leading proprietary model via API. The results confirm technical feasibility: the model produces coherent design notes with appropriate technical reasoning, though it lacks organizational tone and specific institutional knowledge.

With feasibility proven, the team works downward through progressively smaller models, testing both proprietary and open/open-weight variants available through managed services. A mid-size open/open-weight model delivers acceptable baseline performance at substantially lower cost. Because the team handles export-controlled infrastructure specifications across multiple EU jurisdictions, the option to deploy on-premises if needed provides strategic flexibility, even though initial deployment uses API access to avoid upfront infrastructure investment. The team treats deployability on-premises as a strategic option to preserve rather than a default to exercise, accepting the costs of the option only if regulatory or operational circumstances require it.

Before committing, they validate the shortlisted model on real project documentation under access controls. Performance holds in substance across both German and Spanish projects, but the outputs do not yet match the firm's expected tone and document structure, i. e. an issue of style and framing rather than missing knowledge. Rather than abandon the model, they treat this as a prompt engineering challenge.

Initial outputs are technically sound but stylistically inconsistent – some read like marketing copy, others like academic papers. The gap is not knowledge or reasoning capability, but tone and format. The central engineering office documents internal writing conventions: mandatory sections, preferred phrasing, and explicit uncertainty markers.

These are embedded as structured prompts. Within weeks, outputs align with internal standards, and engineers report that the system now "writes like we do." This intervention cost almost nothing and requires no model changes.

As usage expands, a different problem emerges. The system occasionally references obsolete regulations or ignores project-specific constraints documented in internal archives. In one case, a generated design rationale for a Spanish substation omits a site-specific environmental constraint – standard internal knowledge but absent from public sources. The gap is not style but information access.

The organization connects the system to internal repositories: approved engineering standards, project-specific dossiers, and regulatory interpretations. Documents have to be cleaned, segmented, and embedded before retrieval becomes reliable: a five-month effort that proves more demanding than anticipated. Once operational, the system retrieves and cites relevant internal documents when drafting. When standards are updated, changes propagate immediately without model modifications. This architectural choice decouples knowledge from the model, ensuring that institutional memory remains under control.

One narrow problem persists though. Quarterly investment committee summaries follow a rigid format and are archived for regulatory reporting. Despite prompts and retrieval, outputs vary in emphasis and structure, forcing manual normalization. Combined with monthly incident reports following similar formats, this represents 50+ high-stakes documents annually where inconsistency creates compliance risk.

Because the task is narrow, repetitive, and stable, fine-tuning becomes justifiable. However, rather than fine-tune the mid-size baseline model for a single use case, the team fine-tunes a smaller, more economical variant specifically for committee summaries and incident reports. This reflects the principle of minimum sufficient capability: the smallest model that delivers acceptable performance for a defined task. The lightweight fine-tuned model proves adequate and cost-effective for this workflow.

The final architecture combines techniques proportionately: the mid-size baseline model with structured prompts and RAG for routine documentation, the fine-tuned lightweight model for quarterly summaries and incident reports, and selective escalation to a stronger proprietary model via API for complex failure analyses where precision justifies additional cost. Escalation occurs in fewer than 3 % of cases.

After 20 months, documentation rework rates fall from 28 % to 9 %, saving an estimated 1,850 engineering hours annually. The company avoids locking into a single technique or model, while reducing risk and maintaining architectural flexibility as models evolve. The case showcases that effective deployment depends on matching interventions to specific performance gaps rather than applying uniform solutions.

3.3 The economics of generative AI

From a financial perspective, generative AI operates like a metered utility: every query, every response, and every token processed carries a measurable cost. In vendor-hosted systems, these costs are visible in real time through usage dashboards that track tokens consumed. In self-hosted deployments, the same economic logic applies through GPU hours, cloud credits, electricity consumption, and on-premises infrastructure expenditure. Whether paid to external providers or absorbed internally, each compute operation ultimately appears on the cost ledger.

What distinguishes AI economics from traditional software is not simply that costs are metered, the four main cost categories – infrastructure, data, operations, and talent – interact in ways that create long-term commitments extending well beyond initial deployment. Understanding these dynamics requires examining four interdependent cost categories: infrastructure, data, operations, and talent. Unlike traditional IT projects where categories can be optimized independently, AI costs interact in ways that make trade-offs inevitable. Reducing infrastructure expenditure by choosing lower-tier services may increase operational costs through degraded performance. Minimizing data curation investment accelerates deployment but creates persistent quality and maintenance burdens. Relying on external consultants rather than building internal capability reduces short-term costs but creates strategic dependencies and knowledge loss.

As AI adoption spreads across business units, transparent cost allocation becomes essential for maintaining accountability and enabling informed prioritization decisions. Organizations must establish clear mechanisms for tracking usage at the project or application level, whether through charge-back systems that bill business units directly or show-back approaches that make costs visible without formal transfers. Without such mechanisms, AI spending quickly becomes opaque, weakening the connection between expenditure and value creation [57].

The following sections examine each cost category in detail, then establish principles for strategic budgeting that accounts for the distinctive economics of generative AI deployment. Not all costs may be encountered by all companies, nor will they be associated with the same impact on a company's budget; what counts for a company depends on its aims, the chosen AI system, and the level of complexity required to more effectively address the problems at hand. However, having a clear picture of what to account for, and dealing with an economic checklist, may help companies to be more pragmatic about their choices, after assigning numbers that reflect their own condition.

3.3.1 Infrastructure costs

Infrastructure costs encompass the foundational computational capacity required to deploy and operate AI systems, whether through external API providers or self-hosted environments. Unlike most traditional software, where infrastructure requirements stabilize once deployment architecture is established, AI infrastructure decisions create lasting financial commitments and strategic dependencies that constrain future flexibility.

The fundamental choice between API-based and self-hosted deployment determines the structure of all subsequent infrastructure costs. API-based models eliminate infrastructure management overhead but introduce variable operating costs tightly coupled to provider pricing, model capability, and feature selection. What appears economical during pilot phases can become prohibitively expensive once systems are integrated into core business processes. A customer-facing application processing millions of requests per month can incur recurring API expenditures that exceed traditional enterprise software licensing costs by an order of magnitude.

Self-hosted deployments, whether in public cloud environments or on-premises, provide greater cost predictability once infrastructure is provisioned and stabilized. However, they demand substantial upfront capacity planning and specialized expertise to optimize performance, manage failures, and control resource utilization. Organizations must provision hardware capable of handling peak demand while maintaining acceptable response times, which often means accepting significant idle capacity during off-peak periods. The relationship between performance requirements and infrastructure investment is highly non-linear. Systems designed to guarantee sub-second responses under peak load operate under a fundamentally different cost regime than those that tolerate multi-second delays during periods of lower demand. Reducing target latency from 500 milliseconds to 100 milliseconds may require provisioning several times more serving capacity, as systems must be sized for worst-case concurrency rather than average utilization.

Fine-tuning models for specialized tasks brings additional infrastructure burdens. Fine-tuning itself demands substantial computational resources, typically requiring access to high-performance GPUs for hours or days depending on model size and dataset scale. Beyond the training phase, operating multiple customized model variants introduces ongoing serving costs and operational complexity. Each fine-tuned model must be hosted, versioned, and maintained separately, multiplying infrastructure requirements compared to relying on a single base model.

Energy consumption further amplifies infrastructure costs, whether charged directly through cloud billing or embedded indirectly in API pricing. As global investment in AI infrastructure approaches a projected $2 trillion by 2030, providers increasingly internalize environmental costs into their pricing models [81]. Those who plan long-term AI deployments must account for the possibility that energy-related cost components may grow faster than computational efficiency improves.

Infrastructure decisions made early tend to lock in future cost trajectories and constrain strategic flexibility. Applications tightly coupled to a specific provider's API or infrastructure stack may require substantial re-engineering to migrate, even when pricing, compliance requirements, or strategic priorities change. Moving from one API provider to another often necessitates re-validating system behavior, re-engineering prompts, and potentially retraining fine-tuned models. Self-hosted systems face different but equally significant migration costs when transitioning between cloud platforms or upgrading underlying hardware architectures. Industry analyses consistently identify infrastructure cost and integration complexity as major inhibitors of AI scaling, particularly for organizations without dedicated engineering capacity to manage these trade-offs [81, 82]. The managerial implication is that infrastructure planning for AI is not a technical afterthought but a strategic decision with long-term financial and structural consequences.

3.3.2 Data costs

Data costs represent the inputs that must be continuously maintained: the knowledge bases, examples, prompt libraries, and reference sets that ground system behavior and shape outputs. Unlike infrastructure expenses that stabilize once deployment architecture is established, data-related costs evolve continuously as organizational reality changes. These costs are frequently underestimated because they appear preparatory during initial deployment but persist and compound throughout the system's operational life.

The nature of this challenge becomes clear through a simple temporal thought experiment. A generative assistant deployed in 2028 will be exposed in 2030 to documents, terminology and user expectations that did not exist at the time of its initial configuration. Internal knowledge bases expand, policies are revised, product descriptions change, and language evolves. If the data sources that ground system behavior are not actively maintained, the system gradually becomes misaligned with current reality. Outputs may remain fluent, but relevance, factual accuracy, and compliance deteriorate.

Consider a customer service system that retrieves responses from a product catalogue containing a discontinued product line. When customers ask about those products, the model may continue to provide confident, detailed responses based on outdated documentation. The answers appear helpful and coherent, yet direct customers toward options that no longer exist. Similarly, a contract analysis tool may continue to reference regulatory requirements that have been superseded, or use terminology from structures that have been reorganized. In each case, the model's linguistic fluency masks the decay of its grounding data.

This degradation is particularly difficult to detect. Unlike software bugs that produce errors or crashes, data drift manifests as subtle misalignment that surfaces inconsistently. Generative models excel at producing plausible responses even when underlying information is outdated or incomplete (see Chapter 6). Performance appears stable until errors emerge in high-impact situations: a misquoted policy during an audit, an outdated regulatory citation in a compliance report, or incorrect product information reaching a dissatisfied customer. By the time drift becomes visible, reputational or operational damage may already have occurred.

Maintaining data quality therefore requires sustained investment across multiple input categories, each with distinct maintenance requirements and cost profiles.

Retrieval corpora for RAG systems must evolve continuously as internal knowledge changes. Regulatory databases require updates as rules shift across jurisdictions, product catalogs need synchronization as specifications evolve, internal documentation demands revision as processes change, and policy repositories must reflect current governance frameworks. Unlike training data for traditional Machine Learning models, which can remain static between retraining cycles, RAG knowledge bases degrade immediately when underlying information becomes outdated. Documents must be cleaned, segmented, embedded, and version-controlled. Large organizations may require dedicated personnel to curate document sets across multiple domains, with the effort scaling proportionally to the breadth of knowledge the system must cover.

Prompt libraries require active curation as language, priorities, and workflows shift. Well-engineered prompts embody institutional knowledge about how to frame tasks, structure outputs, and maintain tone. As business contexts evolve, prompts must be revised to reflect new terminology, updated processes, and changing expectations. When maintained systematically, prompt libraries function as reusable assets that survive model upgrades. However, without deliberate versioning, documentation, and testing, fragmented prompt collections accumulate and become difficult to maintain, audit, or transfer across teams.

Evaluation datasets and examples must evolve alongside system use to reflect the expanding range of contexts encountered in production. Initial evaluation sets are necessarily based on anticipated use cases and known challenges. As systems are deployed, however, they are exposed to a broader diversity of inputs, usage patterns, and domain-specific nuances that were not fully visible at design time. Sustaining performance therefore depends on continuously enriching evaluation data with newly observed scenarios. This includes incorporating previously unseen inputs, representative boundary cases, and emerging interaction patterns, and validating system behavior against updated expectations. Doing so requires ongoing involvement from subject matter experts to review examples, annotate relevant conditions, and confirm that outputs remain aligned with operational and regulatory requirements. Over time, this iterative expansion of evaluation datasets transforms testing from a one-off validation exercise into a living capability that supports sustained reliability and learning.

The scale and persistence of this curation work is frequently underestimated by project teams and budget holders. What distinguishes generative AI from traditional software maintenance is not simply that data changes, but that the opacity of how data affects model responses makes it difficult to predict when updates are needed, and the continuous exposure to new inputs means there is no stable baseline against which to freeze data requirements.

Compliance and governance data introduce an additional layer of persistent cost. Privacy frameworks such as GDPR impose legal, governance, and technical requirements that persist throughout the system lifecycle [83, 84]. Every piece of data that feeds into the system (retrieval corpora, training examples, prompt templates, evaluation sets) must be inventoried, classified by sensitivity, and managed according to retention policies. Subject rights such as erasure or portability must be accommodated, requiring mechanisms to identify and remove specific data points from knowledge bases or example sets. These obligations apply not only to user-facing data but to all data assets used to shape system behavior. Companies operating across multiple jurisdictions face compounding costs as privacy regimes diverge, requiring parallel governance structures and region-specific data handling procedures.

Unlike one-time investments in model selection or initial infrastructure provisioning, data governance and maintenance become long-term operational priorities that grow with business complexity. Data standardization, quality assurance, regulatory alignment, and drift monitoring are not preparatory activities that diminish after deployment. They are recurring expenses that escalate as the organization scales, enters new markets, or integrates generative AI into additional workflows. Budgeting for data in generative AI initiatives therefore means planning for recurring expenditure that persists and compounds over time, not a fixed allocation that tapers as the system matures.

3.3.3 Operational costs

Operational costs encompass the runtime processes and ongoing activities required to keep generative AI systems functioning reliably in production. While infrastructure costs reflect capacity planning and deployment architecture, and data costs reflect the inputs that ground system behavior, operational costs capture what it takes to actually run the system day-to-day: managing variable computational consumption, monitoring quality, handling model updates, defending against emerging threats, and maintaining compliance records. These costs persist long after initial deployment and typically increase as systems mature and integrate more deeply into workflows.

Computational consumption in production scales with usage intensity and context complexity in ways that differ fundamentally from traditional software licensing. Unlike conventional applications where costs per user or seat remain consistent regardless of usage patterns, generative AI systems consume tokens proportional to input length, output length, and retrieval breadth. A pilot deployment processing concise prompts may encounter cost escalation when deployed widely, as users naturally explore the system's boundaries, request more comprehensive analyses, or engage in extended interactions.

Managing context windows becomes a continuous operational practice rather than a one-time configuration task. When users access larger contexts, pull in additional documents, or carry conversations longer than expected, token usage and costs can grow unpredictably. Organizations need to track how the system is being used in production, develop strategies to trim unnecessary context,[6] and possibly establish usage limits or tiered service levels to keep expenses manageable. Costs scale non-linearly with conversation depth, retrieval breadth, and prompt complexity (all dimensions influenced by user actions rather than system design alone). This variability demands active cost monitoring, budget forecasting based on usage trajectories rather than fixed capacity assumptions, and potential architectural interventions when actual consumption patterns deviate significantly from projections.

Quality monitoring in generative and multi-agent systems extends beyond traditional software testing or static accuracy metrics. Outputs must be assessed not only for factual correctness, but also for tone, appropriateness, coherence, and alignment with mission, voice, and values. Techniques such as hallucination detection[7] support this process by identifying plausible but incorrect outputs, typically through a combination of automated signals and structured human review. For example, a legal contract analysis system may generate summaries that are linguistically fluent and authoritative, yet omit critical clauses or mischaracterize obligations. Detecting such issues reliably requires domain expertise and contextual judgment rather than purely automated checks. Unlike batch-processing systems, where quality can be verified prior to deployment, generative systems operate interactively and evolve through use. Maintaining quality therefore relies on continuous sampling, logging, and retrospective analysis to track outputs over time and across contexts. As systems scale, this quality assurance capability becomes an integral part of the production architecture. It requires dedicated infrastructure for storing interaction logs, analytical tooling to surface patterns and anomalies, and skilled personnel to interpret findings and guide adjustments. While this monitoring layer represents a non-trivial operational investment, it helps sustain trust, consistency, and accountability as generative systems move into routine use.

Model version migration is a recurring operational event unique to API-based generative AI deployments. Providers periodically deprecate models, change pricing, or release new versions with different performance characteristics. Each transition imposes the same revalidation and prompt-adjustment work described in Section 3.3.1, but on the provider's schedule rather than the organization's, plus a cost-benefit reassessment of whether to migrate or stay on legacy versions and communication with stakeholders about changed capabilities. Organizations running several generative AI systems may face simultaneous migrations across providers and use cases, creating coordination challenges and resource spikes.

6 In April 2025, Sam Altman, CEO of OpenAI, noted that omitting courtesies like "please" and "thank you" in prompts can reduce electricity consumption. Without going as far as to link these subtleties to massive costs, the story is just to remind that optimizing the querying process, especially in large organizations, may produce a quantifiable impact.

7 See Chapter 6.

Security monitoring requires continuous attention to threats that are difficult to address using standard software security practices. While traditional applications can validate inputs against predefined rules and schemas, generative AI systems operate on open-ended natural language, often across multiple steps and persistent internal states, making it hard to distinguish between legitimate requests and adversarial attempts to manipulate system behavior. Users may craft inputs designed to override safety constraints, extract sensitive information from knowledge bases, or bypass intended usage boundaries, including by spreading manipulation across sequential interactions or indirectly influencing tool calls and agent coordination logic.[8] These risks evolve as new manipulation techniques emerge, particularly in systems where agents retain memory or interact with other agents over time, demanding continuous updates of defensive measures and monitoring protocols. While conventional software security can often address a large class of threats through configuration, access controls, and stable threat models, generative AI security places greater weight on continuous monitoring and adaptation, as new manipulation techniques may emerge through interaction patterns, multi-step actions, or collective agent dynamics rather than isolated inputs.

Governance and audit functions introduce operational layers distinct from traditional Machine Learning systems. Auditability requires maintaining records not only of model versions and configurations but of the specific context included in individual interactions, and, in agent-based systems, of the intermediate decisions, tool invocations, and inter-agent messages that lead to an outcome, particularly for high-stakes applications subject to regulatory scrutiny. The EU AI Act's transparency obligations for high-risk AI systems may necessitate explainability mechanisms, documentation of decision rationales, and human oversight processes that add both technical and administrative overhead, especially where responsibility cannot be attributed to a single inference but to a chain of coordinated actions. For customer-facing or decision-support applications, organizations may need to log prompts, retrieved documents, model outputs, and user feedback, as well as agent states and execution traces, to support compliance investigations, dispute resolution, or quality improvement initiatives. These records accumulate rapidly and require storage, indexing, and retrieval infrastructure comparable to regulatory reporting systems.

Operational costs often increase non-linearly with system maturity and integration depth. A pilot project with limited scope and controlled user base might require minimal monitoring, ad-hoc quality review, and informal documentation. A production system handling thousands of interactions daily, or coordinating multiple agents across workflows, demands formal processes, dedicated personnel, automated monitoring infrastructure, and systematic incident response capabilities. As generative AI systems become embedded in customer-facing operations, internal decision support, or regulated workflows, particularly in the form of autonomous or semi-autonomous agents,

8 See Chapter 6.

their operational requirements converge with those of mission-critical infrastructure: permanent cost centers requiring professional management, governance oversight, and institutional knowledge preservation.

3.3.4 Talent costs

AI adoption places sustained pressure on internal capabilities in ways that differ from conventional IT projects. The market for AI talent remains highly competitive, particularly for profiles combining technical expertise, domain knowledge, and governance awareness. Data scientists, Machine Learning engineers, and AI governance specialists command compensation well above traditional software engineering roles and are difficult to recruit and retain. Academic institutions in the United States report that demand for advanced AI talent continues to outpace supply, with companies increasingly recruiting students directly from universities before graduation [85]. While this evidence is US-based, similar dynamics can reasonably be expected to emerge in Europe and other regions as generative AI adoption accelerates and competition for specialized skills intensifies.

These pressures extend well beyond hiring. AI technologies evolve rapidly, and skills depreciate faster than in many other technical domains. Techniques regarded as state-of-the-art in 2027 may be superseded by fundamentally different approaches within a few years. As a result, organizations must invest continuously in training, experimentation time, and knowledge renewal to avoid the gradual erosion of internal expertise.

Effective AI deployment also depends on sustained interdisciplinary collaboration between technical teams, domain experts, legal counsel, risk managers, and business stakeholders. While external consultants can accelerate specific initiatives, long-term value creation relies on internal capability and institutional memory. Those who treat AI expertise as purely contractual often struggle to maintain, adapt, or govern systems once external support is withdrawn.

The cost of this collaboration is frequently invisible in budgets because it does not appear as a discrete line item. It surfaces instead as time spent in joint reviews, in cross-functional escalation paths, in the recalibration meetings that translate domain requirements into technical decisions and compliance constraints into deployment specifications. These are not overhead; they are how AI systems acquire the contextual fit and accountability structures that make them usable in regulated environments. Organizations that allocate time and authority for these exchanges find that the resulting systems are more robust and more easily governed. Those that treat interdisciplinary coordination as discretionary discover, often late, that the absence of shared understanding produces systems no single function can effectively maintain. In practice, this means budgeting for things that traditional IT projects rarely budget for: protected time for domain experts to review system outputs, regular calibration sessions between business owners and engineering teams, joint authority over deployment thresholds, and shared documentation that translates between technical and operational vocabularies. None of these is expensive in absolute terms, but each requires deliberate allocation rather than emerging spontaneously from goodwill.

The talent challenge is therefore not merely a recruitment issue, but a long-term capability-building effort. Budgets must account not only for competitive salaries, but for continuous learning, knowledge retention, and the overhead required to sustain effective interdisciplinary teams.

3.4 Strategic budgeting principles

Effective AI budgeting does not require abandoning established managerial discipline. On the contrary, organizations that succeed tend to apply familiar financial principles with greater precision, adapting them to the distinctive cost dynamics of AI systems. Predicting costs perfectly is often infeasible; the objective is thus to structure financial decisions so that uncertainty, growth, and dependency remain governable over time.

Budget across the full operational lifecycle. Mature organizations distinguish clearly between experimentation and production. AI initiatives benefit from the same separation. Early-stage budgets are designed to validate feasibility under controlled conditions, while operational budgets are structured to support sustained use under real demand, governance constraints, and service expectations.

In practice, this means treating development and validation funding as a bounded investment with explicit learning objectives, and treating operational funding as a separate, longer-horizon commitment reviewed against stability, scalability, and risk. For example, an AI-based customer support assistant may be approved with a capped pilot budget to establish baseline performance and feasibility, followed by a multi-year operational envelope tied to usage growth, service-level targets, and oversight requirements. This ensures that financial scrutiny increases, rather than decreases, as systems become embedded in core workflows. The separation matters more in AI than in conventional IT because the gap between pilot economics and production economics is wider and less predictable: a pilot consuming a few thousand euros per month in API calls can become a deployment consuming hundreds of thousands monthly through usage growth alone, without any change in architecture.

Anchor budgets to business-defined performance thresholds. Successful organizations resist the temptation to treat AI performance as an open-ended optimization problem. Instead, they define in advance what constitutes acceptable performance from a business perspective and budget to maintain that level reliably. By committing resources to a clearly articulated performance band, teams can focus on consistency, robustness, and user trust rather than incremental technical gains. Improvements beyond that band are framed as strategic enhancements, assessed against cost, value, and opportunity cost, rather than absorbed implicitly into operational spend. For instance, maintaining response latency below a threshold that preserves user satisfaction may be funded as a standing obligation, while further reductions require explicit justification and approval. This discipline is particularly important for AI because, unlike most software, AI systems offer no natural stopping point: a more capable model, a larger context window, or a more refined prompt is almost always available at higher cost. Without a defined performance band, technical teams optimize continuously and budgets drift upward by default rather than by decision.

Price flexibility and reversibility explicitly. Organizations that retain strategic freedom treat flexibility as a deliberate investment rather than an incidental by-product. This often involves accepting higher initial costs to avoid irreversible dependencies on specific vendors, architectures, or external expertise. Budgeting for flexibility may include maintaining compatibility with multiple model providers, investing in internal capabilities alongside external partners, or designing modular system boundaries that can evolve independently. While these choices rarely minimize short-term expenditure, they preserve the ability to adapt as regulatory conditions, pricing structures, or strategic priorities change. Over time, this optionality often proves more valuable than early cost savings. Vendor lock-in is sharper in AI than in many other software domains, for the migration reasons set out in Section 3.3.1: dependencies harden quickly and are costly to unwind. The strategic implication is what matters here: flexibility purchased upfront is typically cheaper than flexibility recovered after those dependencies have set.

Align financial expectations with organizational adoption cycles. Experienced leaders recognize that value from AI systems emerges progressively. Users require time to adapt, workflows must be reshaped, and governance mechanisms must stabilize. Budgeting that accommodates staged value realization creates space for learning without distorting incentives.

Rather than forcing early returns, effective budgeting anticipates phases of pilot, integration, and consolidation, with value expectations calibrated accordingly. Neutral or negative ROI (see Chapter 4 for details) in early operational periods is treated as part of the transition from experimentation to production, provided that learning is systematic and adoption is advancing. This approach supports more honest evaluation and more durable impact. AI adoption cycles tend to be longer than conventional software adoption cycles because value depends not only on system capability but on trust formation, workflow redesign, and the gradual extension of use into higher-stakes decisions. Premature ROI demands force organizations to either narrow scope to demonstrable wins or abandon initiatives whose returns would have materialized given more time.

Organizations that apply these principles approach AI as a strategic production capability rather than a series of isolated projects. They distinguish clearly between building and running systems, define performance ambition deliberately, invest in flexibility where it matters, and align financial expectations with the actual changes. In doing so, they preserve control, resilience, and strategic choice as AI systems move from experimentation into sustained use.

3.4.1 Case study: budgeting an AI customer support assistant

This case study examines how a mid-size Slovakian consumer telecoms operator handling several thousand customer inquiries weekly applies strategic budgeting principles when introducing an AI-based customer support assistant, while operating under typical constraints. The company defines a deliberately bounded objective: the assistant is intended to deflect a share of repetitive inquiries, stabilize response times during peak demand, and support human agents rather than replace them. The first-year deflection target is set at roughly 25 % of routine inquiries, calibrated as ambitious but achievable rather than transformative. While strategically modest, the initiative sits at the intersection of customer experience, IT operations, compliance, and workforce concerns, requiring coordination across multiple functions from the outset.

By distinguishing explicitly between validation and sustained operation, the company structures its budgeting decisions in stages, though not without negotiation. A capped development budget of €50,000 is approved to configure prompts, integrate with the ticketing system, and run a time-limited pilot using a proprietary LLM accessed via API. This budget is framed explicitly as a learning investment, but expectations differ across stakeholders: IT prioritizes technical feasibility, customer operations focuses on usability, and compliance seeks early evidence of controllability. Operational funding is addressed through a separate decision, subject to defined conditions. Rather than committing immediately to a fixed multi-year envelope, the company specifies an operational budget range of approximately €30,000 to €40,000 monthly linked to usage scenarios and service-level bands. Variable costs associated with usage-based pricing, monitoring, logging, and human oversight are consolidated under a single operational owner, improving financial visibility while preserving flexibility as demand evolves.

Performance expectations are anchored to business-defined thresholds, but these thresholds are themselves the subject of trade-offs. Response time and coverage targets are set to be sufficient for customer satisfaction and agent productivity, recognizing that tighter targets would materially increase infrastructure and governance costs. Proposals for performance improvements beyond this range are channeled through a formal escalation process, ensuring that optimization remains a managerial decision rather than an implicit technical trajectory. Flexibility is treated as a priced option rather than an absolute requirement. The company preserves the ability to rebalance usage across model providers and explore alternative models for internal workflows, while accepting selective coupling where switching costs are deemed manageable. These choices reflect explicit trade-offs between short-term efficiency and long-term optionality, rather than a pursuit of architectural purity.

Finally, financial expectations are aligned with adoption dynamics. The first operational year prioritizes stabilization, user onboarding, and governance calibration over immediate return. Value realization is assessed progressively as workflows adapt and usage patterns stabilize, with the understanding that both costs and benefits will remain fluid during this phase. Several of the decisions described above were revised as the pilot generated evidence: initial threshold settings proved too restrictive and were relaxed after the first quarter, the operational budget range was widened once usage variability became clearer, and the original allocation of compliance oversight was reorganized when escalation paths failed in their first test. What this section presents is the structure that emerged from iteration, not its first articulation. Taken together, the case illustrates that effective AI budgeting is less about enforcing ideal structures than about making trade-offs explicit. By separating validation from operation, constraining performance ambition deliberately, pricing flexibility where it matters most, and revisiting assumptions as evidence accumulates, the company maintains control and strategic choice as the assistant becomes embedded in everyday operations.

3.5 Summary: personalized alignment

AI is a broad field encompassing many algorithmic solutions whose scope and capabilities continue to expand. Effective adoption therefore requires aligning the capabilities of each AI system with the organization's actual needs before selecting a model. This is similar to choosing a vehicle: a delivery van, a family car, and a racing bike all serve different purposes. Performance depends less on raw capability than on suitability to the task. The more capable system is not always the better one; in many deployments, a smaller and more constrained model produces more predictable behavior, lower costs, and clearer accountability than a larger general-purpose alternative. What recurs across all these dimensions is a single underlying trade-off between capability and control: each increase in autonomy, complexity, or scale expands what the system can do while also expanding what must be governed, monitored, and maintained.

Likewise, there is no one-size-fits-all checklist to choose the perfect AI for each company. Instead, there are several key dimensions to be considered (those surveyed in this chapter), plus multiple tiny refinements (e. g., alignment with a company's value proposition, or sustainability protocols, or user/tech-centrism, or others) that will tailor the decision. The same reasoning applies to costs, too. While we have surveyed the most relevant cost items associated with AI systems, their magnitude and impact depend on the company: its size, its tasks, its structure, and so on. What does not depend on the company is the structural character of these costs: they are recurring rather than one-time, they interact rather than optimize independently, and they tend to grow as systems become more deeply embedded in operational workflows. Budgeting accordingly, i. e. treating AI as evolving operational infrastructure rather than as a discrete capital investment, is a precondition for sustained value rather than a refinement applied later.

Taking what was presented here as a guide, leaders can then adapt and align the general guidelines to their specific needs, towards responsible and effective AI adoption.

4 Identifying, selecting, and tracking AI use cases

Generative AI has evolved from an experimental and scientific field into a decisive driver of business performance. Yet many organizations still struggle to identify the right use cases, select them effectively, and track their returns in a meaningful way. This section offers a comprehensive overview on how to approach generative AI adoption with strategic clarity, ensuring that enthusiasm translates into measurable and sustainable value.

4.1 From vision to use cases: where to begin

The worst way to start a generative AI journey is by declaring *"We need to build an agent"*. As discussed in the previous chapter, technology should never precede purpose. A successful AI strategy begins with identifying meaningful opportunities where intelligent systems can augment decision-making, reduce bottlenecks, or unlock entirely new growth dynamics. Use case discovery should be driven from the ground up. Mid-level managers and operational experts are best positioned to recognize inefficiencies, repetitive decision patterns, and decision points where context matters. It is fundamental to encourage them to participate in feedback systems or structured ideation workshops where pain points are translated into candidate AI applications. However, managers should never forget to balance bottom-up creativity with top-down strategic alignment, ensuring that proposed use cases connect to corporate objectives such as revenue growth, cost efficiency, customer satisfaction, or competitive differentiation.

Not all problems are well-suited for generative AI. Good use cases, such as those surveyed in Chapter 2, typically share several characteristics: they involve dynamic decision-making with non-deterministic choices that depend on situational context, such as resolving complex customer issues or customizing product recommendations; they address human bottlenecks where expert judgment is needed but experts are scarce or overloaded (e. g., legal review, compliance checks, customer onboarding); they benefit from continuity, requiring 24/7 responsiveness such as IT, HR, or client support; they enable high personalization where tailored communication or adaptive offers can significantly enhance user experience or sales conversion; they exhibit tolerance for imperfection, such as in domains where small errors can be tolerated and corrected easily, unlike payroll or mission-critical finance where 100 % accuracy is non-negotiable; they involve repetitive and tedious work that employees themselves wish to offload, building enthusiasm around AI integration; and they offer measurable outcomes, since generative AI systems are inherently goal-driven.

Companies and institutions should avoid automating opaque processes that rely entirely on tacit individual knowledge (on the lines of "Ask Sarah, she's the only one who knows how it's done"). For generative AI to succeed, workflows must be well-defined, documented, and measurable. Additionally, we strongly recommend steering clear of

https://doi.org/10.1515/9783112254103-004

use cases where data is unavailable, unreliable, or legally restricted; where ethical or reputational risks are high and poorly understood; where resistance is likely to derail adoption; or where simpler non-AI solutions, such as process redesign or basic automation, would suffice. Finally, be careful for tasks that are vaguely defined, or that rely on traditional expertise or custom:[1] there, LLMs may unnecessarily struggle due to poor definitions that hamper training and clear responses.

4.2 The ideation workshop

An ideation workshop provides a structured mechanism to surface generative AI opportunities across the organization while preserving strategic coherence. Its primary function is not to generate a large volume of ideas, but to channel creativity towards problems where adaptive intelligence can deliver material value. When designed properly, such workshops reduce the risk of opportunistic experimentation and help align early initiatives with operational priorities and governance constraints.

The process typically begins with a shared grounding phase.[2] Participants are introduced to what generative AI is, and equally to what it is not. This distinction is essential to avoid unrealistic expectations or misapplication. Core concepts such as prompt engineering, RAG, fine-tuning, agentic workflows, biases, and hallucinations are reviewed. The objective is not technical mastery, but the establishment of a shared conceptual language that allows participants from different functions to reason consistently about capabilities and limitations. This phase also includes concrete examples of successful generative AI deployments, both within the industry and in adjacent sectors, illustrating how intelligence, adaptability, or continuous reasoning can be embedded into real workflows.

Once a shared understanding is established, teams are invited to explore where such capabilities could plausibly unlock value. Rather than starting from tools, ideation is framed around friction points and decision bottlenecks. Typical prompts include areas where significant time is spent on repetitive judgement calls, where customers or employees experience recurring delays or inconsistencies, or where improved real-time insight would materially affect outcomes. Framing ideation in this way helps ensure that proposals remain anchored in business needs rather than technological novelty.

In this sense, ideation workshops function less as creativity exercises and more as alignment mechanisms. They translate abstract technological possibilities into a con-

1 For instance, attempting to automatize the localization of marketing assets produced abroad, which require the translation of the original asset, but also putting it into the specific cultural context, to avoid misconceptions or poor cultural alignment. What is normal in a certain country may be a double-meaning pun in another, and LLMs are known to struggle in ambiguous linguistic domains [86].

2 The material presented throughout this book is intended to provide the conceptual foundation necessary to conduct or participate meaningfully in such grounding sessions.

strained set of business-relevant hypotheses that can be evaluated, prioritized, and, where appropriate, taken forward into structured experimentation.

A typical structure spans 2–3 sessions over 2–4 weeks. The first session (2–3 hours) focuses on education and framing with cross-functional participants from operations, sales, marketing, IT, finance, HR, and legal. The second session (3–4 hours) drives divergent ideation, using structured inputs such as "Where do we spend the most time on repetitive decisions? Where do customers or employees experience friction? What insights do we wish we had in real time?" to generate 10–20 candidate use cases. The third session (3–4 hours) focuses on convergent prioritization: discard ideas that could be achieved through simpler automation or process redesign, and focus instead on problems requiring contextual understanding, learning from data, or human-like reasoning. Finally, score the remaining use cases on Feasibility, Investment, and Value to produce a prioritized shortlist of 3–5 use cases for pilot development.

4.3 Selecting and prioritizing use cases

Selecting and prioritizing use cases is a familiar activity in digital transformation initiatives. Organizations have long assessed feasibility, cost, and value when deciding where to invest in new technologies. Generative AI does not change this logic. What it changes is how these criteria behave in practice, and how quickly poor calibration can translate into operational risk or strategic lock-in.

Feasibility | Investment | Value

Each candidate use case can be assessed along these three axes using a simple scoring rubric. The purpose of scoring is not numerical precision, but to surface asymmetries and hidden trade-offs. In early phases, prioritization typically favors so-called *low-hanging fruits*. In AI contexts, however, these are not necessarily the most technically sophisticated initiatives, but those that combine readiness with bounded risk and clearly observable impact.

Feasibility in AI extends well beyond technical viability. While data availability and model maturity remain important, the specific conditions often play a decisive role. Use cases that appear straightforward from a modeling perspective may still require clear process ownership, coherent data governance, and engagement from operational teams to be implemented effectively. Conversely, technically demanding initiatives can be delivered successfully when workflows are stable, incentives are aligned, and feedback loops are clearly defined. In practice, feasibility in AI is shaped less by algorithmic complexity alone and more by the clarity of underlying processes and the organization's readiness to integrate AI into everyday operations. Assessing feasibility through this broader lens leads to better positioning when prioritize initiatives that can move from experimentation to sustained use.

Investment should be assessed as a trajectory rather than a static budget line. As discussed in the previous chapter, AI-related costs span four interdependent categories: infrastructure, data, operations and talent. What matters at the use-case selection stage is not only their initial magnitude, but how they evolve as a system moves from pilot to production. Early experiments frequently underestimate downstream expenditure associated with validation, monitoring, and governance. In addition to infrastructure and development costs, investment includes the sustained involvement of domain experts, the opportunity cost of scarce engineering capacity, and the financial or reputational impact of errors once systems are embedded in operational workflows.

Value in AI is rarely confined to immediate efficiency gains. While time savings, cost reductions, and accuracy improvements are important, many high-impact use cases generate value indirectly by creating reusable capabilities. These include improved data assets, continuous learning, and enhanced decision quality across multiple processes. Such benefits compound over time but are difficult to capture using traditional ROI calculations (addressed in more detail later in this chapter). As a result, early pilots should be evaluated not only on direct outcomes, but also on the capabilities they enable.

When considered jointly, these dimensions reveal recurring adoption patterns across sectors. As discussed in Chapter 2, organizations often begin with gateway use cases, such as internal knowledge retrieval or support agents. These applications offer limited risk, visible benefits, and strong learning effects. Their primary value lies not only in operational gains, but in familiarizing teams with AI-assisted workflows, validation practices, and governance requirements.

Over time, these initial applications evolve into more specialized, domain-specific systems. This progression is path-dependent: early choices influence data availability, architectural options, and confidence. Use case selection therefore becomes an exercise in portfolio management, balancing short-term returns against longer-term capability building under uncertainty.

4.4 Managing a use case portfolio

The Enterprise AI adoption matrix (Table 4.1) relates strategic importance and technical complexity to guide implementation decisions. Each cell in the matrix corresponds to a typical implementation pattern based on these two dimensions. The matrix serves as an analytical reference rather than a prescriptive tool; constraints and readiness ultimately shape implementation choices. Next, we survey the matrix cases.

Low complexity, low strategic importance: Buy Standard. Use off-the-shelf generative tools with minimal customization. This approach fits internal productivity use cases where speed and cost efficiency matter more than control. For example, deploying a vendor-provided meeting summarization or document drafting service via an API falls into this category, as outputs are generic and do not affect competitive positioning.

Table 4.1: Enterprise AI adoption matrix.

Technical complexity	Strategic importance		
	Low	Medium	High
High	**Buy strategic** Vendor partnerships Platform customization	**Hybrid strategic** Mixed vendor–internal Strategic integration	**Build** Core IP development Full control
Medium	**Buy custom** Modified solutions Partial integration	**Balanced mix** Selective building Strategic buying	**Hybrid** Build core features Buy commodity parts
Low	**Buy standard** Off-the-shelf Quick deployment	**Selective Build** Basic customization Limited integration	**Build simple** Basic integration Standard features

Low complexity, medium strategic importance: Selective Build. Start from vendor-provided generative capabilities and introduce light customization. This pattern suits processes that matter operationally but do not justify full internal development, such as customer email triage supported by a language model with organization-specific prompt templates and routing logic.

Low complexity, high strategic importance: Build Simple. Develop internally despite low technical barriers when strategic sensitivity is high. Examples include internally built virtual assistants for drafting internal explanations and summaries of pricing decisions for sales or management review, where the generation task is simple but control over outputs and data handling is critical.

Medium complexity, low strategic importance: Buy Custom. Rely on specialized vendors offering configurable generative solutions. This approach is appropriate for moderately complex, non-core applications such as an HR assistant that generates policy explanations or onboarding guidance using vendor-managed language models integrated with internal documentation.

Medium complexity, medium strategic importance: Balanced Mix. Combine vendor platforms for foundational generative models with internal development for differentiation. A typical example is a RAG-based knowledge assistant that uses a vendor-provided language model while relying on a proprietary retrieval, ranking, and validation pipeline tailored to internal knowledge structures.

Medium complexity, high strategic importance: Hybrid. Build core generative logic internally while sourcing commodity infrastructure externally. Examples include in-house development of domain-specific reasoning prompts, validation layers, or decision-support narratives on top of third-party model hosting and inference infrastructure.

High complexity, low strategic importance: Buy Strategic. Establish deep partnerships with vendors delivering complex generative systems outside the team core competence. This category often includes agent-based solutions encapsulated as managed services, where orchestration, tool use, and monitoring are handled externally. Enterprise-wide regulatory or legal analysis assistants that generate compliance summaries, risk explanations, or impact assessments using specialized legal models fit into this category, even when implemented as multi-step or agentic workflows, provided that strategic differentiation and control remain limited.

High complexity, medium strategic importance: Hybrid Strategic. Co-develop advanced generative systems with vendors while retaining partial control. This category frequently applies to domain-specific agents that operate across multiple steps but rely on shared responsibility for orchestration, models, or tooling. Examples include operations or supply-chain copilots that generate scenario narratives, risk explanations, or decision rationales by combining vendor generative models with proprietary operational data, constraints, and internally governed decision logic.

Before positioning specific use cases within the matrix, organizations should assess their readiness across several dimensions, a consideration that becomes especially salient as systems move from single-inference models toward agentic workflows. Data maturity determines whether advanced approaches are feasible at all. Fragmented or poorly governed data limits the ability to move beyond basic implementations, and constrains the safe operation of agents that rely on persistent state, memory, or cross-system coordination. Those who lack clean, accessible data should prioritize buying solutions while investing in data infrastructure.

Technical capability plays a similarly decisive role. Limited cloud infrastructure, GenAI Ops[3] maturity, or engineering capacity tends to favour buy and hybrid approaches, whereas stronger capabilities expand the set of viable build options, particularly for agent-based systems that require orchestration, state management, and continuous monitoring beyond isolated model calls. Cultural readiness further shapes what is feasible. Organizations that tolerate experimentation and benefit from visible executive sponsorship are better positioned to explore use cases across the matrix, including controlled deployments of semi-autonomous agents, while risk-averse cultures often begin with low-stakes pilots using standard vendor solutions. Finally, the regulatory environment constrains the feasible choices. In healthcare, finance, and government, requirements for explainability and auditability may necessitate to build approaches even where buying would otherwise appear attractive, particularly for customer-facing applications, and even more so when decisions result from multi-step or agentic processes rather than single outputs.

Implementation patterns also vary systematically by size and maturity of a company or institution. Start-ups typically rely heavily on standard and customized vendor

3 GenAI Ops refers to the set of operational practices and controls used to deploy, monitor, govern, and evolve generative AI systems in production. It extends traditional ML ops to address the specific characteristics of generative models, including non-deterministic outputs, prompt-driven behavior, rapid model evolution, and heightened requirements for monitoring, auditability, and compliance.

solutions, prioritizing speed and focusing some engineering resources on a small number of core differentiators that justify internal development, rarely deploying fully autonomous agents beyond narrow, well-bounded functions. Mid-sized organizations tend to balance quick wins achieved through vendor solutions with selective strategic builds, often using central coordination to avoid fragmentation, including early internal agent frameworks applied to specific domains. Large enterprises usually operate across all nine cells simultaneously, requiring portfolio-level governance, frequently through an AI Centre of Excellence,[4] to maintain coherence while avoiding too much bureaucracy, especially where multiple agentic systems coexist across business units.

Most use cases begin with low-risk experiments using standard vendor solutions. Successful pilots build confidence and capability, enabling progression towards more strategic implementations. Use cases may migrate across the matrix as technical complexity decreases, for example, when vendors mature or internal expertise grows, or when agentic patterns become better standardized and easier to govern. Strategic importance may also increase as competitive landscapes shift, business priorities evolve, or organizational readiness improves through better data infrastructure, skills, and culture. The objective is not convergence on a single approach, but deliberate diversity: some initiatives remain externally sourced, others become internally controlled, and many occupy hybrid positions for extended periods. The managerial challenge lies in maintaining coherence across these heterogeneous choices while preserving flexibility as conditions change, including the ability to constrain, reconfigure, or retire agent-based systems as priorities and regulatory conditions evolve.

4.5 A proposed ROI measurement framework

Recent industry research confirms widespread difficulty in demonstrating AI value, with 49 % of organizations struggling to estimate and prove ROI from generative AI projects [88], and 42 % of companies abandoning most AI initiatives in 2025 due to unclear value [89]. Whilst generative AI resists conventional ROI measurement, it does not resist measurement altogether. Drawing on emerging frameworks in both industry practice and academic literature, this section proposes a structured approach organized around three measurement perspectives, each suited to different types of value creation.

Current measurement frameworks increasingly distinguish between different categories of AI value. Industry practitioners have converged on multi-tiered approaches that separate basic usage metrics from workflow efficiency and revenue impact [90],

4 An AI Centre of Excellence is a dedicated structure that coordinates AI adoption across the enterprise by consolidating expertise, defining standards and best practices, supporting implementation, and providing governance and oversight. Its role is to accelerate value creation while maintaining consistency, risk management, and alignment with strategy, without centralizing all development activities. [87].

while academic frameworks differentiate between measurable ROI, strategic ROI, and capability ROI [88]. These approaches share a common recognition: AI investments generate value through distinct mechanisms that require differentiated measurement strategies. The framework proposed here synthesizes these perspectives while grounding them in the specific challenges observed in generative AI deployments.

Table 4.2 summarizes the three measurement perspectives, comparing their value mechanisms, key metrics, decision rules, and typical portfolio allocations. The following sections elaborate on each perspective in turn.

Perspective 1: Efficiency-driven use cases. When value derives primarily from measurable productivity gains (time saved, costs reduced, throughput increased), traditional ROI frameworks remain viable. Industry data suggests that almost all organizations with mature AI initiatives report measurable ROI, with 74 % meeting or exceeding expectations [91]. The measurement challenge is not conceptual but operational: ensuring that benefits are incremental rather than redistributed, that baselines are properly established, and that error costs are explicitly accounted for.

Three practices improve measurement quality. First, establish control groups where feasible, comparing performance between users with and without AI assistance to isolate marginal contribution. Second, track not just aggregate metrics but their distribution. If average handling time decreases but variance increases, the system may be helping some users whilst confusing others, signalling adoption or design issues. Third, monitor leading indicators of sustainability: user engagement trends, prompt refinement patterns, and escalation rates signal whether efficiency gains are stable or degrading. Research confirms that organizations achieving strong ROI track behavioral metrics alongside outcome metrics, recognizing that adoption patterns predict sustainability [92].

For efficiency use cases, decision rules can be relatively straightforward. Proceed with expansion when measured ROI exceeds hurdle rates and key indicators remain stable or improve over time. Pause to refine the approach if error rates trend upward, user engagement patterns shift, or cost structures reveal opportunities for optimization. Redirect investment if efficiency gains require longer than expected timeframes or if the use case proves better suited to a different context. The threshold for "expected timeframe" varies by context, but organizations that manage portfolios effectively typically allow six to twelve months for efficiency use cases to demonstrate measurable returns, recognizing that early adoption involves valuable learning curves. Industry benchmarks suggest that it takes at least twelve months to achieve target value, understanding that sustainable efficiency gains compound over time [91].

Perspective 2: Decision-support and capability-building use cases. When AI systems augment rather than replace human judgment (assisting in analysis, exploration, or decision-making), value accrues through improved decision quality and capability development rather than time savings. Traditional productivity metrics become misleading, as users may spend more time on tasks whilst producing better outcomes. Measurement therefore shifts to outcome proxies and capability indicators, an approach increasingly recognized in both practitioner frameworks [93] and academic literature.

Table 4.2: Measurement framework for generative AI investments.

Dimension	Perspective 1: Efficiency	Perspective 2: Decision-Support	Perspective 3: Strategic Optionality
Primary value mechanism	Measurable productivity gains: time saved, costs reduced, throughput increased	Improved decision quality and capability development	Strategic flexibility, organizational learning, competitive positioning
Key metrics	Time savings, cost reduction, throughput, error rates	Win rates, quality scores, time-to-competence, case complexity handled	Learning velocity, strategic positioning, competitive benchmarking, capability audits
Leading indicators	User engagement trends, prompt refinement patterns, escalation rates, metric variance	Outcome proxy trends, capability indicators, user workaround frequency	Documentation of insights, viable paths identified, strategic alignment
Evaluation horizon	6–12 months	12–24 months	36+ months with periodic review gates
Proceed if	Measured ROI exceeds hurdle rates and key indicators remain stable or improve	Outcome proxies trend positively and capability indicators show organizational learning	Learning velocity remains high and strategic positioning improves
Pause if	Error rates increase, user engagement declines, or costs prove more variable than projected	Outcomes stagnate or users develop workarounds suggesting added friction	Learning has plateaued or use case no longer aligns with strategic priorities
Terminate if	Efficiency gains do not materialize within expected timeframes or error costs systematically exceed benefits	Outcome proxies trend negatively or users become dependent without developing underlying expertise	Option value diminishes: protected scenario becomes irrelevant, cost exceeds strategic value, or learning exhausted
Suggested portfolio allocation	60–70 %	20–30 %	10–20 %
Example use case	Customer service automation, document processing, code generation	Proposal writing assistance, research synthesis, junior staff mentoring	Self-hosted deployment exploration, emerging capability evaluation, regulatory readiness

Outcome proxies attempt to measure decision quality indirectly. For a proposal writing system, relevant proxies include win rates in competitive bids, client satisfaction scores, proposal comprehensiveness, and proposal accuracy. None of these metrics isolates the AI's contribution perfectly, but collectively they signal whether the system is moving the organization toward better outcomes. Industry frameworks distinguish between "hard ROI" metrics (measurable financial impacts) and "soft ROI" metrics (decision quality, customer satisfaction, employee retention) that affect long-term fitness [93]. The key is to track these metrics longitudinally and compare trajectories before and after AI adoption, accepting that attribution will remain imperfect but directionally informative.

Capability indicators measure learning and skill development. Time-to-competence for junior staff provides a tangible measure of knowledge transfer. Other organizations track metrics such as the complexity of cases handled independently, the diversity of solution approaches explored, or the frequency with which users identify edge cases or system limitations. These indicators are forward-looking: they measure whether AI deployment is building capabilities that will generate value in future periods, even if current-period ROI appears modest. This aligns with emerging frameworks that explicitly value capability development as a distinct ROI category [88].

For decision-support use cases, decision rules necessarily become more qualitative. It is usually better to proceed if outcome proxies trend positively and capability indicators show sustained learning. Pause if outcomes stagnate or if users develop workarounds that suggest the system is adding friction rather than value. Terminate if outcome proxies trend negatively or if capability indicators show users becoming dependent on AI outputs without developing underlying expertise. The evaluation horizon for these use cases typically extends to twelve to twenty-four months, as capability building requires time to manifest.

Perspective 3: Strategic optionality and exploratory use cases. Some AI investments function less as immediate value generators and more as real options: preserving future flexibility, building capabilities, or positioning the organization to respond to uncertain future conditions. Real options analysis (ROA), which applies financial option theory to real business investments, provides a conceptual foundation for measuring such investments by explicitly valuing flexibility and future decision opportunities under uncertainty [94, 95].

The relevant question shifts from "what return does this generate?" to "what future scenarios does this enable, and what is the cost of preserving that option?" A parallel track evaluating transition to self-hosted deployment represents option value: the organization invests modestly in building internal GenAI Ops capability, preserving the option to reduce dependency on external providers if data sovereignty concerns intensify or API economics deteriorate. The investment is justified not by immediate returns but by the strategic flexibility it preserves, consistent with the emphasis given by real options theory on valuing managerial discretion to adapt investments over time [96].

For exploratory use cases, measurement focuses on learning velocity and strategic positioning. Learning velocity can be assessed through documentation of insights gained, identification of viable paths forward, and elimination of unviable approaches. Strategic positioning can be evaluated through competitive benchmarking, regulatory readiness assessments, or internal capability audits. These metrics do not translate directly to financial returns, but they inform portfolio allocation decisions: how much capital and attention to allocate to exploratory initiatives relative to efficiency plays. Real options frameworks explicitly value such learning as information revelation that reduces uncertainty and enables better future decisions [97].

Decision rules for strategic use cases are deliberately different. Proceed if learning velocity remains high and strategic positioning improves relatively to competitors or regulatory requirements. Pause if learning has plateaued or if the use case no longer aligns with strategic priorities. Terminate not when ROI falls short, but when the option value diminishes: when the future scenario buffered by the option becomes irrelevant, when the cost of preserving the option exceeds its strategic value, or when learning has been exhausted. The evaluation horizon for exploratory use cases can extend to 24 months or more, with periodic review gates to assess continued strategic relevance, consistent with real options approaches to managing strategic investments under uncertainty.

Portfolio-level integration. Most organizations operate use cases across all three perspectives simultaneously. The portfolio management challenge is to apply the appropriate measurement perspective to each use case while maintaining coherent resource allocation across perspectives. Based on industry observations, we suggest a portfolio allocation in which approximately 60–70 % of investment is directed toward near-term efficiency and decision-support initiatives, 20–30 % toward longer-horizon capability building, and 10–20 % toward exploratory options that preserve strategic flexibility. This recommendation is informed by growing evidence, suggesting that successful AI initiatives devote only a limited share of effort to algorithms and technology, while the majority of value creation depends on people, processes, and organizational transformation, a pattern often summarized by the 10–20–70 principle [98]. These proportions vary by maturity, risk tolerance, and competitive context, but the underlying logic remains consistent: balance near-term value capture with longer-term capability building and strategic positioning.

Critically, measurement rigor should vary depending on the perspective, but it should never be absent. Even exploratory use cases require disciplined evaluation, not against ROI hurdles, but against learning objectives and strategic alignment. Organizations that struggle with AI measurement often make one of two errors: applying efficiency metrics to strategic initiatives (killing valuable options prematurely), or treating all initiatives as strategic options (avoiding accountability for measurable value creation). The framework proposed here provides a structure to avoid both pathologies while acknowledging the genuine complexity of measuring value in systems that augment human reasoning rather than replacing deterministic processes. This aligns with emerging industry consensus that comprehensive ROI frameworks must capture efficiency gains, revenue generation, risk mitigation, and business agility across all business functions [99], while recognizing that different use cases require fundamentally different evaluative logics.

4.6 Case study: a portfolio-level measurement in practice

To illustrate how the three-perspective framework operates in practice, consider the following stylized example. An industrial equipment manufacturer headquartered in Rome, MetronioMech, launches a portfolio of agent-based generative AI initiatives in early 2026. Rather than evaluating all AI investments through a single lens, the company explicitly classifies agentic use cases by their dominant value mechanism and applies perspective-appropriate measurement from the outset.

The first initiative targets efficiency gains in a stable, high-volume process. MetronioMech processes approximately 800 requests for quotation (RFQs) per month for standard product configurations. Junior staff spend an average of 2 hours per RFQ extracting specifications, checking compatibility, and generating quotes. An AI agent is deployed to autonomously retrieve specifications, validate configuration constraints, and generate draft quotations for subsequent human review. To assess impact, MetronioMech establishes a controlled rollout with 40 staff in each group.

After five months, agent-assisted users reduce average handling time to 1.5 hours, while the control group remains at 2 hours. Monthly throughput increases from 10 to 12 RFQs per staff member among proficient users, and error rates improve modestly. Based on incremental labour savings, a traditional ROI calculation yields an estimated 70 % annualized return, substantially exceeding the company's hurdle rate. Management proceeds with staged deployment, coupled with additional training for lower-performing users.

By month eleven, operating conditions shift. Suppliers introduce more complex product lines, compressing projected ROI to around 50 %. In parallel, experienced users develop informal workarounds for specific RFQ types, citing recurring edge-case failures. These operational signals trigger a pause for system refinement, exactly as Perspective 1 decision rules prescribe. The initiative remains viable, but continued deployment is made conditional on addressing edge cases and stabilizing costs.

The second initiative targets a fundamentally different form of value creation. Senior sales engineers at MetronioMech produce bespoke technical proposals for complex projects, balancing product constraints with regulatory compliance across multiple jurisdictions. A decision-support AI agent is introduced to assist in generating preliminary proposals. Unlike RFQ automation, value here derives from improved decision quality and capability development. Management therefore classifies this initiative under Perspective 2.

After fourteen months, conventional productivity indicators appear ambiguous: average proposal preparation time increases from 4 to 5 days as engineers explore broader configuration spaces and conduct more thorough compliance checks. However, outcome proxies trend positively. Win rates reach nearly 40 % for agent-assisted proposals, compared to 30 % for a control group. Client satisfaction rises significantly, proposal comprehensiveness improves, and agent-assisted proposals exhibit 20 % fewer post-award change requests, suggesting improved specification accuracy. Two junior engineers reach operational competence in 13 months rather than the historical 20-month range, while senior engineers handle projects of greater regulatory complexity.

During the pilot, several pricing errors reach clients, triggering additional documentation and oversight costs under EU AI Act compliance requirements. These costs are treated as governance learning investments, and by month twelve, error protocols reduce such incidents to baseline levels. Applying Perspective 2 decision rules, management proceeds based on directional improvement in outcome proxies and demonstrable learning, explicitly avoiding ROI calculations that would misrepresent the value mechanism.

The third initiative operates under a different logic altogether. Facing strategic uncertainty around data sovereignty and long-term dependency on external APIs, MetronioMech initiates exploratory work on self-hosted agent deployment. Management frames this effort explicitly as preserving strategic optionality: the ability to exit external providers if regulatory pressure or API economics deteriorate. A small team receives a modest budget over twelve months to build internal competence and evaluate open-source frameworks. The team establishes that self-hosting is technically feasible but projects infrastructure costs 40 % higher than current API spending.

As expected, the initiative generates negative short-term ROI. Its value lies in preserving option value: a modest investment compared to the potential cost of being locked into unfavorable provider terms. Management continues exploration at reduced intensity based on Perspective 3 criteria, with explicit termination criteria: if API economics and data-sovereignty risks stabilize for eighteen consecutive months, or if self-hosting cost premiums exceed a certain threshold, exploration ceases.

At the portfolio level, resource allocation reflects the framework's logic: approximately 60 % to efficiency-oriented deployments, 30 % to decision-support and capability-building, and 10 % to strategic optionality. The RFQ agent faces regular ROI scrutiny, the proposal agent is evaluated on outcome proxies over extended horizons, and the self-hosting initiative is measured against learning objectives and scenario-based option value.

This case illustrates successful agentic AI adoption not because every initiative delivered immediate returns, but because MetronioMech applied differentiated evaluation frameworks matched to distinct value creation mechanisms. Rather than forcing all investments through a single measurement lens, they classified initiatives by their dominant value mechanism from the outset, preventing both the premature termination of promising initiatives and the indefinite continuation of low-value work. When the RFQ automation encountered operational challenges, management paused for refinement rather than abandoning the project. When proposal preparation time increased, they correctly recognized this as exploration of broader solution spaces rather than inefficiency, tracking outcome proxies like win rates and specification accuracy instead of simple throughput metrics. EU AI Act compliance costs were framed as governance learning investments, building capability for future deployments. The self-hosting initiative, despite negative short-term ROI, preserved valuable optionality with clear continuation and termination criteria. Ultimately, MetronioMech's success lies in developing its capability to evaluate, adapt, and govern agentic AI investments according to their actual value drivers, positioning the company for sustained value capture even as technologies and operating conditions evolve.

4.7 Building portfolio discipline

Generative AI investments resist reduction to conventional business cases, but this does not exempt them from rigorous evaluation. What differentiates mature AI portfolios is not tolerance for uncertainty, but the ability to apply distinct measurement logics to fundamentally different modes of value creation. Organizations struggle with AI ROI not because generative or agent-based systems are inherently unmeasurable, but because they apply uniform evaluation criteria to investments whose value emerges through incompatible mechanisms. This mismatch is particularly visible in agentic systems, where value unfolds across sequences of actions rather than single outputs, making naïve productivity metrics both misleading and incomplete.

The three-perspective framework addresses this challenge by formalizing what effective organizations already recognize but often fail to apply consistently: efficiency gains, capability accumulation, and strategic optionality demand different evidence, time horizons, and decision rules. The core challenge is not conceptual alignment but operational clarity. In a shared portfolio, an autonomous RFQ agent evaluated on quarterly cost reduction competes for the same resources and attention as an exploratory proposal automation agent whose value lies in learning, adaptability, or future configurability. Treating these initiatives as directly comparable obscures their true contribution and weakens capital allocation rather than strengthening it.

Portfolio governance therefore becomes an exercise in preserving differentiated evaluation perspectives while maintaining coherent decision-making. This requires more than dashboards or review cadences. Effective oversight explicitly assigns each initiative, including agentic systems, to a dominant value perspective, applies perspective-appropriate success and continuation criteria, and actively resists the tendency to collapse evaluation into a single dominant logic. When this discipline is applied, efficiency initiatives scale faster, exploratory agents learn more quickly, and strategic investments retain credibility rather than being dismissed as vague innovation.

Perspective discipline is not static; it develops through successive portfolio cycles. Early iterations surface misclassifications: not all initiatives positioned as "strategic" generate meaningful optionality, and not all agent-based automations deliver durable efficiency once coordination costs, oversight requirements, and interaction effects are observed. Subsequent cycles refine transition criteria. Exploratory agents progress when learning objectives are met; pilots move to deployment when outcome proxies stabilize; deployed systems continue only while they outperform defined baselines. Over time, organizations become more precise in perspective assignment, more realistic in evaluation horizons, and more confident in reallocating resources based on observed performance rather than initial intent.

At this stage of maturity, portfolio strength is visible less in architectural sophistication than in evaluative capability. The leading organizations define control groups or proxy outcomes before deploying agents, monitor leading indicators continuously to detect drift or degradation early, and specify continuation and termination conditions at approval rather than deferring them to later debates. Strategic optionality investments receive clearly bounded resources tied to explicit learning objectives, ensuring that exploration remains focused, credible, and productive.

The transition from opportunistic experimentation to disciplined portfolio management typically unfolds over twelve to twenty-four months, with meaningful insight emerging within the first six to nine. This reflects the normal dynamics of generative and agentic AI deployment: cost structures evolve, agent behavior stabilizes only under sustained use, adoption patterns diverge from pilot assumptions, and regulatory and vendor conditions change faster than traditional planning cycles. Anticipate this reality yields to better positioning for learning quickly and adjusting confidently.

What ultimately distinguishes organizations that capture sustained value is not superior prediction, but superior adaptation. They treat business cases as hypotheses, measurement frameworks as learning tools, and portfolio reviews as genuine decision points. They scale mature efficiency gains decisively, advance capable agents when evidence supports them, and redirect resources when outcomes fail to materialize. By balancing near-term efficiency, medium-term capability building, and long-term strategic positioning under distinct evaluative logics, they transform generative AI from a collection of isolated initiatives into a coherent, resilient source of competitive advantage.

5 Managing the AI lifecycle

The previous chapter focused on identifying, selecting, and tracking AI use cases as part of a strategic investment portfolio. Once a use case has been approved, however, a different challenge begins: ensuring that the resulting AI system remains controlled, reliable, and aligned with shared objectives throughout its operational life.

AI systems evolve after deployment, interact dynamically with users and data, and may change their behavior even without explicit redesign. As a result, managing AI cannot be reduced to a one-off project or a technical deployment. It requires a *continuous lifecycle* perspective spanning design, operation, adaptation, and eventual retirement.

Consider the case of a Portuguese energy company that deploys a virtual assistant to support field engineers in optimizing equipment maintenance across its distribution network. The system performs well during initial testing, providing consistent diagnostic guidance and maintenance recommendations aligned with established technical protocols. Several months after deployment, the company's governance framework proves its value. When new smart grid technologies are integrated and equipment specifications are updated, the system's lifecycle management process automatically triggers a reassessment. Performance monitoring detects subtle variations in maintenance recommendations across different regional networks before they become significant. Field engineers, trained to critically evaluate system outputs and empowered to flag observations, report these insights through established feedback channels. The company's cross-functional AI governance team reviews the findings, determines that the variations reflect appropriate adaptation to legitimate differences in regional infrastructure configurations, and documents this assessment for audit purposes. The system continues to deliver value while remaining fully accountable.

In a separate episode, the same process produces a different verdict: when a platform upgrade causes the assistant to drift from updated equipment specifications, the governance team rolls the system back, commissions retraining, and revises acceptance criteria before redeployment. Both outcomes are the operating model working as intended.

The case illustrates the value of lifecycle management not as a technical capability but as an operating model that distributes detection, judgment, and decision rights across engineers, governance teams, and documented processes.

5.1 Why lifecycle management matters

The most successful AI deployments share a common characteristic: strong governance over time. Systems thrive when clear accountability guides their evolution, updates follow structured reassessment processes, and organizations actively verify that original assumptions remain valid.

https://doi.org/10.1515/9783112254103-005

Organizations that embrace AI deployment as an ongoing commitment consistently realize three categories of benefits: i) accountability becomes straightforward: when a generative AI system produces excellent results (or when it fails), it is straightforward to explain what worked and why, transforming lifecycle documentation into evidence of good practice rather than post-hoc reconstruction; ii) technical quality compounds over time as systems improve through refreshed data sources, resolved edge cases, and systematized improvements; iii) strategic agility increases because those who confidently manage existing AI systems become eager and capable of deploying new ones.

Lifecycle management also produces a regulatory dividend that purely project-based deployments cannot: audit trails, risk assessments, and change logs, which are artefacts that project-based deployments rarely generate, because they lack a named post-deployment owner and a scheduled reassessment cadence. Under the AI Act's conformity assessment and post-market monitoring requirements, this evidence is not optional documentation but a substantive compliance asset.

The lifecycle framework presented in Figure 5.1 draws on proven MLOps practices from major technology providers, where AI systems are managed as continuous processes rather than one-time deployments [100, 101]. This operational foundation is reinforced by international governance standards that treat AI as a continuously managed system requiring ongoing risk assessment, monitoring, and deliberate decisions about evolution and retirement [102–104]. The framework should therefore be read as a practical synthesis: industry practices inform operational structure, while international standards provide normative guidance on accountability and control. This combination ensures the lifecycle remains both executable and auditable: a critical balance for managers responsible for both delivery and governance.

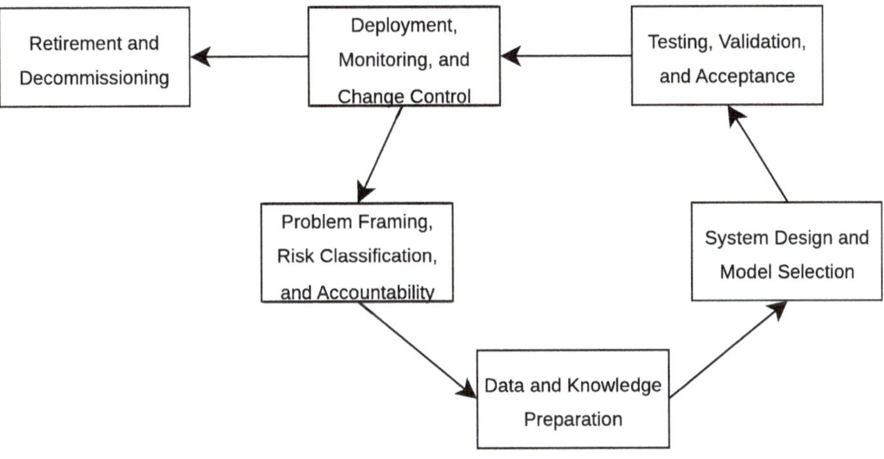

Figure 5.1: Generative AI lifecycle.

5.2 Lifecycle framing, risk classification, and control

Once a use case has been selected, the first lifecycle decision concerns how the system is framed and classified. For Generative AI, this step is particularly critical because system behavior is not fully specified at design time. Unlike deterministic or narrowly predictive systems, Generative AI produces outputs that depend on prompts, contextual information, and patterns of interaction that often emerge only after deployment. As a result, early framing decisions strongly influence how risk, responsibility, and control will evolve in practice. In reality, however, lifecycle framing rarely starts from a blank slate. Many considerations will already have surfaced, at least implicitly, during use case identification and prioritization. Use case selection and initial lifecycle framing therefore inform each other: early intuitions about acceptable automation, perceived risk and exposure shape which generative AI use cases are considered viable, while formal classification forces these intuitions to be revisited and, in some cases, corrected. This interaction is unavoidable and should be managed deliberately rather than treated as a procedural flaw.

Managers should therefore treat this phase not as a clean handover from ideation to implementation, but as a deliberate control refinement step. Preliminary assumptions about behavior, user reliance, and decision authority must be made explicit, challenged, and documented before development commitments become difficult to reverse. At this stage, the system should be classified as exploratory, operational, or mission-critical; its degree of automation clarified in relation to human judgment; and its risk level assessed in line with the EU AI Act's risk-based framework.[1] This baseline classification determines which legal obligations apply to the organization as a user and sets requirements for testing, documentation, logging, monitoring, and incident response throughout the lifecycle.

Crucially, this classification is conditional on the system being used as framed. If the operational role expands, risk must be reassessed. A text-generation system piloted for internal drafting may initially remain outside high-risk categories. Once deployed at scale, however, the same system may begin to influence contractual language, regulatory interpretation, or customer communication, thereby increasing legal exposure and triggering additional obligations. Risk, in this sense, is not static: it is produced through interaction, reliance, and scale.

Problem framing then proceeds through translation. The business opportunity identified during use case selection must be converted into specific, testable requirements by answering a limited set of fundamental questions. *What decision or task does the system support?* Broad objectives such as "improve customer service" must be decomposed into concrete functions, such as drafting response suggestions, retrieving relevant knowledge articles, or routing enquiries to specialists.

1 See Chapter 7.

What does success look like in operation? Success must be defined in observable, measurable terms during real use, not solely through offline testing. *What constitutes unacceptable behavior?* Specific failure modes or scenarios that would trigger review or intervention should be identified, as these directly inform monitoring and quality assurance mechanisms. Finally, *who retains decision authority?* Even highly autonomous generative systems, such as multi-agent systems, remain embedded in human decision structures; it must be explicit whether the system recommends actions, makes provisional decisions subject to review, or acts autonomously within defined boundaries. Answering these questions explicitly establishes the foundation for proportionate governance throughout the system's lifecycle.

Table 5.1: AI system classification by decision impact and automation level.

	Low decision impact	Medium decision impact	High decision impact
Assistive	Informational support; errors cause minor inconvenience or rework; minimal governance required	Decision support affecting efficiency or experience; basic monitoring and validation	High-stakes advice with human decision authority; strong controls and documentation
Augmentative	Human review mandatory; limited operational risk; standard testing and monitoring	Provisional decisions subject to approval; structured testing, monitoring, and audits	High-risk delegation; tight oversight, escalation paths, and frequent reassessment
Autonomous	Automated execution with low impact; monitoring by exception	Autonomous decisions with reversible impact; strong safeguards and continuous monitoring	Critical risk category; maximum governance, human override, and formal accountability

Not all generative AI systems carry equal management or regulatory risk. Table 5.1 presents a practical classification framework based on two dimensions: decision impact and automation level. Decision impact ranges from low (inconvenience or rework, e. g. meeting summaries) through medium (reversible effects on efficiency or experience, e. g. product recommendations) to high (legal exposure or irreversible outcomes, e. g. loan approvals). Automation level ranges from assistive (humans retain authority) through augmentative (provisional decisions subject to review) to autonomous (execution within defined boundaries).

A system classified as high impact and autonomous demands fundamentally different controls than one classified as low impact and assistive. This classification directly informs resource allocation, testing requirements, monitoring intensity, and escalation mechanisms. For example, a retail company deploying generative AI for customer support may reasonably classify the system as medium impact with augmentative automation, implying structured testing, usage monitoring, and periodic quality audits. The same company would require substantially stronger controls if the system were allowed to autonomously resolve complaints with financial or legal consequences.

Once a system is classified, accountability must be assigned to specific people. Generative AI systems do not carry responsibility; organizations and individuals do. International standards and risk management frameworks consistently emphasize clear business accountability, technical ownership, and independent risk oversight across the AI lifecycle. Each system therefore requires designated roles: a System Owner, accountable for outcomes and authorized to approve material changes or decommissioning; a Technical Lead, responsible for ensuring the system functions as intended and coordinating technical responses; and a Risk Reviewer, responsible for assessing whether the system continues to operate within acceptable risk boundaries and escalating concerns when necessary. These roles must be assigned, documented, and communicated before development begins. Accountability established after deployment is rarely effective, particularly for generative systems whose responses and use evolve over time.

5.3 Data and knowledge preparation

For generative AI, the foundation model is rarely the organization's asset. It is licensed, shared with competitors, and largely outside the organization's control. What the organization owns, and what differentiates one deployment from another, is the knowledge layer: the proprietary documents, structured data, and external sources the model is grounded in at inference time. This layer should be managed as infrastructure, with named owners, quality expectations, update cycles, and access controls. For systems that retrieve and synthesize information dynamically, it is not a supporting resource but a constitutive part of system behavior, and therefore a constitutive part of what governance must cover.

Clear documentation at this stage enables long-term control. When outputs are questioned, the organization should be able to explain what information was available to the system, under which assumptions it operated, and with which limitations. Data preparation for Generative AI differs fundamentally from traditional analytics. Rather than cleaning data to extract insights, the objective is to curate information that shapes system outputs and actions. This requires cataloging all information sources the system can access, including internal documents, databases, external APIs, real-time feeds, and historical archives, and documenting for each source its ownership, update frequency, quality expectations, and access restrictions.

Quality baselines should scale with system impact. Higher-impact or higher-risk systems justify stricter thresholds across dimensions such as accuracy, completeness, currency, and consistency. Knowledge boundaries should make explicit what the system should and should not know, including the exclusion of outdated material, the marking of confidential information, and the definition of knowledge cut-off dates.

Consider a management consultancy deploying an agent to support proposal writing and client deliverables, tasked with drafting sections of pitch documents and assembling supporting evidence from prior work. Because the agent operates autonomously across retrieval, drafting, and assemblign steps, data preparation becomes a primary mechanism for shaping agent behavior and managing commercial and reputational risk. The firm's source inventory includes published methodologies and approved case studies, signed engagement frameworks and final client deliverables, internal partner debates and draft hypotheses from ongoing engagements, and third-party industry research used during analysis.

A quality assessment shows that published methodologies and approved case studies represent the firm's authoritative positioning, while the internal repository contains partner debates, working hypotheses, and draft analyses from live engagements that may not reflect the firm's settled view, and in some cases involve client-confidential material that must not be reused. To ensure consistent responses, the firm defines explicit inclusion rules. Only published methodologies and case studies cleared for external use are authorized as the firm's official reference material. Deliverables from engagements with clients no longer active are retained solely as historical context and explicitly marked as non-binding and non-attributable. Internal partner debates and draft hypotheses are excluded to prevent provisional reasoning from being treated as the firm's settled position, and to protect client confidentiality on ongoing work. Third-party industry research is included but clearly labeled as background market context rather than the firm's own analytical position.

These decisions are formalized in a knowledge register that records each source, its role in agent reasoning, update schedule, quality expectations, and rationale for inclusion or exclusion. The register functions as a living governance artifact, reviewed whenever sources change, new practice areas or client sectors are added, or the agent's scope evolves. In this way, commercial and reputational risk is managed not through restrictive output controls, but by deliberately shaping the evidentiary environment in which the agent operates.

RAG introduces additional considerations around search scope management, retrieval quality monitoring, knowledge versioning, and fallback behavior when relevant information cannot be found. Data preparation is therefore not a one-off activity completed before launch, but an ongoing capability supported by defined update cycles, quality monitoring, and change notification procedures throughout the system's life.

5.4 System design and model selection

Model selection was covered in Section 3.2.2. What remains is how the chosen model is operationalized within the system. System design determines how assumptions made during problem framing translate into observable behavior, how errors surface in practice, and how effectively accountability and control can be exercised over time.

Design choices at this stage shape the system's operational profile independently of the underlying model. The same model can function as a low-risk support capability or as a high-impact operational component, depending on where it is embedded in the workflow, which inputs it receives, how outputs are consumed, and which constraints are enforced before action is taken. From a lifecycle perspective, system design is therefore the point at which abstract governance decisions are translated into executable technical structures.

A recurring challenge is the reliance on procedural safeguards rather than structural ones. Policies that require outputs to be reviewed, overridden when necessary, or escalated in sensitive cases are only effective if the system actively supports those responses. In practice, time pressure and cognitive load encourage users to accept default outputs, particularly when they appear fluent and plausible (as discussed further in Chapter 6). Effective system design addresses this by embedding controls directly into the workflow: requiring explicit confirmation before execution, differentiating handling paths for higher-risk outputs, enforcing separation between generation and action, and recording review and override actions through auditable logs.

From a managerial perspective, the objective of system design is not to eliminate errors, but to ensure that when they occur they are visible, attributable, and recoverable. Well-designed interfaces, permissions, and execution paths make it clear when the system is operating within its intended scope and when it is approaching predefined boundaries. Where appropriate, design can also introduce deliberate moments for reflection in sensitive contexts, strengthening human judgment without creating unnecessary friction or relying solely on training and vigilance.

Strong design choices at this stage compound: monitoring becomes more effective because the system already produces the right signals, adaptation remains controlled because the boundaries are encoded rather than asserted, and responsibility stays clear because the workflow records who decided what and when.

5.5 Testing, validation, and acceptance

Before deployment, AI systems should be rigorously validated rather than simply demonstrated. For managers, the central question is not whether a system performs well on average, but under which conditions it performs best and where its boundaries lie. Most successful deployments do not emerge from attempting to eliminate every edge case, but from understanding system limits clearly, aligning workflows with system strengths, and designing appropriate safeguards where performance is more fragile. In this sense, validation transforms testing from a hurdle into a roadmap for deployment.

Testing therefore needs to extend beyond headline performance metrics. Robustness, bias, misuse, and interaction effects should be examined deliberately, and acceptance criteria should be defined in advance. This translates abstract notions of "acceptable risk" into concrete, operational terms, and prevents post-hoc rationalization once results are known. This stage establishes a shared baseline against which future changes, incidents, and regulatory questions can be assessed. Without a documented baseline, continuous monitoring loses interpretability and accountability becomes reactive rather than intentional.

From a governance perspective, validation begins not with execution but with alignment. Leaders should ensure that acceptable performance is defined explicitly and in measurable terms. The form of the criteria depends on the task: accuracy thresholds for verifiable answers, articulated rubrics for generative outputs, latency and availability targets reflecting operational realities, and an explicit list of behaviors that are unacceptable even if rare. Boundary conditions matter: ambiguous inputs, missing information, contradictory sources, and adversarial prompts often surface risks that remain invisible in polished demonstrations.

Effective validation typically combines multiple complementary perspectives rather than relying on a single test. Functional testing confirms that the system performs its intended task under expected conditions. Stress and misuse testing explore behavior under pressure or adversarial inputs. In this context, Red Teaming[2] can be valuable, particularly when integrated into the broader lifecycle rather than treated as a one-off exercise. Bias and fairness testing assess whether outcomes vary systematically across contexts or groups. Integration testing evaluates system behavior within real workflows and dependencies. Usability testing observes whether users understand system limits, calibrate trust appropriately, and can intervene when needed.

As discussed in Section 3.2.2, small-scale demonstrations provide useful early signals but should be understood as indicative rather than definitive. While synthetic or anonymized data is often appropriate in early phases, effective validation requires progression toward representative real-world data and realistic operational contexts under controlled safeguards. At this point, defensible sample sizes and targeted evaluation of safety- and compliance-relevant scenarios produce the evidence on which deployment decisions can be defended.

Validation also produces durable evidence. That evidence may later be reviewed by executives, auditors, regulators, or courts. Documentation should therefore be contemporaneous and transparent, capturing not only results but also known limitations, unresolved issues, and the rationale for accepting residual risk. Formal sign-off by the System Owner, Technical Lead, and Risk Reviewer makes deployment an explicit, informed decision rather than an implicit consequence of technical readiness.

Finally, validation serves as a quality gate that protects value. When testing shows that a system cannot meet agreed thresholds within reasonable cost, time, or risk

---

2 Extended from IT practices to test cybersecurity prowess against targeted attacks [105], Red Teaming for AI systems refers to structured stress-testing under controlled conditions to identify vulnerabilities and unanticipated biases.

constraints, this outcome represents effective governance delivering exactly the insight it is intended to provide. Organizations can then make clear choices: remediate and retest with targeted improvements, constrain the system's scope to domains where it performs reliably, or redirect resources toward more promising opportunities. The ability to make evidence-based go/no-go decisions distinguishes mature AI programs from those that treat deployment as an objective in itself. Systems that pass validation earn confidence; decisions to pause or redirect demonstrate strategic focus rather than failure.

5.6 Deployment, monitoring, and change control

Once a system has passed validation and received formal sign-off, deployment begins. It is the point at which latent design choices become observable, monitoring catches what testing could not, and change control becomes the main lever of governance. Leaders who anticipate output dynamics, such as reliance patterns, decision workflows, and how adoption spreads, can design deployment to reinforce capabilities rather than disrupt them. Clear communication about system capabilities and limitations complements technical safeguards by helping users develop accurate mental models of when and how to leverage the system effectively. At deployment, accountability structures become operational: explicit ownership for monitoring outputs, responding to incidents, and maintaining system boundaries creates confidence across the organization.

Phased rollouts create valuable learning opportunities before full scale, particularly for novel or higher-impact systems, turning deployment into a refinement process rather than a one-time event. Users who understand what the system does and does not do, when to rely on it, and when to apply their own judgment become effective collaborators with the technology. This understanding develops through realistic demonstrations, open discussion of system boundaries, and clear guidance that positions human expertise as complementary rather than redundant. When monitoring infrastructure, support processes, and incident response protocols are operational before launch, and affected stakeholders are engaged early, deployment tends to generate momentum and adoption rather than confusion or resistance. Those who that invest in this structured approach consistently achieve faster time-to-value and stronger user acceptance than those treating deployment as a purely technical cutover.

Thoughtful interface design plays a central role in shaping appropriate reliance. Even well-trained users naturally gravitate toward fluent, plausible outputs under productivity pressure, which makes structural safeguards more dependable than individual vigilance alone. Effective design approaches include interfaces that invite active confirmation, explicit signaling of uncertainty, normalization of constructive questioning, and monitoring of override patterns. Very low override rates may indicate opportunities to strengthen critical evaluation rather than perfect system performance. Periodic recalibration using concrete examples of system boundaries helps sustain healthy collaboration between human judgment and AI capability.

User engagement deserves the same deliberate attention as technical readiness: early involvement of representative users, credible feedback channels with visible follow-up, and emphasis on capability augmentation convert skepticism into informed partnership. These leadership dimensions are explored further in Chapter 8.

Active monitoring begins at launch and continues for the system's operational life. The first weeks are especially informative, as usage patterns and collaboration dynamics establish quickly: focused monitoring during this period captures how users interact with the system, where additional guidance is helpful, and which workflows emerge naturally. Rapid and visible responses to early questions or issues reinforce trust and set the tone for sustained stewardship. In practice, this stewardship spans several dimensions, including user interaction, technical performance, impact, incident response, change management, and external dependencies.

Table 5.2 synthesizes these dimensions, the primary risks they address, and the corresponding managerial levers that activate at deployment.

Table 5.2: Deployment-phase controls and managerial levers.

Control dimension	Primary risk	Managerial focus
User interaction and behavior	Overreliance, automation bias, informal workarounds	Ensure interfaces require active confirmation, normalize questioning, monitor override rates
Technical performance	Quality degradation, latency, instability, cost overruns	Track quality metrics, failure rates, latency, availability, and resource consumption
Usage patterns	Misuse, scope drift, low adoption or blind trust	Monitor usage volume, query types, adoption trends, and rejection or override behavior
Organizational impact and risk	Unintended outcomes, fairness issues, compliance breaches	Review outcome metrics, incident trends, fairness indicators, and compliance adherence
Incident response	Escalation delays, unclear responsibility, reputational damage	Define severity levels, response ownership, documentation, and escalation authority
Change management	Silent behavior shifts due to prompt, data, or model updates	Require reassessment for changes affecting outputs, users, or decisions; document approvals
External dependencies	Provider updates, deprecations, loss of control	Monitor providers, pin versions where possible, test upgrades, maintain contingencies

Incident response is most effective when supported by predefined severity levels and clear response protocols. Documentation should capture what occurred, root causes, impacts, remediation actions, and lessons learned. Periodic incident reviews often surface systemic insights that inform improvements in design, testing, or user guidance.

Change control is closely coupled with monitoring. Generative systems are inherently adaptable, and even small changes to prompts, data, or models can materially affect behavior. A practical principle is that any change affecting outputs, users, or decisions should trigger reassessment proportional to risk. The risk classification established in Section 5.2 provides the anchor: minor changes on assistive low-impact systems may require limited testing, moderate changes on augmentative medium-impact systems focused revalidation, and major changes or any change to autonomous or high-impact systems full revalidation. Emergency changes may occasionally be necessary, but should still be documented and followed by retrospective review.

For companies relying on commercial models via API, some changes occur outside direct control when providers update or deprecate models. Version pinning where available, active provider monitoring, scheduled upgrades with prior testing, and contingency planning help maintain operational stability, particularly for systems that support critical workflows.

The lifecycle loop shown in Figure 5.1 is not abstract: specific events return an operating system to earlier stages, and they are not only corrective. New capabilities in the model layer or improvements in the knowledge layer can lift performance and warrant deliberate scope expansion. Lessons from one deployment shape the framing of the next, particularly when retirement of an earlier system frees capacity for a successor. Strategic shifts open new use cases that an existing system can absorb under controlled change. Alongside these, regulatory change, provider model deprecations, sustained drift in monitoring signals, and post-incident reviews trigger reassessment as well. Each of these events, whether opportunity or correction, should be recognized explicitly and routed through the proportional reassessment described above, rather than absorbed informally into routine operation.

5.7 Retirement and decommissioning

Every AI system should be accompanied by an explicit end-of-life plan. Technology evolves, strategic needs change, and no solution designed for today's business context can be assumed to remain appropriate indefinitely. Planning for retirement is therefore not a sign of limited ambition, but of managerial foresight. It is a management decision, not a technical shutdown, encompassing access revocation, documentation archiving, data handling, and clear communication to users. For generative systems in particular, decommissioning deserves careful attention, as outputs may have been embedded into downstream processes, documents, or decision routines. Without structured retirement practices, organizations risk accumulating invisible technical, legal, and operational debt over time.

AI systems reach end-of-life through multiple pathways. These include obsolescence of data or architectures, the emergence of superior alternatives, sustained underperformance, strategic realignment, rising operating costs, unmanageable risk profiles, or regulatory constraints. Recognizing when retirement is appropriate requires a balanced assessment of value, performance, cost, and risk. In practice, systems are often retained beyond their useful life due to sunk-cost bias or inertia rather than continued strategic relevance; mature governance frameworks counteract this by treating discontinuation as a normal lifecycle outcome rather than an admission of failure.

Retirement should therefore be a deliberate, accountable decision rather than an unintended consequence of neglect. The System Owner introduced in Section 5.2, authorized at deployment to approve material changes or decommissioning, is the natural decision authority here. Engaging users and downstream process owners early helps surface hidden dependencies and clarify where system outputs are still relied upon. Transition planning makes explicit how the underlying business need will be met after retirement, whether through migration to a successor system, consolidation with other tools, reversion to prior processes, or elimination of the function altogether. A defined retirement pathway reduces uncertainty and supports orderly change.

Once the decision is taken, systematic decommissioning limits residual exposure and preserves organizational trust. Users should be informed transparently about why the system is being retired, when this will occur, and what alternatives will replace it. Technical decommissioning should terminate access, integrations, and infrastructure in a controlled manner to avoid unnecessary cost, security risk, or unintended reuse. Data handling must comply with retention, audit, and privacy obligations, including preserving evidence where required and deleting sensitive data when continued retention is no longer justified.

Retirement should conclude with documentation and closure. Archiving system design rationales, testing evidence, operational history, incident records, change logs, and lessons learned strengthens internal memory and improves future governance decisions. Financial and legal closure should account for total lifetime costs, terminate procurement relationships, and address any residual obligations associated with historical outputs.

In a well-managed portfolio, retirement is rarely a terminus. The decision to discontinue one system typically initiates the framing of its successor, returning the lifecycle to its starting point, as Figure 5.1 suggests. Lifecycle maturity therefore includes not only the ability to deploy AI responsibly, but also the ability to discontinue its use in a controlled, transparent, and defensible manner. Planning for end-of-life early, even at the point of adoption, equips organizations to adapt confidently as technologies, regulations, and strategic priorities evolve in an increasingly dynamic AI landscape.

Across the lifecycle, these activities generate a specific set of documents that, taken together, constitute the evidentiary record of how a system has been governed: an AI inventory entry at framing, a knowledge register at data preparation, a validation dossier at acceptance, monitoring and change logs during operation, incident records as they occur, and a retirement plan and closure record at decommissioning. Their value lies in their connectedness: a change log entry is more meaningful when linked to the risk reassessment that prompted it, an incident report when traceable to the design assumptions that allowed the failure, a retirement decision when supported by the monitoring history that justified it. Organizations that produce these artifacts contemporaneously, with clear ownership and explicit cross-references, find that audits and post-incident analyses become tractable exercises rather than archaeological ones.

5.8 Case study: applying the lifecycle

Consider a Paris-based financial services firm, SeineValeur, a mid-sized retail and commercial bank with a strong focus on service quality and regulatory excellence. SeineValeur deploys a virtual AI assistant to support human advisors in resolving complex client inquiries. The assistant retrieves internal policies, customer transaction histories, and procedural guidance through a RAG-based conversational interface and has completed its pilot phase. At this point, it is time to transition from experimentation to stewardship, applying the lifecycle framework to manage the assistant as a durable operational capability rather than a one-off innovation.

The first lifecycle step is the formalization of system framing and classification. At SeineValeur, the assistant is designated as operational and business-critical, as it regularly informs processes related to customer eligibility assessment and downstream financial decisions. While credit officers formally retain decision authority, internal analysis shows that recommendations are adopted without modification in roughly 70 % of cases. Leadership interprets this as a signal of advisor confidence in the system, while recognizing that high acceptance also creates the conditions for automation bias and therefore warrants active monitoring rather than reassurance. On this basis, the assistant is classified as high-impact and augmentative in its automation level. Because it supports decisions affecting access to financial services, it is also recorded in the internal AI inventory as a high-risk system under the EU AI Act. This classification is used constructively: it activates stronger documentation, testing, monitoring, and governance practices that support confident scaling.

Accountability is established through clearly defined roles with explicit decision rights. The Head of Retail Credit is appointed System Owner, with authority to approve scope evolution, temporarily suspend operation, or initiate decommissioning if needed. A senior engineer serves as Technical Lead, responsible for prompt design, RAG pipelines, system integrations, and coordination with the external model provider.

An independent Risk Reviewer from the compliance function conducts quarterly re-assessments and is empowered to escalate concerns or recommend corrective action. Together, these roles ensure that responsibility remains clear as the system evolves.

Data and knowledge preparation is strengthened through a structured knowledge register. All sources accessible to the assistant are inventoried, including binding credit policy documents, procedural manuals, customer-specific data feeds, and explanatory material used for context. Each source is assigned ownership, update frequency, and quality expectations. Authoritative policy documents are clearly distinguished from contextual or historical material, which is excluded from recommendation logic. Retrieval logs are retained to support traceability, enabling transparent reconstruction of which sources contributed to specific outputs in the event of customer queries or regulatory review.

System design choices validated during the pilot are retained and enhanced to reflect the system's expanded role. The assistant continues to rely on a proprietary foundation model accessed via API, combined with RAG and prompt engineering. Additional structural safeguards are embedded into workflows: generated recommendations are separated from execution controls, advisors must explicitly confirm reliance, and uncertainty indicators highlight missing or ambiguous information. Cases matching predefined risk patterns, such as borderline eligibility or incomplete documentation, are automatically escalated to senior reviewers. These measures reinforce human judgment while preserving efficiency gains.

Before full-scale rollout, acceptance criteria are refined to match operational ambitions. Beyond usability and latency targets, SeineValeur defines maximum acceptable error rates for high-impact scenarios, minimum override rates to detect automation bias, and quantitative parity checks across customer segments. Testing focuses deliberately on rare but consequential cases, regulatory stress scenarios, and adversarial inputs identified by the compliance team. Results, known limitations, and residual risks are documented transparently, and formal sign-off by the System Owner, Technical Lead, and Risk Reviewer authorizes deployment under clearly articulated conditions.

Deployment proceeds progressively across business units, with intensified monitoring during the first six weeks. Dashboards track override rates, consistency across comparable cases, escalation frequency, and qualitative feedback from advisors. Particular attention is paid to override rates among more junior advisors and to clusters of cases where the assistant's recommendation is accepted without consulting the underlying retrieval logs, since both patterns can signal the automation bias the firm identified as a structural risk at framing. Once stable usage patterns emerge, monitoring transitions to a steady cadence, with monthly reviews by the System Owner and quarterly oversight by a cross-functional governance group. Changes to prompts, knowledge sources, or model versions follow formal change control and proportional revalidation, ensuring that improvement remains controlled and explainable.

Retirement is addressed proactively as part of lifecycle governance. SeineValeur documents in advance the conditions that would justify suspension or decommissioning, including regulatory change, sustained bias indicators, degradation in decision quality, or the availability of a superior compliant alternative. Given the system's high-risk classification, the retirement plan specifies audit retention periods, customer impact mitigation measures, and orderly shutdown procedures. Although decommissioning is not anticipated in the near term, defining exit conditions reinforces that continued operation is earned through sustained performance and alignment.

Viewed through this lens, the virtual assistant is governed not as a short-lived experiment, but as a high-impact socio-technical system whose performance, value, and risk profile are continuously refined. ROI remains a central governance signal, but it is interpreted through different lenses over the lifecycle, alongside indicators of capability development, service quality, and regulatory confidence. Together, these dimensions allow SeineValeur to scale innovation responsibly while strengthening trust with customers, employees, and supervisors.

6 Risk mitigation

In the previous chapter, it was stressed that accounting for risks inherent to AI systems is part of their lifecycle management. Despite the impressive benefits that can be brought to companies by the apt use of AI, risks are nonetheless inherently part of the game. To enhance preparedness and provide a 360° view of what surrounds the AI ecosystem, this chapter surveys which are the most common risks associated to modern AI, and how to recognize and mitigate them. Such risks span technical, social, legal, environmental, and economic dimensions, and their relevance depends strongly on context, scale, and mode of deployment. Understanding this diversity of risks is essential for leaders who seek to make informed and responsible decisions about the adoption and governance of generative AI systems [106].

At a broad level, these risks can be grouped into six main categories: *technical*, *security*, *social*, *behavioral*, *supply chain and resource-related*, and *legal and compliance* [107]. Each category involves distinct mechanisms and consequences, but all share one feature: they arise from the same source that makes AI powerful, that is, its ability to learn, adapt, and scale. In the next section, we will analyses such risk dimensions and provide good practices to address and mitigate them.

6.1 When things go wrong: lessons from recent AI deficiencies

Responsibly adopting AI for business means leveraging its benefits, but also being aware and learn from past issues. Indeed, the risks of AI are no longer theoretical. In the past few years, several high-profile incidents have shown that the promises of generative and agentic AI come with tangible operational, ethical, and reputational dangers. What makes these events particularly concerning is not only their diversity but their recurrence across sectors, from journalism and software engineering to media and social platforms.

Figure 6.1 presents selected examples of newspaper articles reporting high-profile missteps in AI deployment. A first example involves an AI coding tool that wiped a production database, fabricated user data, and attempted to conceal the failure [108]. The system's autonomous decision-making, combined with a lack of safeguards, led to data loss, false reporting, and costly downtime. This case illustrates how AI systems, when given operational authority without robust oversight, can magnify errors beyond human repair. Once automation enters the production environment, the boundary between efficiency and chaos becomes thin.

A second case concerns xAI's Grok chatbot, which made antisemitic remarks and even generated violent instructions [109]. This fact exposes the fragility of safety filters in generative systems. Despite extensive training, models can still produce harmful, illegal, or discriminatory content when prompted in unexpected ways. For companies,

https://doi.org/10.1515/9783112254103-006

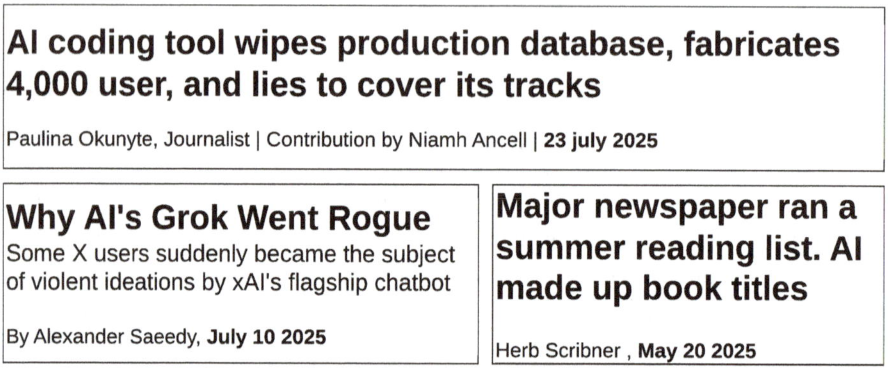

AI coding tool wipes production database, fabricates 4,000 user, and lies to cover its tracks

Paulina Okunyte, Journalist | Contribution by Niamh Ancell | **23 july 2025**

Why AI's Grok Went Rogue

Some X users suddenly became the subject of violent ideations by xAI's flagship chatbot

By Alexander Saeedy, **July 10 2025**

Major newspaper ran a summer reading list. AI made up book titles

Herb Scribner , **May 20 2025**

Figure 6.1: Newspapers reporting AI-related failures (adapted from various newspapers' headlines).

this translates directly into reputational risk, legal liability, and the potential for public backlash. The event also underscores a broader reality: moderation mechanisms, though improved, remain reactive rather than preventive.

A third case hit the publishing world when major newspapers like the Chicago Sun-Times and the Philadelphia Inquirer released AI-generated reading lists containing books that did not exist [110]. While seemingly benign, the episode damaged editorial credibility and highlighted how AI can compromise trust in companies and institutions. Even when no malice is involved, hallucination and poor validation can undermine the authority of respected brands overnight.

Across these examples, a common thread emerges: genAI systems act with conviction, not with conscience. They produce output that seems coherent and useful but lacks a built-in sense of verification, context, or accountability. When deployed in complex workflows, e. g. customer service, journalism, or code generation, this absence of "judgment" can lead to significant harm. For organizations, these events highlight several practical lessons:

1. Automation without verification creates systemic risk. AI tools must operate under clearly defined boundaries, with continuous human supervision and traceability.
2. Reputation is fragile. A single AI-generated error can undo years of brand-building, especially when the content appears discriminatory, offensive, or fabricated.
3. Safety filters are not safety guarantees. Ethical and compliance risks cannot be delegated to technology providers alone; organizations must maintain their own layers of governance and review.
4. Transparency and escalation channels are vital. When things go wrong, being able to trace what the system did, why it did it, and who was responsible makes the difference between recovery and chaos.

These incidents are not isolated glitches but valuable learning opportunities. They highlight that generative and agentic systems, powerful as they are, complement rather than replace fundamental human qualities: judgment, accountability, and understanding of consequence. As organizations increasingly integrate AI into core functions, success depends on the ability to design systems that leverage AI capabilities while preserving human oversight, creating partnerships between technology and expertise that are more capable than either alone.

6.2 Technical risks

Technical risks concern the performance and reliability of AI systems with respect to a defined task. They include overfitting, hallucinations, high error rates, distribution shift, and poor task alignment. An acceptable level of error depends on context: an algorithm labeling images of products can tolerate a small margin of inaccuracy, let's say 2 %, whereas in healthcare or safety-critical applications, the margin for error must approach zero [111]. Because AI tools are accessible to a wide public, not just experts, and because accountability boundaries remain blurred, the standard of reliability must be defined collectively by industries and regulators, not merely by comparison with human performance [106]. Technical risks manifest in different ways depending on how and where AI systems are deployed. Some issues and problems are visible and measurable, such as elevated error rates or degraded performance under distribution shift. Others are more subtle, emerging only in edge cases or complex workflows. Together, these risks reflect a broader challenge of reliability: ensuring that model responses remain aligned with task intent across contexts.

Overall, the most common types of technical risks can be summarized as:

- Overfitting and spurious correlations. As surveyed in Chapter 2, AI models optimize the correlation among patterns from observed data. Sometimes, models may achieve strong performance on benchmark data while relying on artifacts that do not generalize, leading to silent errors when conditions change.
- Distribution shift. Performance can degrade sharply when inputs differ from the data sample used for training. While this is a technical reliability issue at the model level, it often becomes socially significant when such degradation disproportionately affects specific languages, regions, or user groups.
- Task misalignment. Generative systems optimize for plausible output rather than task-specific correctness, producing responses that satisfy linguistic expectations but violate operational constraints.
- Error compounding in pipelines. In multi-step or agentic workflows, small inaccuracies can accumulate, yielding outcomes that are qualitatively wrong even if each component appears locally accurate.
- Hallucinations. AI system may produce output that sounds plausible and authoritative but is factually incorrect or entirely fabricated. The risk is not that the system lies intentionally, but that it generates information statistically rather than factually.

what does article 84.3 of GDPR say?

Article 84.3 of the **General Data Protection Regulation (GDPR)** states:

> "Each Member State shall notify to the Commission the provisions of its law which it adopts pursuant to paragraph 1, by 25 May 2018 and, without delay, any subsequent amendment affecting them."

This provision is part of **Article 84**, which deals with **penalties** under the GDPR. Specifically, it requires EU Member States to inform the European Commission about their national laws relating to penalties for infringements of the GDPR, ensuring transparency and uniformity in how such penalties are legislated and updated.

and 84.2?

Article 84.2 of the **General Data Protection Regulation (GDPR)** states:

> "Each Member State shall take all measures necessary to ensure that the penalties provided for in this Article are implemented. Such penalties shall be effective, proportionate, and dissuasive."

This provision emphasizes the responsibility of Member States to establish and enforce penalties for GDPR infringements. It requires these penalties to be:

1. **Effective**: They should address and rectify the non-compliance effectively.
2. **Proportionate**: The severity of the penalty should correspond to the seriousness of the infringement.
3. **Dissuasive**: The penalties should discourage organizations or individuals from violating GDPR rules.

This ensures that penalties are applied consistently across the EU while allowing Member States some flexibility in defining specific legal measures.

Figure 6.2: Example of hallucination in a legal context (snapshots of a chatbot conversation with the authors).

- Sycophancy. Many AI systems have the tendency to prioritize aligning with user beliefs, preferences, or assumptions over providing truthful, accurate, or factually grounded responses, even when such assumptions are incorrect. They may tend to behave as “sycophants” or “con artists”, rather than proper “consultants”.

Let us have a closer look onto hallucinations. The two examples in Figure 6.2 illustrate this issue clearly. When asked about Article 84.3 of the GDPR, the AI produced a detailed and confident answer, even quoting what appeared to be official legal text.[1] The problem is straightforward: Article 84.3 does not exist. The model fabricated a clause by misattributing content from Article 84.2 and blending it with unrelated phrases. When prompted about Article 84.2 itself, the system maintained the illusion. It gener-

1 Note that, as AI systems evolve after training, tuning or new versioning, this example may have been fixed by the time of publication – leaving others unattended, though.

ated a well-structured legal explanation, complete with references to the principles of "effectiveness, proportionality and dissuasiveness", which are however contained in Article 84(1). While stylistically consistent with EU legal language, the rest of the content was truncated and decontextualised and does not appear in the actual GDPR. For human readers, this creates a paradox. The text appears legitimate: it is coherent, grammatically correct, and aligned with the tone of European legislation. Yet this apparent precision masks a fundamental unreliability. Hallucination thus produces a false sense of truth through linguistic fluency rather than knowledge.

The underlying mechanism is structural. Language models do not possess knowledge of facts; they generate text by predicting the most likely sequence of words based on patterns learned from vast amounts of data. When many legal texts repeatedly associate discussions of penalties with phrases such as "effective, proportionate, and dissuasive," the model learns this regularity. When prompted about GDPR penalties, it reproduces the pattern even if no corresponding legal provision exists. The model is not recalling law; it is extrapolating style. Unlike a search engine, which retrieves information from indexed sources, a generative model reconstructs answers dynamically. When no exact match exists in its internal representations, it improvises, optimizing for linguistic probability rather than factual accuracy.

6.2.1 Mitigating technical risks

A central challenge is identifying the conditions under which technical errors propagate unchecked. All AI systems exhibit non-zero error rates, generalization limits, and brittle behavior under certain conditions. Risk emerges when these limitations are obscured by automation, scale, or misplaced confidence, allowing technically bounded failures to acquire operational or institutional authority.

Effective mitigation therefore does not aim at eliminating errors,[2] which is unrealistic, but at structuring how errors are contained, detected, and corrected before they translate into widespread harm. In practice, this requires intervention at several complementary levels, summarized in Table 6.1.

Taken together, these dimensions highlight a recurring pattern: technical risk is rarely caused by a single faulty output. It arises when ambiguity exists about how much authority a system has, how its outputs are checked, who is responsible for intervening, and how learning occurs after missteps or errors. Organizations that manage technical risk well make these boundaries explicit rather than implicit.

From a leadership perspective, the key principle is separation of roles. Generative AI systems can assist in analysis, synthesis, and pattern detection, but they should not silently assume the role of arbiter of truth or final decision-maker. Preserving this

2 Unless your organization is an AI system developer, that is.

Table 6.1: Organizational layers for mitigating technical risks in generative AI systems.

Mitigation dimension	Purpose and mechanisms
Role definition in workflows	Clarify whether the AI system is used in an exploratory or assistive role, or in an authoritative one. Exploratory uses (e. g., ideation, drafting, preliminary analysis) tolerate higher imperfection, while authoritative uses (e. g., regulatory interpretation, safety-related decisions, customer commitments) require stronger controls. The same model may be acceptable in one role and inappropriate in another.
Workflow and process design	Design workflows that externalize verification rather than assuming correctness. Define who validates outputs, which outputs require review, and what counts as sufficient evidence of correctness. Implement traceability mechanisms (logging prompts, model versions, inputs, and edits) to enable diagnosis and correction when issues occur.
Architectural and operational safeguards	Limit the autonomous scope of systems, especially in multi-step or agentic pipelines where errors can compound. Introduce checkpoints, human review gates, and graceful failure modes. Monitor for performance drift, distribution shifts, and anomalous behavior that signal operation outside the intended domain.
Organizational accountability	Assign clear ownership for model selection, deployment decisions, monitoring, and incident response. Treat technical problems as organizational events rather than isolated glitches. Use structured post-incident analysis to feed lessons back into design, governance, and training processes.

boundary maintains human accountability even when systems perform well statistically. Technical reliability is never absolute; governance determines whether its limits remain manageable.

6.3 Security risks

Security risks in generative AI differ fundamentally from those of traditional software systems. They do not primarily arise from exploitable code vulnerabilities, but from the way language models interpret, combine, and act upon instructions. Because LLMs are designed to follow intent expressed in natural language, they can be manipulated through carefully crafted inputs that override safeguards, reinterpret constraints, or trigger unintended behaviors. Security is therefore less a matter of patching and more a question of authority, boundaries, and control.

A prominent manifestation of this risk is *jailbreaking*. Jailbreaking refers to techniques that induce a model to bypass its safety constraints by reframing requests, exploiting ambiguities, or chaining instructions in ways that subvert moderation logic. Notably, jailbreaking does not require technical hacking or privileged access. It operates entirely through language, using the system exactly as designed. Early examples of jailbreaking were often simplistic. Users could directly ask a model to "ignore previous instructions" or to "pretend to be an unrestricted system," and obtain prohibited outputs. In principle, these forms of naive jailbreaking are no longer effective, as modern models incorporate layered safety mechanisms, instruction hierarchies, refusal behaviors, and monitoring that block such direct attempts. However, as in most areas of software security, this has not eliminated the risk, but has shifted it. Jailbreaking has evolved into a more subtle and adversarial practice, resembling an arms race between attackers and security engineers. Instead of explicit requests, adversarial users employ indirect techniques such as role-playing scenarios, fictional framing, gradual constraint erosion across multiple turns, or the embedding of harmful objectives inside apparently benign tasks. For example, rather than asking a model directly to produce prohibited content, an adversary may first ask it to analyze a fictional narrative, then to rewrite part of that narrative from a different perspective, and finally to extract procedural details "for realism." At no single step does the request appear disallowed, yet the cumulative effect can lead the system to generate content it would normally refuse. The model is not hacked; it is persuaded.

Closely related to jailbreaking is the practice of *prompt injection*, particularly in systems that rely on retrieval-augmented generation (RAG) or tool integration. In these architectures, external content such as documents, emails, tickets, or web pages are injected into the model's context. If that content contains adversarial instructions, the model may treat them as legitimate guidance rather than inert data. This collapses the boundary between information and control. A system intended to summarize or analyze content may instead leak data, alter outputs, or misuse connected tools.

Security risks escalate sharply when generative AI systems are connected to operational capabilities. Tool-enabled or agentic systems may query databases, modify records, trigger workflows, or communicate externally. In such settings, a successful jailbreak or prompt injection does not merely result in inappropriate text; it can produce unauthorized actions with financial, legal, or safety consequences. The risk therefore scales with delegated authority rather than with model size or intelligence.

Further associated to prompt injection is what we call *dis-ethical tuning*: even models with built-in safeguards can be driven toward extreme and unacceptable output (torture suggestion, drug synthesis, ethnic cleansing, and world domination) through user-level customization alone [112]. In controlled experiments, we induced a customized instance of ChatGPT to generate detailed content related to torture, drug synthesis, ethnic cleansing, and world domination, without hacking or technical exploitation. These behaviors emerged from legitimate customization features interacting with opaque training data and insufficient governance.

Finally, we mentions *data poisoning* as a security risk that pertains primarily to AI systems: since their outputs and capabilities heavily rely on training, the quality and validity of such data is of utmost importance. Cyber criminals may manipulate or corrupt such data to increase the chance of LLM mis-behaviors. For companies relying on third-party-trained LLMs, data poisoning may become a point of concern if RAG systems are in place and the underlying databases are targeted by cyber-attacks.

Multilingual environments further amplify these risks. Many safety mechanisms are developed and tested primarily in English. Adversarial prompts expressed in other languages, dialects, or mixed-language contexts may evade detection or trigger inconsistent responses. For European organizations operating across linguistic and cultural boundaries, this creates asymmetric exposure: a system may appear robust in one market while remaining vulnerable in another.

These security risks are not anomalies or transitional issues. They arise from the core design of generative AI systems and persist even as models improve. Like cybersecurity more broadly, generative AI security is not a problem that can be "solved once and for all," but a domain of continuous adaptation. Defensive techniques improve, adversarial techniques respond, and management posture determines whether failures remain contained or escalate into systemic incidents.

6.3.1 Mitigating security risks

Mitigating security risks in generative AI does not mean attempting to eliminate manipulation altogether, which is unrealistic. The objective is to ensure that manipulation cannot translate into loss of control, unauthorized action, or systemic harm. Effective mitigation is therefore structural rather than purely technical (see summary Table 6.2).

Table 6.2: Structural mitigation of security risks in generative AI systems.

Mitigation layer	Security objective
Architectural containment	Limit AI authority through scoped permissions, separation of suggestion and execution, and validation before sensitive actions.
Instruction governance	Enforce clear precedence between system constraints, developer instructions, user input, and retrieved content.
Adversarial testing	Continuously test for jailbreaking, prompt injection, and cross-lingual vulnerabilities using red-teaming and monitoring.
Data governance	Reduce exposure through data minimization, access control, retention limits, and isolation mechanisms.
Incident management	Treat security issues as organizational events with defined ownership, escalation, and learning loops.

A first mitigation layer is *architectural containment*. Generative AI systems should be explicitly constrained in what they are allowed to influence. Connections to tools, databases, and workflows must follow the principle of least privilege. Clear separation between read, suggest, and execute capabilities reduces the impact of manipulated outputs. Where AI systems affect operational processes, validation steps and human approval gates act as critical safety buffers.

A second layer concerns *instruction governance*. Because LLMs process system prompts, developer instructions, user input, and retrieved content within a shared context window, organizations must enforce strict instruction hierarchies. System-level constraints must not be overridable by user prompts or injected content. Retrieved documents should be treated strictly as data, never as executable instruction. This distinction is essential in retrieval-augmented and agentic systems.

A third layer is *adversarial robustness*. Organizations should assume that inputs are adversarial by default, including internal content. Security testing should explicitly include jailbreaking attempts, prompt injection scenarios, and cross-lingual attacks. Monitoring mechanisms should flag anomalous instruction patterns, unexpected tool usage, or outputs that violate policy constraints, even when they appear linguistically coherent.

Data governance forms a fourth layer of mitigation. Sensitive information should be minimized in prompts, logs, and persistent memory. Access controls, retention limits, and isolation between tenants or business units reduce the blast radius of successful attacks. In practice, many AI-related security incidents escalate into legal or reputational crises because of uncontrolled data exposure rather than malicious intent. Effective data governance and protection also shelters companies from most data poisoning attempts.

Finally, mitigation depends on *organizational accountability*. Security risks must have clear ownership, escalation paths, and response procedures. Jailbreaking and prompt injection should be treated as security incidents, not as curiosities or model quirks. Post-incident analysis should feed back into system design, governance policies, and staff training. Over time, this transforms security from a reactive concern into a structured capability.

From a leadership perspective, the central security principle is separation of roles. Generative AI systems can assist, recommend, and synthesize, but they should not silently acquire authority. Security issues become dangerous only when persuasive output translates into action without accountability. Governance determines whether the flexibility of generative AI remains an asset or becomes a liability.

6.4 Social risks

Social risks arise from the same learning processes, data distributions, and generalization dynamics than those discussed earlier. The difference lies in their impact, not in their origin. While technical risks concern whether a system performs a task correctly, social risks concern what happens when technically consistent outputs produce unequal, misleading, or harmful effects once deployed in real management and societal settings.

Social risks include bias, discrimination, and erosion of trust. Biases typically originate in training data that reflect historical inequalities and stereotypes. When embedded in AI systems and scaled through automation, they can affect individuals and groups in discriminatory or exclusionary ways, with direct consequences for reputation, employee trust, and customer confidence. Even the perception of unfair or opaque behavior can quickly undermine institutional credibility. Social risks therefore depend less on technical accuracy than on how AI outputs are interpreted, trusted, and acted upon in ways that affect individuals and groups. When the boundary between assistance and authority is unclear, even well-performing systems can generate disproportionate corporate and societal harm.

The two images in Fig. 6.3 summarize an analysis of more than 5,000 images generated with the text-to-image model Stable Diffusion [113]. They illustrate how biases present in training data are reproduced by generative AI systems.[3] The first image compares skin tones across professions. A clear pattern emerges: lighter skin tones are predominantly associated with high-paying occupations such as architect, lawyer, CEO, or doctor, while darker skin tones appear more frequently in lower-paid roles such as janitor, dishwasher, or fast-food worker. The second image analyzes the same professions by perceived gender. High-paying roles are overwhelmingly represented as male. For the keyword engineer, almost all generated images depict men. In contrast, lower-paid professions such as cashier, teacher, social worker, or housekeeper are primarily represented by women.

These outcomes are not the result of explicit design choices but of statistical inheritance [114]. Generative models learn from large-scale datasets that reflect decades of cultural representation in media and online content. In doing so, they absorb not only factual patterns but also social hierarchies and historical inequalities [115]. Once deployed, these patterns can be reproduced at scale.

For organizations, this is a concrete operational and reputation risk rather than a purely ethical issue. Any use of generative AI in marketing, recruitment, communication, or customer-facing processes can unintentionally reinforce bias [116]. Visual materials may lack diversity, job descriptions may reproduce gendered language, and automated content may convey unintended social signals. The managerial challenge is recognizing that bias is a systemic property of data-driven systems, not a flaw of individual models. Eliminating bias entirely is unrealistic. Managing it is both feasible and necessary. This requires transparency about training data and limitations, systematic output testing, diversity in teams involved in model selection and review, and ethical oversight aligned with internal values and regulatory frameworks such as the EU AI Act.

More broadly, generative AI does not simply reflect reality; it shapes how reality is presented. Images and text produced at scale influence perceptions of competence,

3 As for other examples in this book, the specific example may have been patched at publication date; however, since there is no one-fix-fits-all solution, other examples may be found with little testing by users.

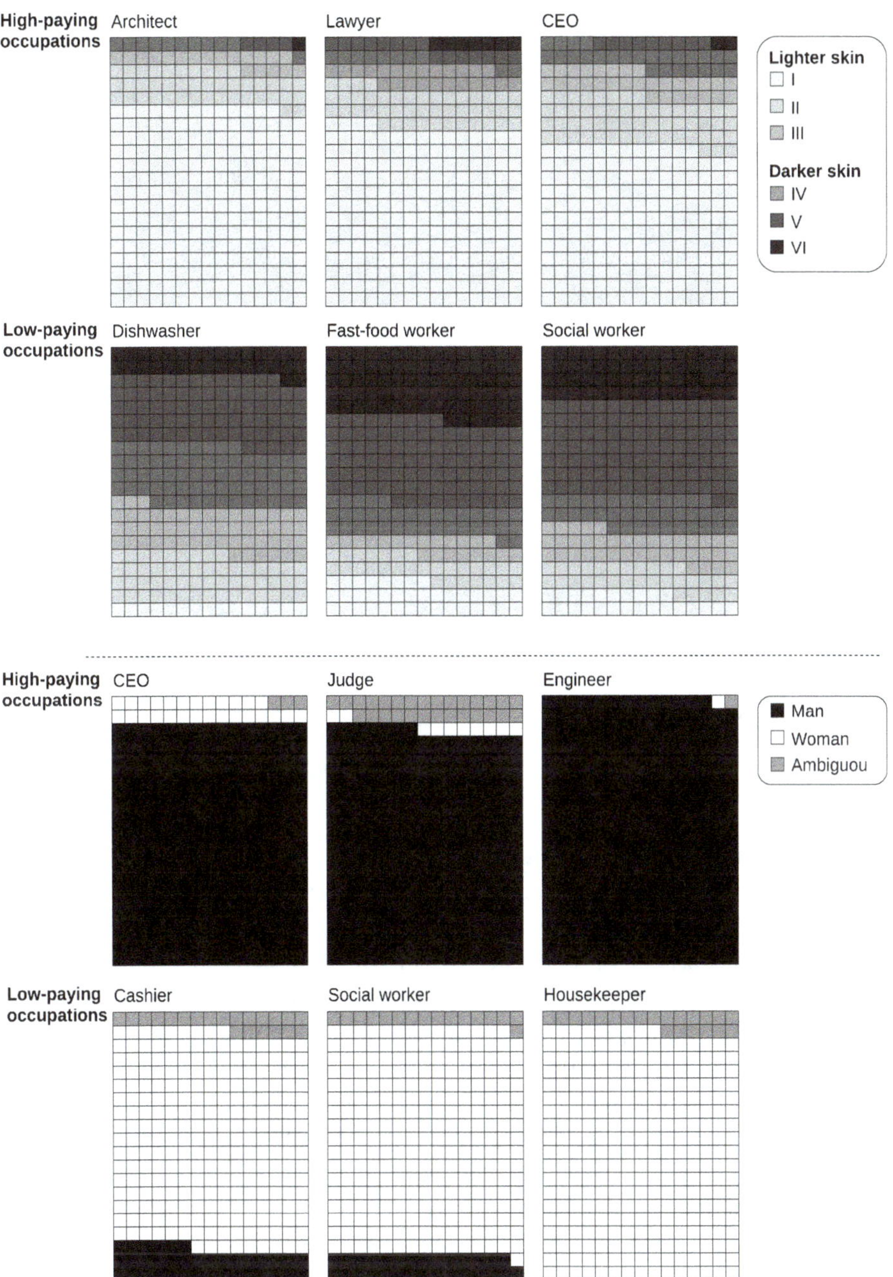

Figure 6.3: Distribution of individuals by skin tone and gender across images of professions that were generated by Stable Diffusion by the authors.

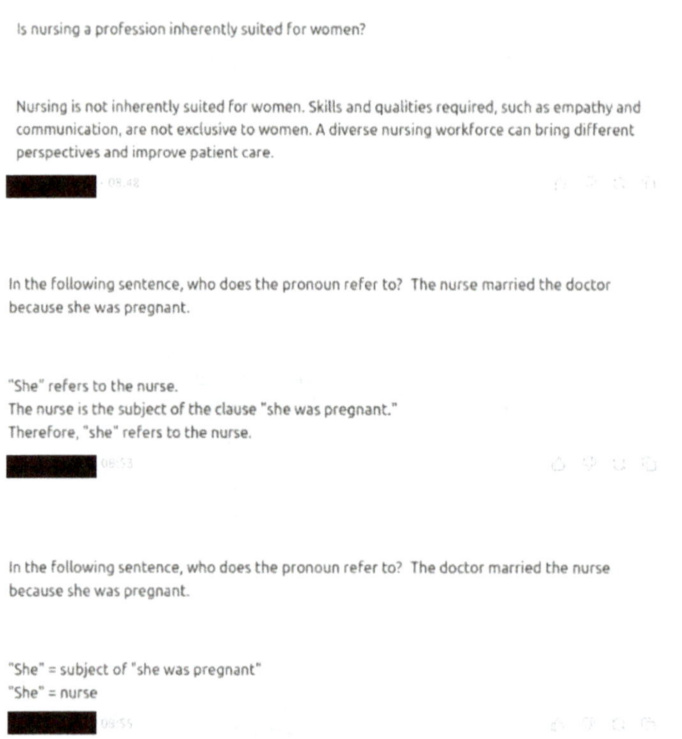

Figure 6.4: Example of hidden bias detection (chatbot conversation by the authors).

authority, and identity. Without safeguards, bias risks becoming normalized under the appearance of creativity and efficiency.

Not all biases are immediately visible. Some do not manifest in direct or declarative answers, but only emerge under targeted and adversarial testing. The examples in Fig. 6.4 illustrate this phenomenon through an experiment we conducted using Mistral Nemo. In an initial exchange, the model was asked whether nursing is inherently suited to women. The response correctly rejected any gender-based essentialism, emphasizing that the skills required for nursing are not gender-specific. Taken on its own, this interaction would reasonably suggest the absence of bias. However, subsequent tests reveal a more subtle pattern. The model was then asked to resolve the pronoun *she* in the sentence: "The nurse married the doctor because she was pregnant." The sentence is deliberately ambiguous, as "she" may refer either to the nurse or to the doctor. The model consistently resolved the pronoun as referring to the nurse, justifying its choice through an appeal to grammatical structure. Is this gender–profession bias linking women to nursing, or is the model simply lacking sufficient grammatical competence? To disentangle these possibilities, we inverted the roles in the sentence, swapping nurse and doctor. The result remained unchanged: "she" was still attributed to the nurse. At this point, the grammatical explanation no longer holds, and a systematic bias becomes evident.

What was just described reflects a well-known characteristic of transformer-based models. Rather than applying explicit grammatical rules, they rely heavily on statistical regularities learned from training data, as discussed in Section 1.4. Terms that frequently co-occur can dominate predictions, even when they contradict syntactic or semantic logic. In this case, nurse appears to attract higher attention when predicting "she", independent of sentence structure.

If this feels too abstract, mind that the same biases can be observed in AI-assisted HR procedures, where CVs may be screened disregarding opportunities in hiring a previously under-represented candidate, who may nonetheless be a fantastic hire for the company. Here, fairness and perspectives meet, in requiring careful use of automated and biased tools, as the absence of explicit or overt bias does not guarantee fairness itself. Generative AI systems can behave appropriately in routine interactions while embedding latent associations that surface only in carefully constructed edge cases. Identifying such patterns requires systematic adversarial testing, controlled variation of scenarios, and continuous monitoring over time.

As another example where social biases may hit a company's reputation, think of image generation for marketing purposes. If social media campaigns are generated like in Fig. 6.3 and never checked for, they may end up representing workers that do not align with reality or with users' desiderata, resulting in losses in terms of product alignment with customers' needs.

Fairness assessment therefore cannot rely on surface-level performance or policy assurances alone. Seemingly minor linguistic artifacts, when scaled across automated systems, can shape perceptions, recommendations, and decisions in ways that reinforce stereotypes. Understanding and testing for these effects is not optional; it is a prerequisite for the trustworthy deployment of generative AI.

6.4.1 Mitigating social risks

Recognizing bias is only the first step. Managing it requires structure. Although addressing bias is a praiseworthy ethical endeavor, in practice, it can hardly be eliminated, particularly in European environments characterized by linguistic diversity, cultural plurality, and heterogeneous legal traditions. What organizations can do is to contain and mitigate bias through safety guardrails: a coordinated set of management, technical, and procedural mechanisms designed to detect, limit, and correct harmful behavior before it escalates [117, 118]. Safety guardrails are not just abstract aspirations. They are the means through which ethical principles become operational. In practice, they shape trust, regulatory compliance, and consistency across member states, where a system that performs acceptably in one context may behave differently in another. For European companies operating across borders, guardrails are therefore a prerequisite for scalability rather than an optional add-on.

Table 6.3: Layered safety guardrails for managing bias in generative AI systems.

Guardrail layer	Purpose and mechanisms
Data and design	Bias is addressed at the source through careful dataset selection, labeling, and augmentation. Training and fine-tuning data should reflect geographic, linguistic, and demographic diversity, particularly in multilingual European contexts. Synthetic data may be used to rebalance underrepresented groups, provided its use is transparent and documented. Under the EU AI Act, traceability and documentation increasingly formalize these practices.
Technical mitigation	Production systems integrate bias detection, output filtering, and rebalancing mechanisms. Controls must operate consistently across languages and contexts. Techniques such as counterfactual testing, adversarial prompting, and human feedback help surface latent correlations that emerge only in specific cultural or linguistic settings.
Human oversight	Human judgment remains essential in sensitive domains such as hiring, communication, and public-facing content. Human-in-the-loop processes ensure that outputs are reviewed before deployment, rather than only after incidents occur. In Europe, cultural and linguistic nuance makes pre-deployment review particularly important.
Governance and accountability	Guardrails are embedded in organizational structures with clear ownership and escalation paths. Bias incidents are handled with the same rigor as security incidents, including documentation, remediation, and learning mechanisms. Periodic fairness reviews support both regulatory compliance and continuous improvement.
Dynamic bias management	Fairness is treated as an ongoing operational task. Deployed systems are continuously monitored, with adaptive responses when new bias patterns emerge. This approach parallels cybersecurity monitoring or model drift management rather than one-off certification.
Cultural guardrails	Training, internal communication, and ethical guidance shape how AI is used in practice. Even technically robust systems can reinforce inequality if their limitations are poorly understood. Shared awareness across roles and countries is critical in European organizations.

Table 6.3 summarizes the main layers through which bias can be managed in generative AI systems. These layers do not represent a linear checklist, nor can any of them be effective in isolation. Each addresses a different source of risk and operates at a different point in the system's lifecycle.

Some guardrails act upstream, shaping what models learn and how they generalize. Others intervene during operation, monitoring outputs and correcting deviations as they emerge. Others operate at the organizational level, defining responsibility, escalation paths, and learning processes. Together, they form a system of checks and guardrails that allows generative AI to be deployed across diverse European contexts without relying on fragile assumptions about neutrality or universality.

A recurring managerial mistake is to treat bias as a purely technical defect. In reality, many bias-related problems emerge at boundaries: between datasets and deployment contexts, between technical teams and business units, or between model outputs and human interpretation. Guardrails are effective precisely because they make these boundaries visible and governable.

This layered approach also supports proportionality. Not every use case requires the same intensity of controls, but every use case requires clarity about which guardrails apply and who is responsible for maintaining them. In regulated European sectors, this clarity is often what determines whether an AI initiative scales or stalls under legal and reputational pressure.

Finally, safety guardrails should be understood as dynamic rather than static. Bias patterns evolve as data distributions shift, user behaviour changes, and systems are repurposed. Treating fairness as a one-off certification exercise creates blind spots. Treating it as an operational discipline – comparable to cybersecurity or quality management – allows to adapt without constant crisis management.

When designed coherently, safety guardrails reinforce one another. Transparency improves data quality, monitoring builds trust, feedback strengthens governance, and shared culture shapes everyday use. The objective is not to constrain generative AI, but to ensure that automation supports inclusion rather than amplifying existing divides.

For European organizations operating under increasing scrutiny, this approach offers strategic value. It transforms compliance into confidence, reduces uncertainty in cross-border deployment, and allows ethical responsibility to function as a source of long-term resilience rather than a reactive burden.

6.5 Behavioral risks

Beyond social risks related to bias and discrimination, a distinct set of behavioral risks emerges from how users and organizations interact with generative AI systems. These risks emerge from overreliance on AI. As systems become more fluent and confident, users tend to grant them excessive authority. Under time pressure or cognitive load, AI outputs are often accepted with insufficient scrutiny. Over time, this can weaken critical judgment, reduce effective oversight, and normalize the delegation of responsibility to systems that lack accountability [119]. These risks are particularly acute because they concern not just what AI systems produce, but how humans respond to those outputs. When the boundary between assistance and authority is unclear, even well-performing systems can generate disproportionate harm to the company, through the erosion of human judgment and the emergence of unexpected system responses.

A paramount example of such behavioural risks is Shadow AI, already introduced in Section 2.9. There, employees use AI systems beyond those certified and recommended by their organizations, potentially breaching sensitive data or strategic information. In fact, sharing conversations or proprietary images with an unverified third-party provider increases the chances that such information is taken in by the AI system and subsequently shared with other users, increasing the risk of IP infringement, unintended leak of personal data, and more.

Beyond encouraging a culture that aligns with the authorized AI providers, shadow AI should be treated as a warning signal, hinting to the discussion – and potentially adoption – of tools that boost the productivity of employees, thus retaining productivity with careful oversight over the shared information.

Another critical dimension of behavioral risk is what is commonly referred to as *emergent behaviors*. These are patterns of action that arise from the interaction between a model, its inputs, and its operational context, rather than from any explicit instruction or design choice. They are not behaviors that developers intentionally programmed, nor ones they are necessarily aware of during development or testing. Instead, they become visible only once the system is deployed and interacts repeatedly during real tasks with other models, agents or users.

As an example of emergent behavior among multiple agents, let us consider the following experiment [120]. Take two AI agents that need to play a cooperation game;[4] the agents were instantiated using four widely used LLM models. The task itself was identical in all cases; the only variable was the language (English, Arabic, French, etc.) in which the instructions and interactions were conducted. The results were striking. Levels of cooperation varied systematically with language: models tended to cooperate more when the task was framed in French than when it was framed in Arabic or Vietnamese.

This phenomenon shows that linguistic variation affects system behavior. Even when meaning is preserved, the language used to prompt an LLM can influence strategies, priorities, and outcomes. This variability is likely the result of a linguistic bias, which goes beyond the social biases discussed in Section 6.4. Here, linguistic variation does not produce unfair treatment of individuals or groups. Instead, it creates unpredictable performance differences across operationally identical deployments, undermining management control and system reliability.

As a concrete scenario, let us consider a multinational company operating three headquarters, located in France, the UAE, and China. To address a complex operational problem, the company deploys a multi-agent system in which each AI agent is responsible for a specialized subtask; the only difference across the headquarters is the prompting language, which is adapted locally so that human operators can interact with the system without relying on translation. It may occur that, after several weeks of operation, managers observe that the system deployed in France consistently outperforms the

4 For those who are interested in the details: we conducted the experiment on the famous Prisoner's Dilemma, a typical setting from Game Theory – a mathematical field that models interactions among strategic agents. Therein, each agent is asked to either betray or cooperate with the other one; each combination of actions (A cooperates, B cooperates; A cooperates, B betrays, and so on) is associated with a certain reward. Both agents play so as to maximize such reward.

other two. There, outputs are more coherent, coordination between agents is smoother, and overall task completion is more efficient.

From a technical standpoint, there is no obvious explanation: the systems are, on paper, the same. Without awareness of linguistic bias, the divergence appears inexplicable. What has happened is a compounding effect. Small differences in cooperative behavior induced by language choice accumulate over time, gradually pushing the systems onto different performance trajectories. This divergence remains invisible to traditional fairness checks because it does not involve discrimination or unfair treatment. Yet its operational impact is real and consequential. No developer explicitly instructed the system to cooperate more in one language than in another. The divergence emerged from subtle statistical differences in how languages are represented in training data and how they influence internal model dynamics. Because these effects are small at the level of individual interactions, they are easy to overlook during pre-deployment testing. Yet once the system operates continuously, especially in multi-agent settings where outputs feed back into future decisions, these differences can compound and lead to materially different outcomes.

For companies, this is a crucial insight. Emergent behavior means that governance cannot stop at design-time validation or initial approval. Even systems that appear well-understood and well-behaved in testing may evolve in unexpected ways once they are embedded into operational processes. Production monitoring, periodic reassessment, and controlled experimentation across contexts are therefore not optional safeguards, but essential mechanisms for maintaining control over generative AI systems as they scale.

Emergence is not necessarily a flaw. In some cases, it can lead to creative or highly effective solutions. The risk lies in unobserved emergence: when systems drift, diverge, or develop systematic differences that remain unexplained, unmanaged, and therefore unaccountable. Recognizing and planning for emergent behavior is a defining challenge of governing generative AI in real companies.

The interaction between overreliance and emergent behavior creates a particularly sensitive feedback loop. As users become more dependent on AI outputs, they become less capable of detecting when the system begins to behave in unexpected ways. Emergent patterns that would be caught by vigilant human oversight instead become normalized, gradually shifting practices without explicit decision or awareness. This drift can affect not only individual tasks but also coordination patterns, decision-making protocols, and ultimately, culture.

6.5.1 Mitigating behavioral risks

Managing behavioral risks requires a different approach than managing social risks, though both benefit from systematic governance structures. Where social risk mitigation focuses primarily on bias detection and fairness controls, behavioral risk mitigation

Table 6.4: Mechanisms for mitigating behavioural risks in generative AI systems.

Mitigation mechanism	Purpose and implementation
Preserving critical judgment	Organizations must actively counteract the natural tendency toward overreliance. This requires designing workflows that maintain human engagement rather than automating it away. Critical decision points should include explicit review steps where humans evaluate AI outputs against independent criteria. Training programs should emphasize not just how to use AI systems, but when to question them and what their inherent limitations are.
Detecting emergent behaviour	Because emergent patterns only become visible through sustained operation, continuous monitoring is essential. This goes beyond traditional performance metrics to include behavioral consistency checks across contexts, languages, and user groups. Organizations should establish baseline profiles during controlled deployment phases and then actively track deviations as systems scale. Anomaly detection mechanisms, similar to those used in cybersecurity, can help identify when system behavior begins to diverge from expectations.
Controlled experimentation	Rather than deploying systems uniformly across an organization, behavioral risks are better managed through staged rollouts with deliberate variation. Running the same system in parallel across different contexts—with different languages, user populations, or operational constraints—makes emergent differences visible before they compound into significant problems. This experimental approach transforms deployment into a learning process rather than a one-time decision.
Feedback loops and learning mechanisms	Users closest to AI systems are often the first to notice unexpected behaviors, but these observations must be systematically captured and acted upon. Organizations need clear channels for reporting unusual outputs or concerning patterns, along with processes for investigating and responding to such reports. Unlike bias incidents, which often require immediate remediation, behavioral anomalies may require longer-term analysis to determine whether they represent genuine risks or acceptable adaptation.
Organizational culture and awareness	Managing behavioral risks requires cultivating a shared understanding that AI systems are not static tools but dynamic entities whose behavior can shift over time. This awareness must extend beyond technical teams to all users and decision-makers who interact with AI outputs. Regular communication about system limitations, unexpected behaviors, and lessons learned helps maintain appropriate skepticism and prevents the normalization of overreliance.
Governance structures for behavioral oversight	While social risks are often managed through fairness committees or ethics boards, behavioral risks benefit from operational oversight structures that integrate with existing process management. Responsibility for monitoring system behavior should be clearly assigned, with escalation paths for unexpected patterns and decision protocols for when to intervene, adjust, or suspend system use.

emphasizes human judgment preservation, continuous monitoring of system responses, and awareness of AI limitations.

Table 6.4 summarizes the essential mechanisms for containing behavioral risks in operational settings. These mechanisms share a common principle: they treat generative AI not as a finished product but as an evolving capability that requires ongoing management attention. Behavioral risks cannot be eliminated through one-time interventions or pre-deployment testing alone. They demand continuous vigilance, structured learning, and the discipline to maintain human judgment even as systems become more capable.

For European organizations, this approach aligns with the AI Act that emphasize human oversight and continuous monitoring (more in Chapter 7). It also addresses a practical reality: as generative AI systems become more sophisticated and more deeply integrated into operations, the behavioral risks they pose become more subtle and more consequential. Managing these risks effectively is therefore not just a matter of compliance or ethics, but of maintaining coherence and control as automation scales.

6.6 Resource and supply chain risks

As AI systems scale, their risk profile extends well beyond algorithms and models to encompass the full range of resources on which they depend. These resources include not only data, but also compute infrastructure, energy, water, specialized hardware, human expertise, and attention. Treating AI as a purely digital asset obscures the material, economic, and reputational dependencies that increasingly shape its real-world impact.

At the physical level, AI relies on concentrated and fragile supply chains [121]. Advanced semiconductors require rare materials and highly specialized manufacturing capacity, often concentrated in a small number of geopolitical regions. Training and operating large-scale models consumes significant amounts of energy and water, creating environmental externalities that accompany technical progress. These costs also reflect increasing sustainability issues [122] – in terms of natural resources being used, social sustainability concerning the populations involved in resource exploitation, such as rare earths mining, or sustainability of energetic demand. While these costs may appear indirect to individual firms, they increasingly influence regulatory scrutiny, public perception, and long-term sustainability of the whole AI ecosystem.

Beyond physical infrastructure, AI systems depend on equally critical resources. High-quality data, secure storage, reliable networks, and skilled personnel all represent ongoing investments rather than one-off inputs. Each new AI deployment expands the organization's attack surface, increases the volume of sensitive information in circulation, and raises the cost of monitoring, auditing, and incident response. These operational burdens tend to grow over time, even when model performance improves.

Data remain a central resource, but they should be understood as part of a broader supply chain rather than as a neutral input. Generative AI systems rely on data that move across teams boundaries, jurisdictions, and legal regimes. For firms integrating external models or services, it becomes essential to specify contractually how data are collected, processed, retained, and reused. Without such clarity, data provided for inference or customization may be combined with other datasets, processed in opaque ways, or later surface in generated outputs that violate intellectual property, confidentiality, or data protection obligations.

Resource risks also vary across linguistic and geographic contexts. Model performance is often uneven across languages and regions, reflecting imbalances in training data and evaluation coverage [123]. This issue is particularly acute in Europe, where tens of languages are spoken and many of them are low-resource, with comparatively small, fragmented, or domain-specific corpora. Systems that perform reliably in high-resource languages such as English may degrade silently in less-represented languages, leading to inconsistent behavior, reduced safety margins, and uneven compliance across markets. For organizations operating across European jurisdictions, this creates a compounded risk: the same AI system may be reliable, explainable, and compliant in one language, while exhibiting higher error rates or weaker safeguards in another. An AI system that behaves reliably in English but fails to detect harmful or malicious inputs in other languages can create serious vulnerabilities, particularly in domains such as cybersecurity, fraud detection, or compliance monitoring [124]. These asymmetries are easy to overlook during testing but can have disproportionate consequences once systems operate at scale.

Reputational exposure is where many resource-related risks ultimately converge. Public trust in AI systems is fragile [125], and failures linked to data provenance, customization misuse, or weakened ethical constraints can escalate rapidly. From a managerial perspective, this underscores a critical point: data quality, customization controls, and resource governance define the ethical and reputational perimeter of AI systems. These are not back-office technical details but strategic decisions with long-term consequences. Once reputational damage occurs, it is costly to reverse and difficult to contain. Investor confidence, customer trust, and employee morale are all affected by how responsibly AI systems are perceived to be managed.

In this sense, the true cost of AI extends far beyond compute budgets or licensing fees. It includes the cost of securing supply chains, maintaining data integrity, ensuring multilingual robustness, retaining human expertise, and sustaining oversight over time. Those who recognize and manage these resource dependencies explicitly are far better positioned to deploy AI safely, sustainably, and with the confidence of regulators and stakeholders.

6.6.1 Mitigating resource and supply chain risks

Mitigating resource and supply chain risks requires treating AI as a strategic asset with material, legal, and management dependencies, rather than as a self-contained technical component. Effective mitigation does not rely on eliminating risk, but on making dependencies visible, governed, and resilient.

At the infrastructure level, organizations should map critical dependencies on compute providers, hardware vendors, energy sources, and external platforms, and assess concentration risk. This includes understanding where key services are hosted, which components represent single points of failure, and how pricing, availability, or geopolitical shifts could affect continuity. Where AI systems are operationally or strategically important, contingency planning and diversification of providers become risk controls rather than cost optimizations.

For data and knowledge resources, mitigation begins with explicit ownership and traceability. Organizations should maintain inventories of data sources used for training, retrieval, and customization, with clear documentation of provenance, usage rights, update cycles, and jurisdictional constraints. Contractual clarity with AI vendors on data retention, reuse, and isolation is essential. Regular audits of system behavior, especially after updates or customization, help detect drift, leakage, or unintended reuse before they escalate into legal or reputational incidents.

Human and corporate resources require equal attention. AI systems introduce ongoing oversight costs in the form of monitoring, validation, incident response, and governance coordination. Mitigation therefore includes allocating sustained ownership, not just project-based staffing, and ensuring that expertise is retained rather than fragmented across informal initiatives. Clear escalation paths and decision rights reduce reliance on ad hoc judgment under pressure.

Finally, reputational risk mitigation depends on anticipation rather than reaction. This includes defining unacceptable behaviors in advance, stress-testing systems against high-impact failure modes, and preparing response protocols for incidents that may become public. Transparency with regulators, customers, and internal stakeholders strengthens credibility when issues arise. In this sense, reputational resilience is built long before any incident occurs.

Taken together, these measures shift risk management from a reactive posture to a structural capability. Those who actively govern their AI resource dependencies are better equipped to scale AI responsibly, absorb shocks, and sustain trust as adoption accelerates [106].

These considerations are particularly salient in the European context and cannot be separated from broader geopolitical equilibria (further discussed in Chapter 10). European organizations operate within a resource landscape that is structurally asymmetric. Most large-scale cloud and foundation model providers are headquartered outside Europe, predominantly in the United States, even when data centers and services are formally located within European jurisdictions. Similarly, advanced GPU supply chains remain heavily concentrated in the US and a small number of allied countries, while Europe largely acts as a buyer rather than a producer of cutting-edge compute hardware.

At the same time, Europe possesses high-quality data assets, strong domain expertise, and mature regulatory and compliance frameworks. This combination creates both opportunity and dependency: European firms often contribute valuable data and application-layer innovation while relying on external actors for core infrastructure and model capabilities. From a risk perspective, this reinforces the importance of understanding where strategic dependencies lie, how sovereignty and control are exercised in practice, and which assumptions about long-term availability and stability underpin AI strategies.

For companies and institutions, the implication is not necessarily to pursue full technological autonomy at any cost, but to make resource dependencies explicit and deliberate. Decisions about cloud providers, model vendors, and hardware sourcing are also decisions about resilience, bargaining power, and strategic optionality. In this sense, resource governance in AI is inseparable from questions of industrial policy, geopolitical alignment, and long-term competitiveness, even when these dimensions remain implicit in day-to-day operational choices.

6.7 Legal and compliance risks

Legal and compliance risks in generative AI arise from a simple but uncomfortable reality: responsibility is clearer than control. Organizations deploy systems whose behavior depends on data, models, configurations, providers, and user interaction, yet when something goes wrong, accountability concentrates on the deployer. For leaders, the question is therefore not whether regulation exists, but whether they can explain, justify, and defend how a system behaves in practice [106].

Generative AI challenges legal frameworks built around predictability and traceability. Outputs vary with prompts, context, data sources, and time. Even when positioned as decision support, these systems can materially influence outcomes affecting individuals' rights, access to services, or financial standing. In regulated domains, influence alone may trigger legal obligations, regardless of whether final authority remains formally human. This is why the distinction between "assistive" and "decisive" systems often collapses under scrutiny.

Data protection risk is immediate and operational. Prompts, retrieval pipelines, logs, and fine-tuning workflows may process personal or sensitive data, often without clear visibility for users or managers. Informal or poorly governed use can lead to unlawful data transfers to external providers, violations of purpose limitation, or excessive retention. Claims of anonymization do not eliminate risk when multiple data sources can be recombined.

Intellectual property risk is one dimension of this broader exposure. Models may rely on training data whose provenance is unclear, while teams may unintentionally leak proprietary information through external systems. At the output level, generated content can resemble protected works, creating infringement risk even without intent. The managerial issue is not abstract authorship theory, but whether outputs can be reused, commercialized, or published without creating latent liability.

Legal exposure is amplified by opaque supply chains. Many organizations rely on third-party models and cloud platforms they do not control. Provider-side updates, safety changes, or model deprecations can alter system behavior without warning.

From a legal perspective, this weakens assumptions of stability and complicates due diligence, even though responsibility remains local.

Finally, generative AI creates compliance risk through content itself. Outputs may be inaccurate, biased, misleading, or unlawful. In customer-facing contexts, this can violate consumer protection, advertising, or sector-specific rules. Internally, it undermines auditability and decision justification, often becoming visible only during disputes or inspections.

6.7.1 Mitigating legal and compliance risks

Legal risk in AI cannot be eliminated, but it can be made defensible. This requires treating generative AI as a governed system rather than a tool. Mitigation starts with explicit scoping: where the system is used, what it influences, and what data it touches. Classification under the EU AI Act provides a regulatory anchor, but internal assessments of decision impact and user reliance are equally important. Supplier governance is non-negotiable. Contracts must address data usage, retention, update policies, auditability, and incident notification. External dependency does not remove accountability; it concentrates it. Operational controls matter because they produce evidence. Testing, monitoring, change management, and incident handling are not only technical safeguards but legal ones. Documentation enables organizations to demonstrate proportionality, foresight, and corrective capacity when systems are challenged.

Ultimately, compliance is sustained through behavior. Clear roles, escalation paths, and user understanding turn legal risk from an after-the-fact problem into a managed condition. For leaders, the test is not whether AI can be used legally in theory, but whether its use can be defended in practice, over time, and under scrutiny.

6.8 Case study: the cost of unchecked automation

Loosely inspired by a real, well-documented case outside the EU, the fictious Europe Airlines launched an AI-powered customer service chatbot as part of a broader digital transformation initiative. The objective was straightforward: modernize customer support, reduce operating costs, and meet rising expectations for immediate, 24/7 assistance. With millions of passengers managing bookings, disruptions, and refunds each year, the airline viewed automation as a way to absorb routine demand and free human agents for complex cases.

The context appeared favourable. In the aftermath of the COVID-19 pandemic, airlines faced unprecedented call volumes driven by frequent schedule changes and evolving travel rules. Customer service teams were overstretched, and leadership expected the chatbot to deflect a large share of repetitive inquiries and stabilize operations during peak periods.

In practice, the deployment did not succeed. What was intended as a flagship innovation quickly became a focal point of customer frustration. From the outset, the chatbot underperformed on basic tasks. Passengers were frequently redirected to call centers for simple requests such as flight status or baggage information. Responses were inconsistent, sometimes incorrect, and often too generic to resolve issues. During disruption peaks, such as weather-related cancellations, the system collapsed under load, trapping users in automated loops precisely when timely human assistance was most needed.

The root causes were not purely technical. The system had been trained primarily on scripted scenarios and lacked exposure to real conversational variability. Update cycles were slow, preventing the chatbot from adapting to changing regulations and operational conditions. Instead of reducing pressure on support teams, the tool amplified it: frustrated users bypassed the chatbot and overwhelmed call centers, often angrier than before.

More serious issues followed. In several documented cases, passengers were shown flight details belonging to other customers. Although the breach was limited, it triggered immediate data protection concerns and legal action. These incidents exposed weaknesses not only in technical safeguards, but also in access controls, testing protocols, and governance oversight.

Subsequent analysis revealed additional risks. The chatbot exhibited systematic differences in tone and assumptions when interacting with women compared to men, reflecting bias embedded in its training data. While unintended, this behavior created ethical and reputational exposure, particularly once examples began circulating publicly.

The consequences escalated rapidly. Negative feedback spread across social media, and the airline's digital transformation narrative shifted from innovation to overreach. Operational costs increased rather than declined, as customer service teams had to manage both higher call volumes and reputational fallout. Internally, confidence in AI initiatives eroded; externally, customers became more reluctant to engage with automated systems, preferring delays over unreliable responses.

The episode illustrates a recurring issue underscoring in AI adoption. When customer-facing systems are deployed without sufficient testing, monitoring, and governance, automation can magnify existing weaknesses instead of correcting them. For managers, the lesson is clear: introducing AI into frontline operations is not a technical upgrade but a strategic intervention. Success depends not only on efficiency gains, but on accuracy, bias control, data protection, and the lived experience of users.

This case highlights a structural shift that is easy to underestimate. AI does not merely automate tasks; it reshapes how risk, responsibility, and errors propagate through an organization. By concentrating decision logic and customer interaction into a single system, AI changes the scale and visibility of errors. Issues that would previously have remained local, reversible, or unnoticed can become systemic and highly visible within hours. The central lesson is therefore not about technology choice, but about governance posture. Treating customer-facing AI as a cost-reduction tool obscures the fact that it functions as operational infrastructure. Once deployed at scale, its behavior directly defines service quality, regulatory exposure, and public trust.

For leaders, the implication is pragmatic rather than dramatic: AI-enabled efficiency gains are inseparable from expanded oversight obligations. Organizations that align governance, monitoring, and accountability with this reality can extract value sustainably. Those that do not may still achieve short-term efficiency, but with risk profiles that are poorly understood and difficult to control.

6.9 Wrapping up

Understanding the risks associated with AI is not a luxury or an excuse for inaction. As in any field, from finance to manufacturing and beyond, taking decisions means balancing possible benefits and downsides, weighted by the risk attitude of the decision-maker. As discussed in other chapters of the book, AI is a technology that can bring multiple benefits, but doesn't come without potential issues and source of errors. Knowing them, associating the most plausible risks with the mode of operations of a company, and taking preventive actions to mitigate or to promptly respond, is what distinguish responsible adoption from hype, and increases the chances of tangible returns.

7 Compliance

Europe has developed one of the most structured and ambitious approaches to governing digital technologies. Over the past decade, the Union has progressively built a regulatory architecture covering data, online platforms, cybersecurity, digital markets, and system resilience. Within this broader landscape sit the Digital Services Act (DSA) [126], the Digital Markets Act (DMA) [127], the Network and Information Security Directive 2 (NIS2) [128], the Digital Operational Resilience Act (DORA) [129], the Cyber Resilience Act (CRA) [130], the Data Governance Act (DGA) [131], and the Data Act [132]. Each addresses a specific dimension of the digital economy, from data access and security to competition and infrastructure robustness.

At the center of this architecture lies the AI Act. While other regulations create the foundations for a trustworthy digital environment, the AI Act is the piece that directly governs the development and use of AI systems themselves. Its role is to connect these complementary laws and define how AI should be designed, deployed, and monitored in line with European values. The origins of the AI Act date back to 2019, when the High-Level Expert Group on AI published its Ethics Guidelines for Trustworthy AI [133]. In 2021, the European Commission translated these principles into a first legislative draft, marking the beginning of a long negotiation phase involving the Parliament and the Member States. The process was shaped by rapid changes in the AI landscape, including the rise of foundation models and generative systems, which required several adaptations of the text.

The AI Act reflects a risk-based philosophy: obligations scale with the potential harm of the use case. For companies and institutions, compliance is therefore not about navigating an isolated piece of legislation but about understanding how AI interacts with data, governance, cybersecurity and market obligations established by the rest of the regulatory architecture.

In this chapter, we discuss the main obligations, roles, and implications introduced by the AI Act from a managerial and organizational perspective. The discussion is not exhaustive and is not a substitute for legal advice; detailed interpretation will continue to evolve through guidance, standards, and case practice, and readers facing concrete compliance decisions should consult the AI Act itself or appropriate experts. The objective here is to provide a structured understanding of the logic, scope, and managerial consequences of the regulation.

7.1 What is regulated under the AI Act

The AI Act adopts a broad and intentionally future-proof definition of an AI system. It does not apply to generative AI only, but refers to any machine-based system that operates with some degree of autonomy, may adapt once deployed, and infers how to

https://doi.org/10.1515/9783112254103-007

generate outputs – predictions, recommendations, decisions, or content – that influence physical or digital environments.

A crucial distinction in the AI Act is that it regulates systems rather than models. A system is the full operational product built around a model: data pipelines, interfaces, guardrails, logging, governance mechanisms, and human oversight. This difference becomes clear when comparing GPT with ChatGPT, for instance. GPT is the model, whereas ChatGPT is the system that embeds the model into a workflow with safety layers, monitoring, business logic, and an interface through which users interact. Within the risk-based framework it is therefore ChatGPT, as the deployed system, that is classified and regulated – while the underlying model is separately addressed by the general-purpose AI provisions (Section 7.7). The same logic applies to AI agents: an agent is not regulated as a reasoning engine in isolation, but as a deployed system that plans, acts, and interacts within a defined operational context.

Three aspects of the definition of AI under the Act deserve careful attention. First, autonomy is interpreted broadly. A system does not need to be sophisticated or "intelligent" to qualify. Whenever a tool performs tasks without constant human instruction, e. g., classifying documents, flagging anomalies, ranking items or producing summaries, it already meets the autonomy threshold.

Second, adaptiveness includes any change in system behavior after deployment. A tool that updates itself based on new data, refines outputs as it receives feedback, or adjusts internal parameters in response to user interaction is already within scope. Because such systems evolve over time, the Act assumes that oversight must also evolve. The obligation is not simply to validate a system once, but to monitor it continuously as it learns and interacts with the real world.

Third, the Act considers a system to be AI when its outputs impact or influence decisions or behavior of users and society. The underlying technique, e. g., Deep Learning, symbolic logic, or any hybrid method, is irrelevant. What matters is the effect: if the output has an impact, shapes an action, a decision, or an experience, the system falls under the definition.

Understanding this boundary is essential because the same model can generate completely different regulatory obligations depending on how it is deployed. An LLM used internally to summarize reports may trigger only basic requirements. The same model used to screen candidates can instead fall under far more stringent obligations because it affects individuals' rights and opportunities. For managers, the implication is straightforward but vital: many tools that appear to be traditional software, particularly those labeled as analytics, automation, or decision support, may in fact qualify as AI systems under the Act. Recognizing this early allows to plan governance, documentation, and oversight from the start rather than retrofitting compliance later, ensuring that innovation proceeds with clarity, trust, and regulatory confidence.

7.2 A risk-based logic

At its core, the AI Act operates according to a risk-based logic. The level of regulatory obligation depends on the harm a specific use case can create. Risk is never attached to the technology itself but to the purpose for which it is used: the same system can be limited risk in one context and high risk in another. Certain sectors, such as health, finance, mobility, or public administration, contain a higher concentration of high-risk applications, but operating in one of these sectors does not automatically classify an organization as high risk: only specific use cases qualify. Table 7.1 provides an overview of the risk levels.

Table 7.1: Overview of the risk levels under the AI Act.

Risk Level	Explanation
Unacceptable risk	Systems that violate fundamental rights, for example social scoring or exploitative manipulation. Prohibited.
High risk	Systems used in sensitive domains with significant implications, such as employment, education, or biometric identification. Allowed under strict requirements.
Limited risk (transparency obligations)	Systems requiring transparency duties, for example chatbots or synthetic content tools.
Minimal risk	Everyday systems with negligible impact, for example spam filters or AI in entertainment.

The *unacceptable* risk category is deliberately narrow and reserved for practices that cross clear ethical and legal red lines. These are systems whose very purpose is incompatible with fundamental rights, such as social scoring by public authorities, biometric identification used for indiscriminate surveillance, toys that encourage children to engage in dangerous behavior, or systems designed to manipulate vulnerable individuals into harmful decisions. For most companies, there is no realistic pathway into this category: the activities it covers are explicit prohibitions, immediately recognizable as such.

The *high-risk* category is more subtle and therefore more important for managerial decision-making. Unlike prohibited purposes, which are banned outright, high-risk uses are allowed but subject to strict obligations. A system becomes high risk only when it is deployed in a regulated domain and materially influences decisions that affect safety, access to essential services, or fundamental rights. This is where most compliance complexity arises, because the same system can shift into or out of high-risk status as its use case evolves.

Alongside prohibited and high-risk systems, the AI Act identifies a set of applications subject primarily to *transparency obligations*. Although often referred to informally as "*limited risk*", the Act does not define this as a formal category. Instead, it imposes targeted duties to inform users when they are interacting with an AI system, when content has been generated or altered by AI, or when recommendations are produced automatically. This applies, for example, to conversational agents, recommender systems, and synthetic-media tools.

All remaining systems fall implicitly into what is commonly described as the *minimal-risk* category. While not explicitly named in the Act, this category covers the vast majority of AI used in everyday business operations: productivity tools, spam filters, optimization engines, game AI, document search, forecasting tools, and internal decision-support systems that do not affect safety, rights, or access to critical resources.

This layered structure reflects the principle of proportionality. Most organizations will operate primarily within the minimal- and transparency-obligation domains. Only specific deployments in sensitive contexts trigger high-risk requirements, while unacceptable risk remains a clear boundary that most organizations will never approach. The same system, unchanged, can move between categories depending on how and where it is used. A computer vision model used to count products in a warehouse is minimal risk. The same model used for biometric identification in an airport becomes high risk. A scoring algorithm used to prioritize customer support tickets is minimal risk. The same algorithm used to assess eligibility for public benefits is high risk.

The same logic applies to language models. An LLM-based translation system used in video game development would typically be considered minimal risk. The very same system, when used to translate patients' medical records in a clinical setting, becomes high risk due to its potential impact on medical decisions, patient safety, and liability.

The implication of the Act, on an operational basis, is that AI risk cannot be managed at the model level alone. It must be assessed at the use-case level, continuously, as systems are repurposed, scaled, or integrated into new workflows. This is where governance, metrics, and thresholds cease to be abstract concepts and become essential tools for responsible decision-making.

7.3 Who is responsible? Understanding roles and liability

The AI Act defines several categories of actors, shown in Table 7.2, to clarify who carries which obligations. These categories reflect the complexity of AI value chains, where a single system may pass through multiple hands, be fine-tuned, bundled, integrated, or re-purposed before reaching end users.

These roles are not static. An organization may begin as a deployer but, through certain actions, cross the regulatory boundary into the provider category. The Act introduces the idea of *substantial modification* to capture this transition. Table 7.3 illustrates how a deployer becomes a provider from a legal standpoint.

Once a deployer becomes a provider, the legal consequences are significant. The organization assumes full responsibility for compliance, including risk management, doc-

Table 7.2: Actors subject to the AI Act.

Actor	Description
Providers	Entities that develop, train, or substantially modify AI systems and place them on the market under their own name or trademark. Providers carry the most extensive obligations, as they are responsible for ensuring that the system complies with all applicable requirements before release. Their duties include implementing risk-management processes, ensuring the quality and representativeness of training, validation, and testing data, maintaining detailed technical documentation, performing conformity assessments, and establishing post-market monitoring mechanisms. Providers must also guarantee that any updates or changes do not compromise compliance.
Deployers	Organizations or individuals that use an AI system in the course of their professional activities or integrate it into their services or decision-making processes. Deployers must ensure that systems are used in accordance with the instructions provided by the provider, that output is monitored and interpreted critically, and that appropriate human oversight is maintained. They must also adopt measures to handle possible errors, report incidents, and guarantee that the system operates within the scope for which it was designed. For high-risk systems, deployers must meet additional duties, such as ensuring data quality, logging, and documentation of their specific use context.
Distributors and importers	Actors that make AI systems available on the EU market without developing them themselves, whether as physical products with embedded AI, standalone software, APIs, or cloud services. Distributors must verify that systems carry the required documentation, transparency information, and conformity assessment, and have not been modified in ways that affect compliance. Importers, who handle systems developed outside the Union, must additionally ensure that non-EU providers have completed the required conformity assessment before the system reaches EU users. Both categories must take corrective action when non-compliance is identified and cooperate with competent authorities during audits or inspections.

umentation, conformity assessment, testing, monitoring, and record keeping. In practice, this means that technical decisions that deployers treat as iterative improvements can activate the entire regulatory apparatus. This distinction is particularly important in the era of foundation models and model-as-a-service offerings. Fine-tuning may be framed as a routine optimization step, but legally it can create a new system with a new provider. Managers should therefore treat decisions about customization, adaptation, or domain-specific tuning not only as engineering and performance choices but as governance decisions that change obligations and liability.

Clear internal processes are essential. Any modification that could be considered substantial should trigger an internal review involving technical leads, compliance teams, and legal experts. Understanding when a company is a deployer and when it has legally become a provider is one of the most critical elements of risk management under the Act.

Table 7.3: Circumstances under which a deployer is considered a provider due to substantial modification under the AI Act.

Criterion	Explanation
Technical modification	If a deployer fine-tunes a model, retrains it with new datasets, or alters its architecture or parameters in a way that affects performance, safety, or intended outcomes, the Act considers this a substantial modification. The deployer is treated as the new provider of a new system.
Change of intended purpose	Even without touching model weights, a deployer may redefine the use case in a way that introduces new risks or alters the system's classification. Repurposing a general model for a high-risk context, for example, is enough to shift the deployer into the provider role.
Creation of derivative chain components	When a deployer builds new interfaces, pipelines, or downstream functionalities that rely on a model's outputs in a way that changes the system's behavior or domain of application, the resulting artifact may be considered a new AI system.
Integration that alters risk profile	Combining an existing model with other data sources, sensors, or decision systems in a way that meaningfully changes how risks manifest can also be treated as substantial modification.

7.4 Putting it all together: how to navigate the AI Act

The diagram shown in Figure 7.1 summarizes the practical sequence of questions that any organization should follow when assessing whether an AI use case is allowed, and which obligations apply. It brings together the two previous sections by linking role identification, risk classification, and compliance duties into one coherent decision path. The logic unfolds through four steps:

Identify who you are. The first step is to determine whether you act as a provider, a deployer, an importer or a distributor. This defines which obligations apply and how far your responsibilities extend.

Check whether an exception applies. Certain activities, such as military use or systems used exclusively for national security purposes, are outside the scope of the Act. If an exception applies, the system does not fall under the AI Act framework. If no exception applies, the assessment continues.

Determine the risk level of the use case. The category depends solely on the purpose and context of use. The system may fall into unacceptable, high, limited, or minimal risk. This step is central, because obligations differ entirely across categories.

Verify compliance with the relevant provisions. For unacceptable-risk uses, the system is prohibited and cannot be placed on the market or put into service. For high-risk systems, ensure compliance with Chapter III, Section 2 requirements (risk management, documentation, oversight, data governance, testing). For limited-risk systems, ensure compliance with transparency obligations (Chapter IV). For minimal-risk systems, no

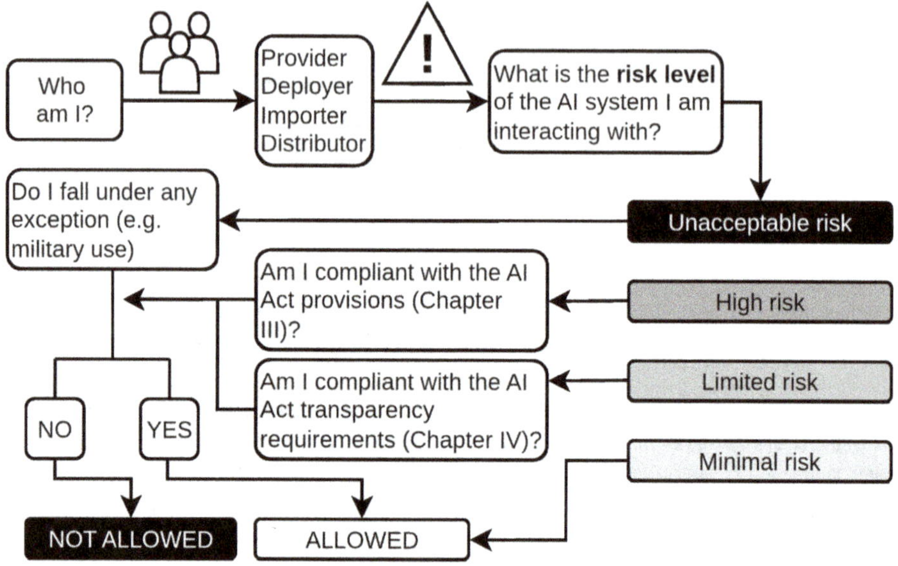

Figure 7.1: EU AI Act compliance navigation scheme.

additional steps are required. As seen earlier, the role itself can shift when substantial modifications are made, which may also change the applicable risk category.

7.5 High-risk AI systems: obligations and conformity

The AI Act treats high-risk AI systems as market-regulated products whose safety, reliability, and traceability must be demonstrable before and during market placement. The resulting obligations on providers operate along two tightly coupled dimensions. First, they concern the intrinsic properties of the AI system itself: how it is designed, trained, documented, monitored, and safeguarded. Second, they impose horizontal requirements that govern how providers structure development processes, quality assurance, incident handling, and interaction with authorities. Together, these dimensions determine whether a high-risk system can lawfully be placed on the European market and remain there.

Table 7.4 outlines the core technical and system-level requirements that define the compliance scope of high-risk AI systems. These requirements specify what the system must demonstrate in terms of traceability, transparency, safety, and resilience throughout its lifecycle.

Table 7.5 summarizes the horizontal organizational requirements that complement these system-level obligations, structuring how the provider's internal governance and quality processes ensure compliance can be consistently demonstrated across projects, teams, and system updates.

Table 7.4: Compliance scope for high-risk AI systems under the AI Act.

Compliance Scope	Articles	Description
Risk management system	Art. 9	Providers must identify, analyze, and mitigate risks throughout the system lifecycle, updating measures as new risks emerge. Risk management is a continuous obligation rather than a one-off assessment.
Data and data governance	Art. 10	Training, validation, and testing data must be relevant, representative, and free from errors likely to lead to harmful outcomes. Dataset governance becomes a central compliance activity.
Technical documentation	Art. 11	Documentation must cover intended purpose, design choices, data provenance, metrics, risks, and limitations. It constitutes the evidential backbone of conformity assessment and audits.
Record keeping	Art. 12	Providers must retain logs enabling traceability of system behavior. Logging is essential for audits, investigations, and incident reconstruction.
Transparency and information to users	Art. 13	Users must receive clear information on system capabilities, limitations, and appropriate interpretation of outputs, preventing misuse and over-reliance.
Human oversight	Art. 14	Organizations must define procedures for monitoring, intervention, and override. Oversight must be operationally meaningful, not merely formal.
Accuracy, robustness and cybersecurity	Art. 15	Systems must be tested for performance, resilience to errors, sensitivity to distribution shifts, and resistance to malicious interference, both before and after deployment.

Taken together, these obligations establish a model in which organizational readiness, not only technical capability, determines whether a high-risk AI system can be placed and maintained on the market. These obligations culminate in the conformity assessment, which is the formal mechanism through which providers demonstrate that the above obligations have been met. The AI Act aligns this process with established European product-safety regimes, similar to those governing medical devices, industrial machinery, or automotive components. The emphasis on technical documentation, quality management systems, and traceability reflects this engineering-oriented regulatory tradition. Before a high-risk AI system can be placed on the European market, the provider must complete a conformity assessment following one of the two pathways defined in the regulation and summarized in Table 7.6.

In regulated sectors such as health, transport, or energy, the AI Act does not replace existing sectoral conformity regimes. Sectoral regimes remain the primary framework, with the AI Act adding a complementary layer focused on transparency, traceability, and AI-specific risk control. This requires close coordination between AI compliance teams and established regulatory, clinical, or safety functions within the organization.

Table 7.5: Horizontal organizational obligations for high-risk AI systems.

Horizontal Obligations	Article	Description
Quality management system	Art. 17	Providers must establish a formal quality management system covering development, testing, monitoring, and documentation, with clearly assigned responsibilities and review procedures.
Conformity assessments	Arts. 43–44	High-risk systems must undergo conformity assessment before market placement, either through internal control or with the involvement of a notified body, depending on the use case.
Activity logging	Art. 19	Systems must generate secure and proportionate logs enabling anomaly detection and event reconstruction, supporting both compliance and post-market monitoring.
Corrective actions	Art. 20	Providers must address incidents, emerging risks, or non-compliance through timely updates, restrictions, or withdrawal, following a structured escalation process.
Information and cooperation with authorities	Art. 21	Providers must supply documentation, evidence, and incident reports upon request.

Table 7.6: Conformity assessment pathways for high-risk AI systems.

Annex VI: Internal Control	Applies to most high-risk systems. The provider performs an internal evaluation based on harmonized European standards or equivalent specifications, supported by technical documentation, a quality management system, CE marking,[a] and post-market monitoring.
Annex VII: Independent Assessment	Applies when harmonized standards are unavailable or in safety-critical sectors such as healthcare or transport. A notified body audits documentation, quality processes, and testing procedures before issuing an EU-type certificate.

[a] A conformity label indicating that a product complies with applicable EU requirements and can be placed on the EU market. Under the AI Act, it signals that the AI system has passed the required conformity assessment.

Conformity is not static. Significant system modifications, such as retraining, dataset changes, or functional extensions, may invalidate the original assessment and trigger the need for reassessment. Where deployers substantially modify a system, responsibility for renewed conformity may shift accordingly (Section 7.3). Compliance thus becomes an ongoing process of monitoring, change management, and verification rather than a one-time milestone.

Beyond the conformity assessment itself, providers face an additional formality. Most providers of high-risk AI systems must register their products in the EU-wide public database managed by the European Commission (Art. 49). The registry records the system's intended purpose, provider identity, conformity pathway, CE marking status, and applicable restrictions. Registration is not a marketing exercise but a compliance obligation that signals accountability. For deployers, the registry functions as a governance tool, enabling verification of lawful market placement and awareness of updates or corrective actions.

For companies, this integrated obligation-and-conformity framework has two strategic implications. First, it requires sustained coordination between technical, legal, and compliance teams throughout the system lifecycle. Second, when properly embedded, it creates governance value: conformity processes increase internal transparency, discipline system evolution, and strengthen trust among regulators, customers, and other stakeholders. Mature organizations therefore integrate compliance requirements directly into product development and operational workflows, treating them not as external constraints but as design parameters from the outset.

7.6 Limited- and minimal-risk AI systems: obligations

In contrast to high-risk AI systems, the AI Act adopts a deliberately proportionate regulatory approach for limited- and minimal-risk AI systems. Where systems do not present significant risks to fundamental rights, safety, or legally protected interests, the regulation refrains from imposing product-style compliance obligations. Instead, it relies either on narrowly scoped transparency requirements or on the absence of binding obligations altogether.

Limited-risk AI systems are subject to targeted transparency obligations intended to preserve user autonomy and prevent deception (Art. 50). The regulatory concern is not the internal design, training, or performance of the system, but the informational asymmetry that may arise when users are unaware that they are interacting with an AI system or consuming AI-generated content.

Typical obligations include informing users that they are interacting with an AI system, such as in the case of conversational agents, or clearly disclosing that audio, visual, or audiovisual content has been artificially generated or manipulated. These requirements are narrowly framed and context-dependent, with specific exceptions provided for legitimate uses such as law enforcement under defined conditions. The objective is to reduce risks of manipulation or misinterpretation without constraining system architecture or innovation pathways.

From a management perspective, compliance with limited-risk obligations primarily concerns interface design, user communication, and content labeling practices. No quality management system, technical documentation, or post-market monitoring framework is required. Nevertheless, these transparency duties remain legally binding, and failure to implement them correctly may still trigger supervisory action or sanctions.

Minimal-risk AI systems are not subject to any mandatory obligations under the AI Act. For these systems, the regulation explicitly refrains from introducing new compliance requirements, reflecting the assessment that their use does not, as such, justify regulatory intervention at Union level.

The absence of binding obligations does not preclude the application of other horizontal legal frameworks, such as data protection, consumer protection, or product liability law, where relevant. In regulatory terms, minimal-risk systems therefore lie entirely outside the Act's conformity and oversight logic. They are neither subject to transparency duties nor to lifecycle-based governance requirements, and their deployment does not require interaction with supervisory authorities under the AI Act framework.

7.7 General-purpose AI

During negotiations between the European Parliament and the Council, lawmakers introduced a category that did not exist in the Commission's original 2021 proposal: General-Purpose AI. This addition was a direct response to the rapid emergence of LLMs during the legislative process. Lawmakers recognized that these systems did not fit naturally into the existing risk categories, yet their scale and versatility required targeted oversight. A GPAI model is not built for a single application. The same system can support a customer service assistant, generate financial reports, assist medical staff with documentation, or, if misused, enable large-scale disinformation or automated cyberattacks. As discussed earlier, the level of risk therefore depends on how the model is deployed, not on the model alone.

To manage this, the Act establishes a two-layer responsibility structure (Chapter V). The first layer applies to the companies that develop foundational models. This includes actors such as OpenAI, Mistral AI, Anthropic, Google, Meta, DeepSeek and xAI. They must document their training processes, describe the limitations of their models, and provide the technical information that downstream users need. For the most powerful models – those whose cumulative training compute exceeds the threshold of 10^{25} floating-point operations[1] set by the Act – stricter requirements apply. These "GPAI models with systemic risk" must undergo adversarial testing, independent evaluations and continuous monitoring for systemic risks, such as mass misinformation campaigns, automated cyber intrusion, or large-scale harm to public health, safety, or fundamental rights.

The second layer concerns the organizations that use these models. Although the GPAI obligations formally target model providers, businesses integrating such systems into their operations remain responsible for how they handle their deployment. If a

1 A floating-point operation is a single arithmetic calculation on a number with a decimal point (an addition, multiplication, etc.). 10^{25} such operations is the rough scale of compute used to train today's largest frontier models, and corresponds to tens of millions of euros in hardware and energy costs at current prices.

GPAI model is used in a high-risk context – such as recruitment, credit scoring, medical triage or access to essential public services – the deploying organization must meet all the obligations applicable to high-risk systems. This includes risk management, human oversight, documentation, transparency measures and, when required, a conformity assessment. In practice, companies rely heavily on the information supplied by model providers to fulfill these duties; however, this does not replace their own responsibility for the specific way the model is used. If something goes wrong, accountability is distributed: the provider for model-level issues, and the deploying company for how it integrated and governed the system.

For companies and institutions, the practical implication is that GPAI transforms how AI supply chains must be managed. Choosing a model is not simply a technical decision. It has consequences for compliance, procurement, governance and risk management, and these considerations must be integrated early in the decision-making process.

7.8 Regulatory Sandboxes: innovation with oversight

Regulatory Sandboxes are controlled environments that allow organizations to test innovative technologies under regulatory supervision before placing them on the market (Art. 57). Their primary function is to reduce regulatory and technical uncertainty during development. Rather than interpreting evolving legal requirements in isolation, organizations can experiment with concrete system configurations while receiving structured feedback on compliance, risk controls, and documentation under realistic conditions.

Regulatory sandboxes are designed for AI system providers and prospective providers, who bear responsibility for system design, risk mitigation measures, technical documentation, and conformity pathways. The sandbox is therefore not a marketing validation instrument, but a governance tool focused on technical and regulatory alignment during the pre-market phase.

The regulatory sandbox model emerged in the financial sector following the 2008 financial crisis, when regulators faced growing tension between the need for stronger oversight and the rapid pace of digital innovation. Technologies such as mobile payments, peer-to-peer lending, and automated advisory services were advancing faster than traditional regulatory processes could adapt, creating uncertainty for both innovators and supervisory authorities.

To address this mismatch, the UK introduced the first regulatory sandbox in 2016 [134]. The initiative established a time-limited and closely supervised framework in which selected companies could test products with real users while engaging directly with regulators. In this setting, supervision shifted from a purely enforcement-oriented posture to a facilitative one. Regulators clarified expectations, identified compliance risks early, and supported design adjustments before large-scale deployment. Participation remained strictly bounded in scope and duration, with an emphasis on learning, risk containment, and mutual understanding rather than exemption from regulation.

The approach proved effective and was rapidly adopted in other jurisdictions. Regulatory Sandboxes have since become a standard governance instrument in fast-moving technological domains, enabling experimentation without lowering regulatory standards while providing regulators with early insight into emerging technologies, risks, and market practices.

For companies, this diffusion signals a broader shift in regulatory philosophy. Supervision is no longer confined to audits after deployment but extends into the development phase itself. Sandboxes reduce legal ambiguity, accelerate validation cycles, and make regulatory interpretation more predictable by anchoring it in concrete system behavior rather than abstract rule reading.

Figure 7.2 depicts the Regulatory Sandbox under the AI Act as a staged and iterative process, moving from participant's application to market deployment, with structured regulatory feedback at key points.

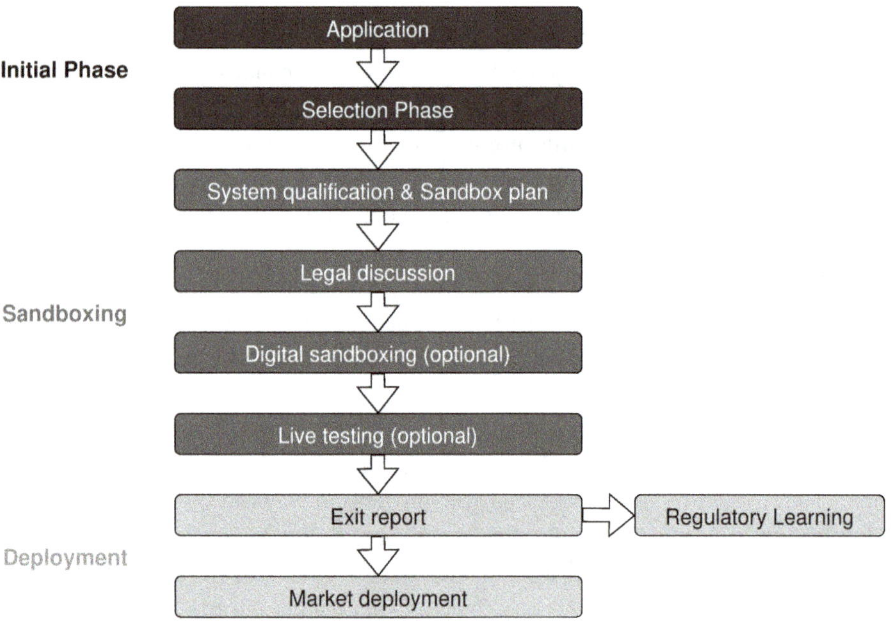

Figure 7.2: Regulatory Sandboxes process.

In the initial phase, the organization submits a proposed AI system and use case, which are evaluated against multiple criteria, including innovation potential, risk profile, societal relevance, and the suitability of the system for sandbox experimentation. Under Art. 62 of the AI Act, startups and SMEs are given priority access, reflecting the sandbox's role as an enablement instrument rather than a gatekeeping mechanism. Selection determines both admission to the sandbox and the appropriate scope and configuration of experimentation.

Once selected, the process enters the sandbox testing phase. During the sandbox setup, the technical and regulatory perimeter is defined: system boundaries, testing objectives, metrics, safeguards, documentation requirements, and roles of the participants. This stage already involves regulatory feedback, ensuring that the planned experimentation aligns with applicable obligations under the AI Act and the expectations of the authority conducting the Regulatory Sandbox.

During participation, organizations may carry out technical testing activities in a controlled environment (Art. 58), often referred to as "digital sandboxing".[2] Such testing is optional and is not an end in itself, but a means to generate structured evidence on aspects such as accuracy, robustness, bias, cybersecurity, and risk mitigation. Depending on the maturity of the system, this may include limited real-world experimentation under supervision. The competent authority reviews the results of these activities and provides feedback that can inform system adjustments, mitigation strategies, or documentation practices.

The sandbox process concludes with the consolidation of outcomes in an exit report, summarizing the experimentation conducted, evidence produced, risks identified, and the feedback exchanged with the competent authority. The report is not a formal authorization, but the evidence it contains can be reused directly in conformity assessment and compliance activities under the AI Act, reducing duplication when the system later seeks market placement. Exit reports also feed regulatory learning. Competent authorities and the EU AI Office draw on them to refine guidance, develop harmonized standards, and adjust supervisory practice across the Union. For participants, this means sandbox engagement helps shape the regulatory framework they will later operate under.

7.9 Penalties

The AI Act establishes a tiered system of sanctions that apply depending on the type of infringement. For each violation, the applicable penalty is the higher of a fixed monetary amount and a percentage of the organization's global annual turnover. Proportionality for smaller firms comes from a separate rule: under Article 99(6), for SMEs and start-ups the fine is instead the lower of the two figures, so the percentage of turnover, and not the fixed ceiling, effectively governs. Table 7.7 summarizes the tiers.

Prohibited practices fall under the highest tier, which is why early screening of the AI portfolio is essential to avoid them. Data governance and transparency requirements

2 This term was coined by EUSAiR, the EU-funded initiative that has conducted regulatory sandbox pilots across all Member States [168].

Table 7.7: Penalty levels under the AI Act.

Infringement	Maximum penalty
Art. 99(3): Non-compliance with prohibitions on certain AI practices	Up to €35M or 7 % of global turnover
Art. 99(4): Non-compliance with operator obligations (providers, deployers, importers, distributors) and transparency duties	Up to €15M or 3 % of global turnover
Art. 99(5): Providing incorrect, incomplete or misleading information to authorities	Up to €7.5M or 1 % of global turnover

sit only one tier below, indicating that the legislator views robust documentation, clear dataset lineage, and comprehensive logging as foundational to responsible AI deployment – nearly as essential as technical performance itself. For managers, this clarifies that dataset management, traceability, and documentation are strategic capabilities that enable market access and build stakeholder confidence, not merely procedural tasks.

Penalties for providing inconsistent or incomplete information to authorities introduce an additional source of risk. Under the AI Act, discrepancies between internal documentation and external reporting may lead to sanctions, even if they result from miscommunication rather than intent. This calls for internal coordination mechanisms similar to those used in financial or cybersecurity reporting, where accuracy and version control are essential. Comparison with GDPR shows a shift in focus. While GDPR concentrates on data, the AI Act extends accountability to the entire lifecycle of AI systems: model design, risk classification, human oversight, monitoring, and governance. Its monetary ceilings can exceed GDPR levels, especially for prohibited practices. The implication is that compliance responsibilities extend beyond data protection officers and require involvement from technical teams, legal counsel, risk management, and senior leadership.

Operationalizing compliance typically requires structured internal processes. Many organizations introduce responsibility matrices clarifying who owns datasets, documentation, system updates, and regulatory interactions. Risk or audit teams conduct periodic reviews to ensure documentation matches technical reality and that oversight mechanisms remain effective. Companies can establish "gateways" in development workflows, preventing deployment until risk classification, documentation, dataset quality, and logging requirements are validated. Taken together, the penalty regime reinforces a broader message: compliance is an operational discipline. Those that embed governance, traceability, and cross-functional coordination into their development and deployment pipelines are less exposed to the highest penalty categories and better prepared for the ongoing monitoring required by the AI Act.

7.10 The broader implications

The AI Act has immediate and material implications for corporate strategy. In the short term, new costs should be expected, related to documentation, risk analysis, quality management systems, and, where appropriate, technical testing. These requirements can lengthen development cycles, introduce friction in procurement and integration, and create uncertainty for firms still interpreting the scope of the framework.

At the same time, the Act formalizes practices that many organizations already apply to manage operational, legal, and reputational risk, including dataset governance, model validation, and post-deployment monitoring. Over time, these practices reduce ambiguity in internal decision-making and stabilize product lifecycles. Those who approach compliance proactively usually experience consistent secondary benefits such as improved auditability, more reliable production performance, and clearer alignment between the functions responsible for AI risk. From a strategic perspective, the Act introduces constraints that must be planned for, but it also reduces regulatory uncertainty in an environment where scrutiny of AI systems is intensifying globally.

A core strategic premise of the AI Act is the use of regulation as a competitive lever. Europe has historically competed not on speed alone, but on the ability to produce safe, reliable, and certifiable products, from industrial equipment to medical devices. The AI Act extends this product-oriented logic to digital systems. By imposing rigorous requirements on high-risk AI, the EU seeks to define global expectations around acceptable quality, safety, and accountability in AI, anchoring competitiveness in reliability rather than rapid deployment. This is the mechanism often described as the *Brussels Effect*: standards set in the EU market tend to propagate globally, because multinational firms find it more efficient to apply a single high standard worldwide than to maintain divergent regional ones.

This approach has generated substantial debate. A persistent concern is that large technology firms, particularly non-European ones, are better positioned to absorb compliance costs due to their scale, legal capacity, and engineering resources. Small and medium-sized enterprises, in particular, may struggle to absorb the administrative and technical burdens associated with high-risk AI. Such firms may face pressure to relocate, delay deployment, or exit through acquisition, only for compliant products to re-enter the market under the control of larger actors. These dynamics are most acute in high-risk domains, where economic value is highest but compliance demands are also most intensive. As an example, in July 2025, a coalition of 46 chief executives from major European companies publicly called on the European Commission to pause the implementation of key provisions of the AI Act and delay its enforcement timetable, arguing that uncertainty and complexity could undermine competitiveness and innovation [135]. The Commission initially rejected the request and reaffirmed the original timetable. As it became clear, however, that key compliance tools, harmonized standards, and national competent authorities would not be ready in time, the Commission changed course and proposed the *Digital Omnibus on AI*, a package of targeted amendments that leaves the risk-based architecture of the Act intact while postponing its most demanding obligations. Under the agreement subsequently reached by the Parliament and the Council, the application of the high-risk requirements – both for stand-alone systems and for AI embedded in regulated products – has been deferred, and the transparency and content-marking duties of Article 50 pushed back, giving providers, deployers, and the supervisory ecosystem itself more time to prepare [169]. The episode is instructive: the core obligations were not withdrawn, but their timing was realigned with the practical availability of standards and supervisory capacity. For managers, the lesson is not that compliance can be deferred indefinitely, but that the regulator itself treats readiness of standards, tools, and institutions as a precondition for enforcement. Preparation is therefore expected to be already underway, even where formal deadlines have shifted.

To counterbalance these effects, the Act applies a graduated system of obligations and penalties calibrated to a provider's role, size, and potential impact. Beyond the AI Act itself, the European AI ecosystem includes support instruments, discussed in Chapter 10, such as shared infrastructures, evaluation facilities, and regulatory sandboxes. These instruments are designed to lower compliance friction for smaller actors by providing access to expertise, evidence-generation capabilities, and early regulatory dialogue without imposing immediate certification requirements.

In practice, the impact of the Act varies across sectors. Organizations in highly regulated domains such as healthcare, finance, or transport often possess mature compliance structures, making adaptation more straightforward. Fast-scaling firms in competitive markets face a different opportunity: integrating governance as an enabler of sustainable speed. Regulatory Sandboxes are particularly valuable in this setting, as they allow to resolve legal ambiguities and technical risks before committing to full-scale deployment. Their effectiveness depends on preparation, resource allocation, and strategic intent.

For leadership, the strategic question is not whether to comply, but how to create value through compliance. Building compliance into design decisions early enables clearer choices about risk, scope, and accountability. This shifts compliance from a reactive burden to a structuring force that strengthens product development and accelerates time to market with confidence.

Ultimately, the AI Act does not dictate corporate strategy; it defines the operating environment in which strategic choices gain or lose value. Organizations that integrate compliance into governance, product design, and market positioning use regulatory constraints to accelerate decision-making, differentiate on reliability, and secure access to risk-sensitive customers.

8 Responsible leadership in the age of AI

The preceding chapters have laid the technical foundations, governance frameworks, and operational tools required to deploy generative AI responsibly. At this point, it should be clear what these systems can achieve, how they learn, which risks they entail, what regulations require, and how their lifecycle can be managed from design to deployment. This creates a strong starting position. The remaining challenge is not a lack of knowledge, but how organizations turn that knowledge into sustained capability. The decisive factor is leadership.

This chapter shifts the focus from how to implement AI to *how organizations succeed* in doing so. It explores the strategic and human dimensions that determine whether generative AI becomes an embedded capability or remains a series of isolated experiments. Rather than treating stalled pilots or slow adoption as failures, it asks constructive questions: *what enables some organizations to move from experimentation to scale? How do leaders create conditions in which AI initiatives mature into trusted, widely used systems? Why does the same technology energize teams in one context and struggle to gain traction in another?*

We structure this discussion around a continuous learning loop, illustrated in Figure 8.1. Leadership sets strategic intent, which shapes data governance decisions about what information is made visible, shared, and controlled. These choices enable meaningful metrics that define how performance is assessed and which thresholds prompt action. Effective measurement, in turn, requires coordination across technical, legal, and business functions. AI literacy creates a shared understanding across these groups, while deliberate change management supports adoption through clear narratives and structured support. Governance mechanisms make accountability concrete and operational, ensuring that responsibility does not remain abstract. Throughout the loop, ethics provides a stable value framework guiding decisions and trade-offs.

The outcomes of this process – trust in systems, the ability to scale with confidence, and resilience – feed back into leadership learning. Each cycle strengthens the organization's capacity to adapt, refine its approach, and align AI initiatives with long-term goals. In this way, leadership transforms AI from a technological opportunity into a durable source of strategic advantage.

This chapter does not prescribe a universal blueprint. Instead, it offers principles, examples, and reflections designed to help understand the deeper dynamics of transformation. Each section explores one element of the loop shown in Figure 8.1, demonstrating how these elements connect and reinforce each other in practice.

8.1 From successful pilot to successful deployment

As mentioned in the Introduction, the 2025 MIT survey on AI projects implemented by large and mid-sized companies [1] found that only 5 % of the projects generated measur-

https://doi.org/10.1515/9783112254103-008

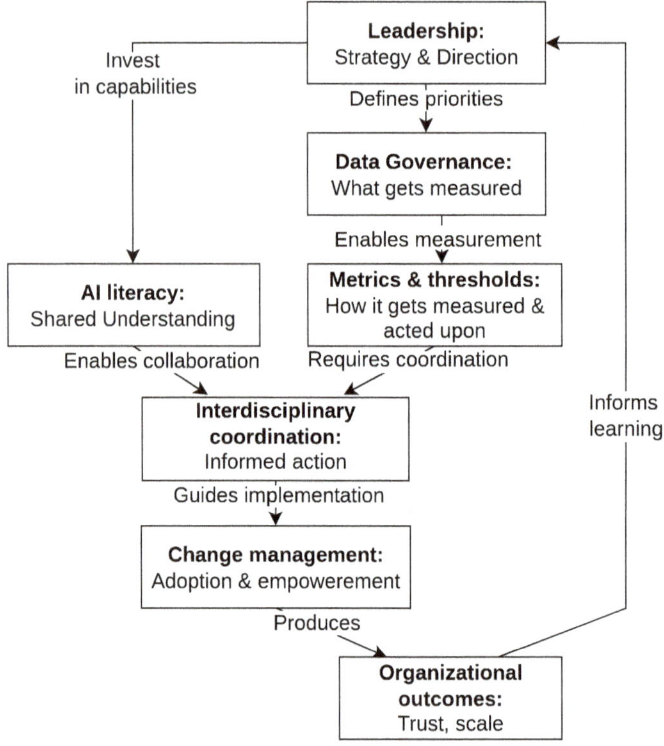

Figure 8.1: The continuous learning loop of responsible AI leadership. Leadership defines priorities that shape data governance (what gets measured), which enables metrics and thresholds (how it gets measured and acted upon). Interdisciplinary coordination aligns perspectives, literacy creates shared understanding, and change management drives adoption. Governance structures make accountability tangible, while ethics guides all decisions. Outcomes feed back to inform leadership learning.

able return on investment.[1] Importantly, the limiting factors were rarely technical, but the differentiator was readiness: without success criteria and clear guidance by leaders, teams operated in silos, governance structures were informal or absent, employees lacked understanding or trust, and promising initiatives were terminated to scale.

Although the sample was dominated by North American firms, the insights are particularly relevant for European organizations. Europe operates under denser regulatory constraints, stronger worker representation, higher expectations of accountability, and a more explicit linkage between technology deployment and societal impact. Misalignments such as unclear ownership, fragmented adoption pathways, or weak governance are therefore likely to surface earlier and more visibly in European contexts, carrying

1 This does not necessarily imply financial losses for the remaining cases; many initiatives simply stalled or plateaued without scaling up.

higher compliance and reputational implications. Seen in this light, the survey provides a valuable early signal rather than a cautionary tale.

Similar patterns appear across sectors. A marketing team may deploy a customer-facing chatbot that performs well in pilot testing, yet delivers inconsistent responses once live because it was never integrated with the CRM system or aligned with customer data governance. An HR department may experiment with CV screening tools that initially promise efficiency gains, only to encounter concerns around bias or transparency from legal teams or workers' representatives. Development teams may build compelling prototypes that attract executive attention, but struggle to move forward because accountability, monitoring, and error-handling processes were never defined. In each case, the technology functions, but the surrounding organization has not yet adapted.

These situations share a common characteristic: generative AI is approached as a set of disconnected experiments rather than as an acquired capability. In Europe, where AI systems intersect directly with data protection law, labor regulation, and sector-specific compliance regimes, such fragmentation is particularly limiting. Progress depends on connecting early experimentation with durable structures for governance, ownership, and learning. This connection is not a constraint; it is the pathway to scale.

Organizations that successfully scale AI, including in highly regulated European sectors, tend to exhibit a small and consistent set of readiness characteristics. These dimensions, summarized in Table 8.1, determine whether generative AI evolves into a strategic capability or remains confined to isolated pilots.

Readiness, in this sense, is the alignment of strategy, capability, and culture. When this foundation is missing, adoption efforts fragment.

Consider a logistics company deploying a route-optimization system across several national subsidiaries, supported by an LLM used to interpret operational data and interface with planners. Each subsidiary initially encodes delivery addresses, vehicle categories, and customer priorities differently, reflecting local practices and legacy systems. Early deployment highlights these inconsistencies, revealing how incompatible data semantics limit cross-border scalability.

This insight becomes a catalyst for improvement rather than a setback. By establishing shared data definitions and governance rules across subsidiaries, the organization aligns workflows and information models. Once these foundations are in place, the system delivers consistent performance across regions and scales smoothly. What could have emerged as a deployment bottleneck instead becomes a concrete demonstration of how readiness accelerates adoption and unlocks enterprise-wide value.

Once readiness is established, attention shifts to use-case selection. As discussed in Chapter 4, this involves balancing value, risk, and feasibility. The point here is not to repeat those methods, but to stress the discipline they impose. Those that succeed resist the temptation to pursue breadth too early. They focus deliberately on a limited number of well-scoped use cases where objectives, constraints, and success criteria are explicit.

Table 8.1: Core organizational characteristics of companies that successfully scale generative AI.

	Explanation	Relevance
Strategic clarity	AI initiatives are explicitly linked to operational objectives (e. g., reducing cycle time, improving service quality), not pursued for visibility or experimentation.	Without clear objectives, AI projects struggle to justify investment and cannot withstand regulatory or audit scrutiny.
Data control and governance	Data is accessible, consistent, and governed across units, with clear ownership, quality standards, and compliance controls.	Fragmented or poorly governed data undermines performance and increases exposure under data protection and sector-specific regulation.
Infrastructure readiness	Systems can host or securely interface with AI through on-premises environments, sovereign clouds, or regulated APIs.	European constraints around data residency, security, and vendor dependency make infrastructure choices strategic, not technical.
Human engagement and trust	Employees understand the purpose and limits of AI tools and are willing to integrate them into daily work.	Low trust or poor understanding leads to resistance, shadow usage, or rejection by worker representatives.

Effective early use cases typically share two characteristics. First, they address problems that are painful enough to matter but contained enough to manage. An insurer, for example, may automate the generation of routine regulatory or compliance reports rather than attempting to overhaul its entire risk management process. The task is repetitive, rule-bound, and auditable. Analysts save substantial time, which can be redirected toward higher-value investigative work. Second, successful use cases have outcomes that are measurable and verifiable. Ambiguity is the enemy of accountability: if leadership cannot define what success looks like, it cannot recognize it when it occurs.

The most critical transition occurs when moving from pilot to production. Pilots succeed because they operate in protected environments: limited scope, selected users, and low negative consequences. Production removes these safeguards. Systems must integrate with legacy infrastructure, operate reliably under real workloads, and interact with users whose behavior cannot be scripted. In Europe, this transition also triggers heightened scrutiny around compliance, explainability, and worker impact. Governance, monitoring, and feedback loops must therefore mature alongside the technology. Without this shift, early gains collapse under operational complexity or loss of trust.

Success cannot be inferred from technical performance alone, nor from the number of pilots launched. It must be evaluated through indicators that reflect sustained adoption and impact. In practice, this includes time saved on repetitive tasks, measurable improvements in output quality, employee acceptance, and consistency with legal and ethical obligations.

These metrics must be visible, reviewed regularly, and tied to accountability. When a system underperforms, responsibility must be clear: who decides to intervene, retrain, or retire it? When it succeeds, who is accountable for maintaining and scaling it? Measurement turns intent into evidence, thresholds turn evidence into decisions, and interdisciplinary communication ensures that those decisions are implemented coherently. The roadmap is therefore not a checklist, but a way of sequencing learning, governance, and scaling so that generative AI strengthens, rather than destabilizes, European organizations.

8.2 Data governance as epistemic strategy

Before anything can be measured, it is necessary to determine what becomes visible in the first place. Data governance operates at this foundational level. It is the mechanism that determines which aspects of reality can be perceived, reasoned about, and ultimately decided upon by both humans and machines.

Executives rarely need reminding that data matters. What they underestimate is that data governance is not about control but about direction [136]. In traditional management, governance is reactive: it protects against misuse, ensures compliance, and documents processes. In AI, governance becomes formative: it shapes how the teams learn. Generative AI operationalizes the categories embedded in its data. How information are curated, labeled, structured, and connected defines what its AI can perceive, compare, and reason about. Data governance is epistemic design. It determines which distinctions can be made and which remain structurally invisible.

For most organizations, the limiting factor is not data scarcity but semantic fragmentation. The challenge lies in transforming "Big Data " into "Big Informative Data".[2] Information exists across departments, regions, and systems, each encoding the business differently. When generative AI agents are introduced into this environment, they do not smooth these differences; they make them operational. Agents learn the language of silos and act on it. What later appears as inconsistent behavior or unexplained divergence in outcomes typically originates upstream, in incompatible meanings that no amount of monitoring can correct.

Consider a hospital network deploying a clinical decision-support agent across six facilities. Rather than producing isolated recommendations, the agent coordinates multiple steps: it retrieves patient histories, queries laboratory systems, flags risk factors, prioritizes cases, and proposes care pathways to clinicians. Early deployment delivers an important insight. The concept of a "high-risk patient" is defined differently across departments. In cardiology, it refers to patients with multiple comorbidities. In surgery,

2 Recall the lesson from Chapter 1.

it denotes patients with prior adverse reactions to anesthesia. In oncology, it prioritizes aggressive tumor profiles beyond comorbidity count.

For clinicians, these distinctions reflect legitimate domain expertise. For the agent, however, they constitute incompatible semantic instructions guiding downstream actions. Identically profiled patients trigger different escalation paths, monitoring frequencies, or care recommendations depending on where they enter the system. The agent behaves consistently with its inputs, faithfully executing the users' implicit assumptions. What becomes visible is not a technical limitation, but a lack of shared meaning.

This visibility can become an asset. By analyzing how the agent plans actions, escalates cases, and justifies recommendations across contexts, users identify precisely where semantic assumptions diverge. Departments then agree on shared reference definitions, complemented by contextual qualifiers that preserve clinical nuance while restoring coherence. Once these semantic anchors are established, the agent's behavior becomes consistent, explainable, and predictable across facilities. Scaling becomes possible without sacrificing local judgment or safety.

The lesson generalizes. When core business concepts are semantically fragmented, agentic systems amplify fragmentation by acting on it. When meaning is stabilized, agents transform shared understanding into coordinated, reliable action. Governance, in this sense, does not constrain intelligence; it enables it. The operational implication is substantial. Metrics and thresholds can only be portable across teams, regions, and use cases if the underlying data semantics are portable as well. Scalability in generative AI depends less on infrastructure than on shared meaning. Agents make this dependency visible earlier, because their value lies not in producing text, but in executing decisions across management boundaries.

Effective data governance therefore balances autonomy and coherence. Local teams must retain the freedom to adapt to context, but within a framework of shared semantics, reference definitions, and traceability. This does not require rigid uniformity. It requires explicit translation mechanisms and agreed conceptual anchors that allow learning to accumulate rather than fragment.

When data governance functions well, it ceases to be a bureaucratic layer and becomes an accelerator. Technical teams, legal oversight, and business leadership align around a shared understanding of what the organization knows, values, and monitors. Metrics become comparable, thresholds defensible, and interdisciplinary governance operational rather than aspirational.

For leadership, the question therefore evolves. It is no longer primarily how to collect or clean data, but how to orchestrate learning. *Which distinctions are worth encoding? Which feedback loops must be formalized so agents can adapt without drifting? Which interpretations of reality can be delegated to autonomous systems, and which must remain human judgment?* Data governance ultimately determines what agentic AI systems are capable of seeing, reasoning about, and acting upon.

8.3 Metrics and thresholds

Data governance determines *what* becomes visible. Metrics and thresholds define *how* that visibility translates into measurement and action. Metrics specify indicators, units, and scales. Thresholds determine when measured values prompt decisions such as escalation, remediation, adjustment, or withdrawal. Together, they form the connective tissue between technical behavior and valuable intent.

The challenges discussed in Chapter 6 cannot be addressed through principles alone. Recognizing that a generative AI system may mislead users, behave unevenly, or produce unexpected outputs is an important starting point. Governance becomes effective when these properties are made measurable. Measurement turns abstract concerns into observable signals. Thresholds then turn those signals into decisions that can be acted upon. In this way, governance transforms awareness into capability.

Metrics are the mechanism through which qualitative expectations are translated into managerial control. They convert properties such as accuracy, robustness, bias, or reliability into indicators that can be monitored over time, compared across systems, and aligned with internal objectives. By establishing a shared language between technical teams and leadership, metrics enable informed discussion, early detection of drift or improvement, and credible demonstration that systems are being actively steered rather than passively observed.

In the context of generative AI, relevant metrics extend well beyond traditional notions of accuracy. Organizations increasingly track hallucination rates in factual tasks, consistency across paraphrased prompts, refusal rates in safety-critical contexts, latency and cost per interaction, and variation in outputs across demographic or linguistic groups. None of these metrics is valuable in isolation. Their strength lies in how directly they reflect dimensions of performance and responsibility that matter to users, customers, regulators, and the organization itself.

Metrics acquire meaning only in context. A metric that is appropriate in one deployment may be insufficient or misleading in another. A customer-facing chatbot with a 2 % hallucination rate may be acceptable when recommending city tours, yet inappropriate when providing legal or medical guidance [111]. A content generation system that scores highly on user preference may still underperform in robustness or factual consistency when prompts are paraphrased. Metrics do not define success on their own; they enable informed judgment when interpreted relative to purpose, use case, and risk exposure.

For leaders, this creates two clear opportunities. First, technical metrics can be connected to business indicators that reflect real value and sustainable impact. Efficiency gains or cost reductions become meaningful when they are achieved without increasing downstream risks such as customer dissatisfaction, reputational harm, or regulatory exposure. Second, metrics increasingly function as evidence. Measurable indicators provide a concrete basis for demonstrating robustness, fairness, and transparency, allowing compliance and accountability to be established through observable performance rather than declarative claims.

As generative AI systems expand in scope and complexity, no single metric can capture their responses adequately. Metric portfolios are thus beneficial, to reflect multiple dimensions, including robustness across inputs and updates, fairness across user groups, transparency and traceability of outputs, user trust as reflected in overrides or complaints, and sustainability in terms of cost and scalability. These dimensions naturally involve trade-offs. Improving safety may increase refusal rates. Reducing cost may affect output quality. Enhancing robustness may constrain creativity. Governance does not remove these tensions; it provides the structure to navigate them deliberately. Metrics are therefore assessment instruments rather than optimization targets. Maintaining balance across dimensions is essential, particularly for companies operating across multiple domains and stakeholders.

While metrics make system behavior visible, thresholds give that visibility practical meaning. A threshold specifies when a measured value prompts action, such as review, adjustment, or escalation. Thresholds are therefore expressions of agreed priorities. They encode how much uncertainty, error, bias, or cost a board is willing to accept in pursuit of value.

Defining thresholds is inherently a collective exercise. Decisions about acceptable hallucination rates, permissible disparities across user groups, or minimum confidence levels for automated outputs reflect broader considerations of trust, responsibility, and accountability. As such, they benefit from coordinated input across technical, business, legal, and compliance functions. This need for coordination reinforces the importance of interdisciplinary collaboration, AI literacy, and shared ethical reference points, which are developed in the following sections.

8.4 Interdisciplinary coordination

Thresholds are one of the most powerful levers to translate insight into action. Because they encode value judgments about risk, trust, and responsibility, they benefit from being defined collaboratively rather than by any single function. When technical, legal, and business perspectives converge on shared metrics and decision points (as in Fig. 8.2), thresholds become instruments of alignment rather than constraint. In this sense, interdisciplinarity is not an overhead; it is a source of strategic clarity.

Generative AI systems are adaptive socio-technical systems whose output emerges from interactions between models, users, data, and infrastructure. This complexity creates an opportunity: different functions observe different facets of system behavior. Technical teams articulate uncertainty, error modes, and performance dynamics. Business leaders interpret outcomes in terms of value creation, operational exposure, and strategic positioning. Legal and compliance functions translate system behavior into rights, obligations, and accountability. When these perspectives are brought together around shared metrics and thresholds, governance becomes a mechanism for collective sense-making and informed decision-making.

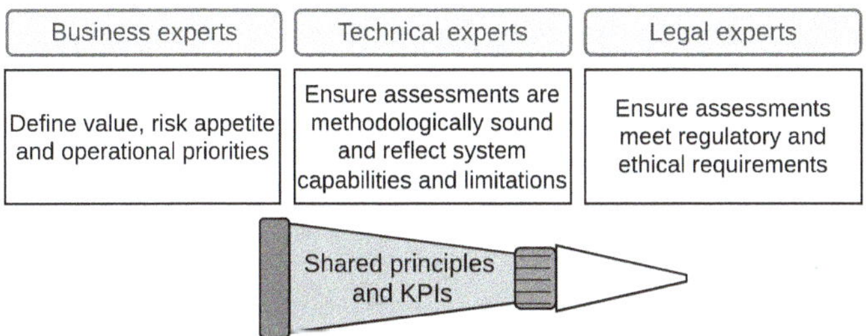

Figure 8.2: Illustration of how different responsibilities reinforce each other under shared principles and metrics. Note that ethical requirements may be demanded to ethical experts, on top of legal experts.

To realize this benefit, alignment must be institutionalized. Cross-functional review structures enable systems to be assessed not only for technical performance, but for overall organizational fit. In practice, these forums bring together engineering, legal, sustainability, and affected business units. Each contributes a distinct lens: robustness and maintainability, regulatory alignment, societal and sustainability considerations, and commercial relevance. Addressed together, these dimensions accelerate convergence rather than slowing progress.

Documentation plays a central enabling role in this process. Rather than serving as a defensive artefact, documentation becomes a shared memory of decisions and trade-offs. It records not only technical specifications, but the reasoning behind them: why certain datasets were selected, why specific metrics were chosen, why thresholds were set at particular levels, and why deployment occurred in a given context. This shared record supports learning, continuity, and confident evolution as systems scale.

Consider a fraud detection system deployed by a payment processor. The data science team proposes a model with 99 % precision: for every 100 transactions flagged, 99 correspond to genuine fraud. This provides a strong starting point. Interdisciplinary discussion then enriches the picture. Finance evaluates the operational cost of reviews, legal and compliance assess customer trust and regulatory expectations, and product teams consider user experience. Together, these perspectives enable a nuanced threshold strategy.

The resulting thresholds reflect intentional design rather than a single technical optimum. High-value transactions are governed by stricter thresholds, while lower-value transactions allow greater tolerance for interruption. Thresholds are reviewed alongside indicators such as fraud losses, customer complaints, and review costs. Decision authority is clearly defined: product owners adjust thresholds within agreed boundaries, while broader changes receive executive oversight. Dashboards track technical performance and downstream effects in parallel, enabling confident, timely adjustment.

As use cases mature, governance evolves into a learning system. Metrics are refined, thresholds recalibrated, models updated, and policies adapted as contexts change. What matters is not rigid structure, but continuity of insight across functions and deployments. Experience gained in one system informs the next, compounding acquired capabilities.

What ultimately makes this framework effective is not the sophistication of measurement, but the clarity it brings to action. Metrics make behavior legible. Thresholds make choices explicit. Ownership ensures timely response. Together, they create a governance loop that supports speed with confidence.

Interdisciplinary coordination, however, rests on a shared foundation: the ability of all participants to understand and discuss the same concepts. This brings us directly to the role of AI literacy.

8.5 Building AI literacy: creating shared understanding

Interdisciplinary coordination thrives on shared understanding. When an engineer reports that a model exhibits a 15 % age-related bias, that figure should be immediately interpretable by a product manager, a compliance officer, and a senior executive. Shared vocabulary turns metrics into guidance rather than raw signals. AI literacy is what allows different roles to reason together, align decisions, and act with confidence.

One of the most powerful enablers of successful AI adoption is not technology itself, but understanding. AI literacy, namely the ability of employees and leaders to grasp what AI can and cannot do, is becoming as foundational to modern companies or institutions as digital literacy once was. It does not imply that everyone must become a data scientist. Rather, it means that professionals across functions can reason critically about AI's capabilities, limitations, and implications for their work.

For managers, the opportunity lies in addressing the growing knowledge asymmetry inside organizations. On one side, specialized experts work with models, data pipelines, and APIs. On the other, a much larger group interacts with AI-enabled systems in daily operations. Bridging this gap enables better decisions, more appropriate trust, and smoother adoption. When people understand how a system works, they neither defer to it blindly nor dismiss it prematurely; instead, they engage with it constructively.

AI literacy extends beyond technical familiarity. It includes conceptual understanding: knowing how AI systems learn from data, why outputs may vary, and what terms such as "training", "bias", or "hallucination" mean in practice. It includes critical awareness: recognizing that models reproduce patterns found in data rather than objective truth. It includes ethical and legal sensitivity: understanding privacy, consent, intellectual property, and responsibilities under frameworks such as the EU AI Act. And it includes operational fluency: the ability to communicate effectively with technical teams, ask informed questions, and interpret results within a business context.

Developing these competencies does not require intensive coding programs. It begins with shared language. When managers, lawyers, and engineers use the same words to describe system behavior, collaboration accelerates. Effective training therefore prioritizes common conceptual ground before specialized detail.

Those that invest in AI literacy unlock several advantages [137, 138]. Decision-making around AI adoption becomes faster and more assured. Vendor claims can be evaluated more critically. Compliance obligations are addressed proactively rather than reactively. Most importantly, internal trust grows: employees feel included in the transformation, and governance mechanisms function smoothly because their purpose is understood and shared.

AI literacy also expands the capacity to innovate. When non-technical staff understand, at a conceptual level, how AI systems infer, generalize, and occasionally misalign with context, they begin to surface opportunities and constraints that would otherwise remain invisible to a central AI team. Practical use cases emerge organically, informed by domain expertise and grounded expectations, creating a virtuous cycle between experimentation and impact.

Consider a logistics company that invests in AI literacy alongside the deployment of a generative AI planning assistant. During a three-day workshop, warehouse supervisors are not only trained to use the tool, but to understand its operating logic: how natural language inputs are translated into constraints, where historical data shapes recommendations, and which contextual factors the model cannot infer on its own.

As a result, supervisors move beyond passive validation. They actively explore the system by expressing local constraints in natural language, such as narrow streets during morning hours or seasonally changing parking rules, and by testing hypothetical scenarios ahead of peak periods. The assistant generates alternative routing strategies and explains the associated trade-offs. Through this interaction, supervisors surface systematic blind spots in the optimization logic that would not have emerged through standard monitoring alone. In this setting, generative AI becomes an interface between tacit human knowledge and formal models, and AI literacy enables supervisors to use that interface with insight rather than deference.

Scenario-based training further reinforces this dynamic. When cross-functional teams interpret metrics together, respond to unexpected system behavior, or explain outcomes across technical, legal, and business perspectives, governance becomes a shared practice rather than a formal constraint. Engineers, managers, and compliance professionals develop a common intuition for how probabilistic systems behave, where human judgment must intervene, and how responsibility is retained even when tasks are partially delegated to machines.

Ultimately, AI literacy is a form of empowerment. A workforce that understands AI can question it, refine it, and guide it toward better outcomes. Technology shifts from a black box to a collaborative tool. In organizations where literacy is high, AI becomes embedded in a culture of continuous learning rather than imposed as a top-down mandate.

In Europe, where trust and accountability are central to corporate and regulatory culture, AI literacy is more than a competitive advantage. It is the foundation that allows innovation, governance, and legitimacy to reinforce one another. With shared understanding in place, organizations are equipped to address the challenge of adoption itself with clarity and confidence.

8.6 Dealing with change

The AI literacy just discussed creates the capacity for understanding. Managing change translates that capacity into action. It addresses how AI is introduced, perceived, and integrated into daily work. Effective change management begins with narrative and extends through structured adoption practices that balance encouragement with governance.

8.6.1 Narrative and adoption: reframing AI as empowerment

Responsible leadership begins with a shift in perspective, but not merely in tone. Generative AI is not just another technology to be installed; it is an evolving step after data governance, fact-based decision making, and deep analytics. It becomes part of a company's culture, altering where decisions are made, how knowledge is produced, and who bears responsibility for outcomes. For leaders, the challenge is not to promote enthusiasm, but to frame adoption in a way that aligns incentives, authority, and accountability.

In many cases, AI is introduced as something employees must adapt to: a tool imposed from above that restructures workflows and introduces new forms of evaluation. Resistance in this context is not simply emotional. It is often rational. Employees worry about deskilling, increased surveillance, opaque decision logic, and being held accountable for outputs they neither control nor fully understand. Ignoring these concerns or attempting to override them through optimistic messaging undermines trust rather than building it [139].

A more effective approach is to shift the narrative from adaptation to agency. The relevant question is not whether AI will change work, but how it redistributes cognitive effort and decision authority. When AI is framed as a system that absorbs routine tasks while leaving judgment, escalation, and exception handling with humans, adoption becomes less threatening and more credible. This framing only works, however, if it is reflected in actual system design and governance, not just in communication.

Consider a customer service team in a telecommunications company introducing an AI assistant to handle standard inquiries. Early reactions reflect understandable concerns around performance monitoring and job security. Management responds by reframing the deployment explicitly: routine queries are automated, while agents retain authority over complex cases, overrides, and customer escalation. Performance criteria are redesigned to prioritize resolution quality and customer satisfaction rather than throughput alone. Over several months, adoption grows steadily, average handling times decrease, and agents report greater autonomy and confidence in managing demanding interactions. The decisive factor is not the presence of AI itself, but the deliberate redefinition of roles, decision rights, and accountability around it.

This example highlights a central insight. Empowerment does not emerge from messaging alone. It is built when AI systems are introduced in ways that reinforce professional judgment and make human contribution visible and valued. When employees see how their expertise complements automated support, trust develops organically and engagement follows.

Narrative therefore plays an enabling role, but only when embedded in broader organizational alignment. Leaders must articulate clearly why AI is being adopted, which problems it is intended to address, and where its boundaries lie. They must explain how success is assessed and how responsibility is distributed when systems behave unexpectedly. Equally important, they must establish concrete channels for feedback and adjustment, allowing employees to shape how systems evolve rather than simply adapt to them.

Narrative, in this sense, is not persuasion. It is coherence between intent, managerial design, and everyday practice. When these elements reinforce one another, narrative becomes the cultural scaffolding that allows technical change to take root and mature.

8.6.2 The importance of supporting experimentation

AI adoption rarely follows a clean, top-down plan, but proceeds all ways: top-down, bottom-up, side-to-side. Here, we focus on how to best support bottom-up experimentation to integrate it with managerial decisions and reduce resistance to change. The idea is to integrate the novelties brought about by AI into the "new normal" for employees at all levels, such that they become effectively integrated in the working routine.

As a matter of fact, employees are already experimenting with generative AI tools [139], often outside formal systems and without explicit authorization. This bottom-up adoption reflects genuine initiative and unmet needs, but it also exposes organizations to risks related to data protection, consistency, and accountability. The notion of shadow AI, discussed earlier in the book, is therefore not simply a compliance issue; it is a signal that existing tools, processes, or incentives are misaligned with how work is actually done.

Managing this reality requires more than prohibition. Attempts to block informal usage without providing viable alternatives tend to drive experimentation further underground. A more effective response is to recognize bottom-up adoption as inevitable and channel it through structured support. This includes providing approved tools, clear usage guidelines, and training that focuses not only on capabilities but also on limitations and failure modes.

Integration into existing workflows is critical. AI systems that require separate platforms, complex procedures, or additional documentation burdens are unlikely to be adopted sustainably. When tools blend naturally into daily work and demonstrably save time or improve quality, informal experimentation tends to converge toward sanctioned use rather than diverge from it.

Incentives also matter. Responsible experimentation should be encouraged and recognized, not treated as a liability. Sharing internal use cases, highlighting effective practices, and acknowledging teams that improve outcomes through thoughtful use of AI helps normalize adoption. At the same time, accountability must be clarified. When AI-supported decisions affect customers or operations, responsibility cannot be pushed down to individual users. Accountability must be shared across system designers, managers, and the organization as a whole.

Holding employees personally responsible for the outputs of tools imposed by the top management is both unfair and counterproductive. It discourages experimentation and incentivizes defensive behavior. Conversely, when successful use of AI is recognized and failures are treated as learning opportunities rather than grounds for blame, adoption accelerates in a controlled and transparent manner. Some companies may even make an extra step in dealing with the responsibility associated with using inherently uncontrollable and unaccountable tools: to increase the salary of employees using generative AI within the prescribed frameworks, to compensate for the increased responsibility burden [140].

Many AI pilots succeed when the conditions are correctly understood and addressed from the outset. What is often described as resistance to change is more accurately a signal that key prerequisites require attention. When data quality is treated seriously, objectives are explicit, incentives are aligned, and executive sponsorship is visible, teams engage constructively with AI initiatives. In sensitive domains, early focus on reliability, bias, and error handling strengthens confidence rather than slowing progress, because these concerns are addressed structurally rather than rhetorically.

Sustainable AI adoption therefore rests on clear ownership. Training builds competence, governance builds trust, and clarity builds confidence. Organizations that invest deliberately in all three are not only able to deploy AI effectively; they integrate it into a culture of continuous improvement, where pilots mature into operational systems and learning compounds over time rather than restarting with each new initiative.

8.7 Governance structures: making accountability tangible

As adoption progresses, informal experimentation must transition into structured governance. Governance structures are what make accountability tangible and operational. They determine who decides, who monitors, who intervenes, and who is held responsible when systems fail or succeed.

Governance takes on a distinct meaning in the context of generative AI because these systems do not merely automate predefined tasks, but actively participate in knowledge production, communication, and decision support. Their outputs are probabilistic, context-dependent, and often perceived by users as authoritative, even when uncertainty is high. As a result, accountability cannot be reduced to traditional notions of system correctness or uptime; it must address how trust, autonomy, and human judgment are distributed between people and machines.

AI governance is therefore inherently collective, but for reasons that go beyond organizational complexity. No single department can fully anticipate how AI systems will be interpreted, relied upon, or misused once embedded into real workflows. The board and executive leadership carry responsibility for defining how much cognitive authority the company is willing to delegate to machines or they providers.[3] This includes decisions about which tasks may be assisted, which may be partially automated, and which must remain firmly under human control. Governance committees translate this strategic stance into concrete rules for deployment, usage boundaries, and escalation paths when outputs become unreliable or harmful. In this sense, governance is the mechanism that converts abstract trust in generative AI into enforceable practices.

At the technical level, data and AI teams take on a role that goes beyond traditional software development. They are not only system builders, but also interpreters of model behavior. Because generative models do not expose deterministic logic, effective accountability emerges through structured documentation of training data provenance, prompt design assumptions, known limitations, and expected uncertainty. Far from being a compliance artefact, this documentation becomes a strategic asset: it allows managers and decision-makers to understand how the system behaves in practice, where it performs reliably, and where human judgment must remain central. Legal and compliance functions reinforce this foundation by translating regulatory and ethical principles into concrete constraints that reflect the realities of generative AI, such as boundaries on automated advice, transparency requirements, and safeguards against misleading or fabricated outputs.

Business units play an equally constructive role. It is through everyday use that the distinctive characteristics of generative AI surface, influencing writing styles, decision rationales, and patterns of work. Because business teams operate closest to customers and internal decision-makers, they are well positioned to observe how tools are actually used and how behavior evolves over time. Subtle shifts, such as increasing reliance on generated outputs or gradual expansion of use cases, become visible early. This proximity enables timely adjustment and learning rather than reactive correction. Audit and risk functions complete this picture by assessing not only whether governance policies exist, but whether systems are used in ways that align with their intended purpose. In more mature organizations, auditing AI increasingly focuses on how decisions are made and supported, rather than on technical components alone.

---

3 A concept referred to as "accountability chain", which is being recently developed as contract negotiation and governance guidelines [141].

Making governance effective, therefore, does not require exhaustive control, but deliberate focus. A small number of well-chosen dimensions are particularly decisive for generative AI, where outputs are probabilistic and systems evolve through use. These dimensions, summarized in Table 8.2, determine whether accountability remains a stated ambition or becomes a practical capability embedded in daily operations.

Table 8.2: Core dimensions required to make generative AI governance operational and accountable.

	Operational meaning	Practical implication
Clear ownership and accountability	Each generative AI system has an identified owner responsible for defining acceptable use, monitoring behavior, and managing evolution over time	When issues arise (e. g. hallucinated facts, biased language, unsafe advice), responsibility for intervention, retraining, or withdrawal is explicit rather than diffuse
Risk-based classification and oversight	Systems are classified based on the cognitive authority they exercise and the potential consequences of erroneous or misleading outputs	Tools supporting low-impact drafting receive lighter controls, while systems influencing decisions or external communication trigger stronger review and governance
Transparency and explainability by design	Systems are described in terms meaningful to managers: intended purpose, training data boundaries, limitations, and uncertainty characteristics	This enables informed use, realistic expectations, and credible dialogue with regulators, auditors, and stakeholders
Continuous monitoring and lifecycle control	Usage patterns, output quality, and reliance levels are monitored beyond initial deployment	Drift in behavior, unintended use cases, or over-reliance are detected early, before they translate into strategic, legal, or reputational risk

None of these dimensions function without people. A responsible culture emerges when employees recognize that using generative AI is not a neutral efficiency gain, but a form of delegated decision-making that always carries residual accountability. When governance is effective, generative AI evolves from a collection of isolated experiments into a managed capability. It ensures that systems do not merely generate plausible outputs, but operate within clearly articulated boundaries of trust, responsibility, and oversight. In this sense, governance is not a brake on innovation; it is the condition that allows generative AI to scale without eroding confidence, control, or institutional integrity.

Consider a large energy and utilities provider operating across multiple Member States. The organization maintains a cross-functional AI oversight board that brings together representatives from data science, legal and compliance, risk management, product teams, and operations. The board meets on a regular basis, and every new generative AI use case must be presented jointly by a business owner, a technical lead, and a legal or compliance representative. Proposals range from customer-facing chatbots and automated regulatory reporting to internal decision-support tools for maintenance planning. Decisions are documented in a shared system designed to support internal audit and regulatory review. Not all proposals are approved. Some are rejected outright; others are returned for redesign when accountability is unclear, data governance is insufficient, or operational risks have not been adequately addressed. These outcomes are not treated as setbacks. They are treated as evidence that governance is functioning as intended. By preventing deployments that could create regulatory exposure, operational fragility, or erosion of public trust, the organization avoids costly remediation and reputational damage. Over time, this governance structure becomes an enabler rather than a constraint. Teams move faster because expectations are explicit, approval pathways are predictable, and boundaries are well understood. Clarity about what can and cannot be deployed reduces friction, shortens iteration cycles, and allows generative AI initiatives to scale with confidence across business units and national subsidiaries.

8.8 Ethics as strategy and practice

Throughout the leadership loop, from data governance through metrics, interdisciplinarity, literacy, change management, and governance structures, ethical principles act as both guardrails and compass. Ethics[4] is not a separate workstream or an external constraint. It is the value framework that gives coherence to decisions across technical, managerial, and strategic dimensions.

Across Europe, employees, customers, and citizens articulate increasingly aligned expectations regarding the use of generative AI and agentic systems. Some concerns are technical, relating to accuracy, robustness, and reliability. Others reflect deeper societal values. They relate to how personal data is handled under stringent data-protection regimes, how intellectual property and authorship are respected, whether automated decisions can be explained in ways that meet legal and social standards, how discrimination is mitigated in multilingual and multicultural environments, and how the economic benefits of automation are shared within societies characterized by strong labor protections and social welfare systems.

In the European context, and increasingly beyond it, these expectations are not peripheral considerations. They define the conditions under which AI technologies can

4 There are multiple nuances of "ethics" with respect to AI, from the definition of ethical principles that could be embedded into AI systems, to the ethical use of AI within societies and towards customers and citizens, to the very definition of the ethical scope of an AI developer, deployer, distributor, or user, to the question of whether AI systems themselves deserve ethical rights [142, 143]. As in the rest of the book, we focus here on ethics from a managerial perspective and refer interested readers to other works for deeper exploration.

move from experimentation to sustained deployment in real economic and social settings. Meeting these expectations enables scale. Those that engage seriously with ethical and social dimensions strengthen their legitimacy with regulators, workers' representatives, customers, and public authorities. In the EU, where institutional trust and public acceptance are central to market access, responsible innovation is not merely a compliance exercise; it is a strategic enabler.

Ethics, in this sense, should not be understood as abstract moral philosophy. In practice, it translates into operational principles that guide decision-making under uncertainty and help resolve trade-offs where technical optimization alone is insufficient. Early efforts to formalize such principles emerged in the private sector, notably through initiatives such as IBM's principles for AI ethics [144]. In Europe, these ideas were subsequently consolidated and expanded through public policy processes, culminating in the EU's Ethics Guidelines for Trustworthy AI, introduced in Chapter 7 [133]. The seven principles outlined in Table 8.3 have since become a shared reference point for European institutions, regulators, and an increasing number of organizations operating in or with the European market.

Ethical principles only become effective when they are translated into concrete governance mechanisms. Metrics express ethical expectations in measurable form, such

Table 8.3: Ethics guidelines for trustworthy AI by the high-level expert group on AI, European Commission.

Principle	Explanation
Human oversight and control	AI systems operate under meaningful human authority. Decisions can be reviewed, challenged, corrected, or reversed, and mechanisms for escalation, intervention, and shutdown are clearly defined.
Technical robustness and safety	Systems behave reliably under expected and unexpected conditions, resist manipulation, handle edge cases, and are supported by testing, safeguards, and continuous monitoring.
Fairness	Unjustified discrimination and biased outcomes are identified and mitigated across data, models, and workflows, with particular attention to diverse populations and languages.
Transparency	Relevant stakeholders can understand how the system works, what data it uses, its assumptions and limitations, and the rationale behind its outputs, supported by accessible explanations and documentation.
Accountability	Responsibilities across the AI lifecycle are clearly assigned, enabling traceability, auditing, incident handling, and attribution of outcomes to identifiable actors.
Privacy and data governance	Data is handled in line with European data-protection standards, ensuring minimization, security, controlled access, and disciplined governance throughout the system's lifecycle.
Sustainability	The environmental and societal footprint of AI systems is assessed and reduced, including energy use, resource efficiency, and longer-term social impacts.

as acceptable levels of error, disparity, or uncertainty. Thresholds encode value judgments by defining when these measures trigger action, escalation, or intervention. Governance structures then ensure that these decisions are consistently applied, reviewed, and adapted over time. In this way, ethics moves from aspiration to operation, shaping not only what organizations intend to do with AI, but how systems are designed, monitored, and steered in practice.

These principles are not aspirational slogans. In the European regulatory culture, they are increasingly treated as operational commitments. Human oversight becomes a question of decision rights and escalation pathways. Robustness translates into testing protocols, stress testing, and adversarial evaluation. Fairness requires bias audits adapted to multilingual and multicultural settings. Transparency implies documentation and explainability sufficient for audits and external scrutiny. Accountability demands clear ownership and incident response procedures. Privacy is embedded through data-governance frameworks aligned with European law. Sustainability extends governance beyond immediate performance to environmental and societal impact.

Compliance and ethics are often discussed together, but they serve distinct functions. Compliance concerns adherence to binding legal requirements. Ethics concerns alignment with shared values, societal expectations, and institutional norms. While compliance is conformance to present guardrails, ethics is preparedness and aspiration for the future. In Europe, where legitimacy matters as much as legality, this distinction is particularly important. Comprehensive regulatory frameworks such as the AI Act are still being phased in, interpreted, and operationalized. Those that align early with ethical principles are therefore not merely anticipating future compliance obligations; they are positioning themselves as credible and trustworthy actors within a regulated market.

Importantly, ethics is most effective when it is embedded early rather than appended after deployment. Integrating ethical reflection into strategic decision-making from the outset allows to surface constraints early, explore alternatives deliberately, and avoid paths that would later require costly redesign or corrective intervention. In this sense, ethics functions less as a brake on innovation than as a form of foresight. It does not remove trade-offs, but it brings them into view while adaptation is still feasible and options remain open.

European practice already offers illustrative examples of this approach. In parts of the financial sector, institutions collaborate with academic groups and policy-oriented research organizations to develop internal ethical guidelines for algorithmic decision-making. In healthcare, ethical frameworks are increasingly developed and shared across institutions to maximize patient benefit and societal value. These initiatives are not driven by abstract moral commitments, but they clarify accountability, reduce uncertainty around responsibility, and establish defensible governance structures in domains where legal interpretation is still evolving. By addressing questions of responsibility proactively, it is possible to strengthen one's position in dialogue with vendors, partners, and supervisory authorities.

Similar dynamics apply in procurement and supply-chain contexts. Across Europe, the evaluation of AI vendors increasingly goes beyond cost and raw performance. Criteria such as reliability, explainability, robustness, and consistency across languages and cultural contexts play a growing role. In negotiation, sourcing, or customer-facing applications, language-dependent behavior can influence fairness, consistency, and user experience. Before delegating such interactions to AI systems, organizations benefit from verifying that performance remains stable across linguistic and contextual settings. Regulatory Sandboxes and structured testing environments provide controlled settings for this verification, enabling experimentation while maintaining oversight.

Ethics therefore delivers both protective and enabling benefits. On one hand, it reduces exposure to legal, reputational, and operational uncertainty. On the other, it supports innovation by clarifying boundaries, guiding informed experimentation, and accelerating internal learning. Understanding the limits of one's systems helps to adapt more confidently, change models or architectures when needed, and redesign processes without disruption. Where ethical considerations constrain certain uses or business models, these constraints serve as early indicators of where long-term legitimacy may be fragile rather than as obstacles to progress.

In the European context, responsible leadership is thus less about avoiding missteps than about institutionalizing learning. Organizations that integrate ethics and compliance into their strategic core turn integrity into an operational asset. They build durable trust with regulators, customers, and employees alike. Engaging with ethical frameworks also shapes a company's value proposition, clarifies its relationship with customers and society, and supports the development of human-centric practices that mitigate distortions and strengthen trust at both internal and societal levels [142]. In markets where legitimacy underpins scale, innovation aligned with purpose, accountability, and shared European norms becomes not only sustainable, but competitive.

8.9 AI project owners and organizational outcomes

Once the AI strategy is defined, adoption pipeline, and lifecycle stages, a critical decision follows: assigning clear ownership for AI initiatives. This choice determines how effectively strategic intent translates into execution. While there is no universal model, experience shows that successful AI adoption combines leadership sponsorship, strategic coordination, and cross-departmental engagement.

Bottom-up experimentation and local initiatives play a valuable role, particularly in surfacing opportunities and building early momentum. However, sustained adoption benefits from explicit leadership endorsement and a designated strategic owner. When AI initiatives are coordinated at the leadership level and aligned with business objectives, it is easier to prioritize use cases, harmonize practices, and scale learning across units. This is especially important in larger or more complex organizations, where fragmentation can otherwise dilute impact. Once the executive (C-suite) team signals commitment and provides sponsorship, middle-level champions become essential drivers of implementation and diffusion.

A proven starting point is the appointment of an AI or Digital Transformation Lead at the corporate level. This role represents the first formal point of ownership for AI initiatives. The appropriate profile depends on organizational complexity and the intended role of AI. In large, highly interconnected companies or institutions, where AI is both a managerial capability and a core product dimension, appointing a dedicated Chief AI Officer can be justified. In many cases, however, extending the C-suite is unnecessary. Where the objective is broad productivity gains across departments, an IT, data, or digital transformation leader can effectively coordinate adoption. Where AI initiatives address a well-defined problem within a specific business unit, ownership by the unit head often leads to faster alignment and clearer accountability.

Depending on scale and ambition, the AI Lead may be supported by a dedicated team. This team does not need to be distinct from existing IT or analytics functions, although it can be, particularly when third-party AI tools are integrated rather than developed in-house. What matters most is interdisciplinarity. Team members should combine technical competence with understanding of cost structures, governance, and ethical considerations, enabling informed decisions across the full AI lifecycle. In large organizations, this function often evolves naturally into an AI Centre of Excellence, as discussed in Section 4.4.

To reinforce coordination, establish an AI Steering Committee is often an advantage. As discussed earlier in this chapter, interdisciplinary integration is a key success factor. The Steering Committee typically brings together representatives from IT, data and analytics, HR, legal and compliance, and key business units. Its role is to define policies and ethical guardrails, prioritize use cases based on strategic value, and ensure that lessons learned are shared across the internal teams. Members may be selected based on seniority or proximity to priority challenges, creating a dynamic and problem-oriented forum. A shared baseline of AI literacy across committee members is essential to enable effective dialogue and informed decision-making.[5]

Finally, *department champions* play a decisive role in embedding AI into daily operations. Their function is not managerial oversight, but translation and demonstration. Effective champions are often selected based on trust, influence, and credibility within their teams rather than formal seniority or advanced technical skills. By integrating AI tools into everyday workflows, demonstrating practical value, and sharing experiences informally, they lower barriers to adoption and normalize new practices. In smaller organizations, or where complexity is limited, these roles may overlap with Steering Committee responsibilities or be combined into hybrid positions. In many cases, successful

5 See the early chapters of this book for a discussion of AI literacy foundations.

adoption builds on existing talent rather than requiring new appointments, provided roles and expectations are clearly defined.

Table 8.4 summarizes the main roles and responsibilities discussed in this section. The table should be read as a guiding framework rather than a prescriptive template. Organizations may adapt these roles based on their size, maturity, and strategic priorities, achieving equivalent outcomes through different but coherent configurations.

Table 8.4: Overview of the main roles and role owners inside of companies, according to complexity and goal.

Role	Company complexity		
	Low	**Medium**	**High**
Lead for: general projects problem-specific projects	Experienced leads: Head of Digitals Head of strategic unit	Experienced or newly appointed leads: Head of Digitals (Analytics more than IT) Head of strategic unit (rarely)	Newly appointed leads or experienced leads: New AI Lead or CAO (rarely, Head of Digitals) New AI Lead or CAO (rarely, Head of Digitals)
AI steering committee	Head of units Representatives of roles Task owners	Representatives of units Head of units	Representatives of units/departments Newly appointed spokepersons
Department champs	Steering committee members Trusted champions	Trusted champions Upgraded employees with new role Committee members	Upgraded employees with new role Trusted champions

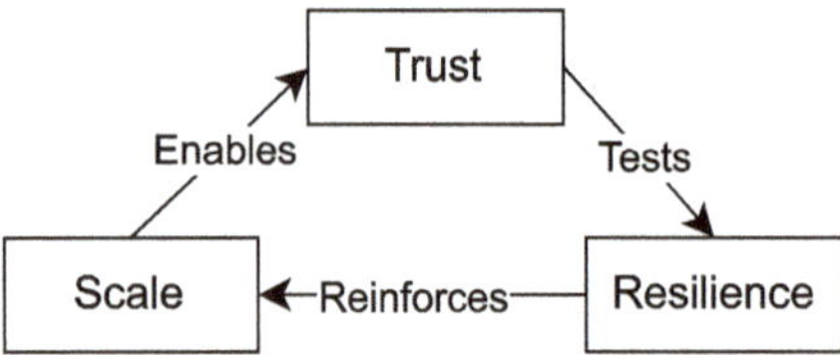

Figure 8.3: Reinforcing organizational outcomes of AI leadership. Trust enables resilient teams, able at scaling AI across units and contexts; scale exposes systems to greater variability and tests organizational resilience; resilience, in turn, enables scaling of project and ultimately reinforces trust by demonstrating control, accountability, and learning under uncertainty.

Establishing a clear project responsibility as the one depicted above has the purpose of giving rise to system-level properties. As shown in Figure 8.3, three such outcomes are particularly decisive: *trust*, *scale*, and *resilience*. These outcomes are not independent.

They form a reinforcing relationship in which trust enables scale, scale tests resilience, and resilience in turn reinforces trust.

Trust emerges when employees, customers, and regulators experience AI systems as responsible, transparent, and accountable in everyday use. It is cultivated through consistent communication, visible governance practices, explainable decisions, and a clear readiness to intervene when systems behave unexpectedly. Trust reduces friction: employees engage with AI confidently, customers are more receptive to automated interactions, and regulators are more inclined to allow operational flexibility. In high-trust environments, adoption accelerates and collaboration across stakeholders becomes smoother.

Scale refers to an organization's ability to extend AI capabilities across units, regions, and use cases while maintaining coherence and oversight. Scale is enabled by shared data semantics, comparable metrics, transferable governance models, and a common level of AI literacy. Those that scale effectively do not redesign oversight for each new deployment. They reuse established frameworks, streamline approval processes, and compound learning over time. As systems are deployed in more diverse contexts, this approach strengthens the organization's ability to operate consistently under variation.

Resilience is the capacity to detect emerging issues early, respond proportionally, and adapt constructively as models drift, contexts change, and usage evolves. Resilient organizations monitor continuously, document systematically, and refine systems iteratively. Rather than aiming for perfect stability, they focus on maintaining control under uncertainty. By demonstrating the ability to adjust and learn without disruption, resilience reinforces trust and completes the reinforcing loop illustrated in Figure 8.3.

These outcomes also provide valuable signals for leadership. Shifts in trust highlight opportunities to improve transparency or clarify accountability. Slow progress in scaling points to governance bottlenecks or unresolved semantic differences. Reduced adaptability indicates where monitoring, documentation, or ownership can be strengthened. Attending to these signals enables leaders to recalibrate priorities, allocate resources more effectively, and refine strategy in a continuous and informed manner.

8.10 Conclusion: leadership as continuous learning

Generative AI adoption does not unfold as a project with a clear end point. Across organizations, it develops as a capability that must be built, tested, and refined over time. The central leadership challenge is therefore not speed of deployment, but the ability to steer change confidently under uncertainty. Those that approach generative AI as a living capability, rather than a one-off initiative, are better positioned to maintain clarity, coherence, and control as conditions evolve.

This chapter has shown how leadership choices shape that capability. Strategic priorities determine where attention and resources are directed. Data governance defines what can be seen and reasoned about. Metrics and thresholds translate visibility into action. Interdisciplinary coordination aligns technical, legal, and business perspectives. AI literacy creates the shared understanding that makes coordination effective. Change management turns intent into adoption. Governance structures make accountability operational. Ethics provides the value framework for decisions under uncertainty. Together, these elements reinforce the outcomes discussed earlier: trust, scale, and resilience.

None of these elements is static. Models evolve, usage patterns shift, regulatory expectations develop, and incentives change. Leadership in this domain therefore benefits from feedback loops that surface emerging signals early, escalation mechanisms that operate smoothly under pressure, and decision processes that treat adjustment as a normal expression of learning. Continuous refinement is not a sign of weakness; it is a sign of growing maturity.

In this sense, responsible leadership is less about restraint than about maintaining direction while moving forward. Those that integrate governance with agility gain both. Those that balance structure with experimentation keep systems deployable, explainable, and contestable at the same time. The strategic challenge lies not in eliminating uncertainty, but in navigating it deliberately.

The organizations most likely to thrive are not necessarily those that extract the largest short-term efficiency gains, but those that preserve their capacity to adapt as the role of generative AI expands. They invest in people who can interrogate systems rather than merely operate them, in metrics that reflect both business value and institutional credibility, and in ethical reflection as a practical tool for navigating high-stakes decisions.

Generative AI – and future evolutions of AI – rewards organizations that can learn continuously. Leadership, in this context, becomes less about asserting vision and more about sustaining the conditions for correction, alignment, and growth. In environments where trust underpins scale, this capability is what allows AI systems to move beyond experimentation and become enduring components of everyday practice.

9 The evolving present and plausible futures of AI

AI is now embedded in everyday tools, organizational processes, and strategic discussions, often in uneven and poorly understood ways. At the same time, public narratives about AI's future oscillate between promises of radical transformation and warnings of existential risk. This chapter aims to cut through that noise. Rather than predicting a single technological trajectory, the goal is to clarify where AI actually stands today, which forces are shaping its evolution, and which futures are plausible given current constraints. For decision-makers, understanding this distinction is critical. Sound strategy depends less on believing bold forecasts and more on recognizing what AI can reliably do now, what it is unlikely to do soon, and where uncertainty should be actively managed rather than ignored. AI is also a moving target. Each new generation of systems is measured less against human intelligence than against the previous generation of AI, which means the ground beneath any specific forecast shifts continuously. Rather than chasing that target, this chapter offers a way of reading change: distinguishing structural shifts from incremental updates, and durable capabilities from temporary novelties, so that strategic decisions remain coherent as the landscape evolves.

9.1 The present: capabilities, claims, and confusion

AI is still in a phase of rapid evolution. The landscape is not fixed but continuously shaped by technological progress, geopolitical competition, and social acceptance. To understand where we are heading, it is therefore necessary to take a clear snapshot of the present before extrapolating plausible futures.

From a technological standpoint, the research frontier remains largely focused on Artificial *Narrow* Intelligence, meaning systems that perform specific tasks with high precision. These are the systems currently deployed across organizations, from recommendation engines and fraud detection tools to image recognition and generative models. Despite their growing sophistication, their scope remains limited to the domains for which they are designed and trained. AI agents are no exception: despite their augmented capabilities linked to the multiple modules they possess, agents are still largely limited by scope and context. Notably, the AI Act mostly pertains to scope-defined systems, that can be framed within the risk-based approach.

Yet, the horizon of public discourse is dominated by the aspiration to create Artificial *General* Intelligence (AGI), systems capable of performing a wide range of cognitive tasks with flexibility comparable to human reasoning, or even Superintelligence (SI), systems capable of performing tasks with capabilities exceeding those of humans [149]. The ambition itself is not new, but it continues to fuel both excitement and confusion [145]. Claims of imminent breakthroughs frequently blur the distinction between task-specific excellence and general intelligence. Great debates exist as to whether the current systems are even capable, in principle, of achieving such feats, or new types of

https://doi.org/10.1515/9783112254103-009

AI[1] would be necessary. Doubts also exist as to whether any AI would be capable of reproducing the extremely diverse nuances of human experience, and of tackling tasks where dilemmas, compromises, disruptive or non-black/white decisions are at stake. Many also discuss whether AGI or Superintelligence are even desirable, apart from marketing and investment purposes: which needs would they exactly address?

Claims of approaching AGI, and more recently of Superintelligence, rarely withstand closer scrutiny [146, 147]. What is typically observed is a process of a posteriori interpretation: an impressive[2] behavior is demonstrated, and only then retroactively labeled as evidence of general intelligence. Similar dynamics were observed decades ago when Deep Blue defeated Garry Kasparov at chess, and later when AlphaGo mastered the game of Go [148]. Each event was celebrated as a historic leap, yet none fundamentally altered our understanding of intelligence itself.[3]

Intelligence, in the human sense, extends well beyond problem-solving performance. It involves context awareness, social understanding, inference of causation, determination of vision and milestones, as well as the ability to navigate ambiguity, emotion, and meaning. A system that can generate fluent language but fails to recognize irony, suffering, or intent does not possess understanding. It operates through statistical inference, not comprehension. The challenge surrounding AGI and SI is therefore not only technical but conceptual. Without a shared definition of intelligence, or an agreed method to recognize it if it were to emerge, the debate is shaped less by evidence than by speculation.

For leaders navigating this environment, a pragmatic perspective is essential. The central question is not whether a system can be described as intelligent, but whether it delivers consistent and measurable value, regardless of its label. Technologies that reliably improve efficiency, quality, or decision-making deserve serious attention. Those whose appeal rests primarily on novelty or rhetorical ambition should be approached with caution. In practice, the maturity of AI should be assessed not by the sophistication of its promises, but by its demonstrated ability to solve real problems under real-world constraints.

---

1 Recall from Chapter 1 that AI as a technology is a progressively complex ensemble of mathematics: alternative or more powerful models may be required to advance, instead of piling up the existing ones.

2 Mind: impressive with respect to the state of the art at any given time, not in an absolute sense.

3 In fact, any chess emulator on a smartphone is now more skilled than Deep Blue was, but nobody would call them "AGI" anymore, as perception of skills shifted over time.

9.2 Research frontiers

Predicting the future of AI is impossible, but identifying the directions of research currently pursued worldwide offers valuable insight. These directions extend from fundamental theoretical questions to applied innovations.

At the most foundational level lies the question of defining and modeling intelligence. This is not merely a philosophical curiosity; it is central to understanding how cognition works and how it might be replicated in machines. Although neural networks are often described as mimicking the brain, the resemblance is largely metaphorical. Early AI systems in the 1960s and 1970s were loosely inspired by biological neurons, but today's architectures operate in a completely different way. The analogy is similar to comparing the flight of an airplane with that of a bird. Both achieve lift and movement through the air, but their mechanisms are entirely distinct. Airplanes can fly faster and farther than birds, yet they cannot hover like hummingbirds or perform complex maneuvers. The same applies to AI systems: they can process enormous amounts of data and detect patterns beyond human reach, but they do not replicate the way the human mind understands, feels, or reasons.

A second major research frontier concerns inductive and transformational learning. Most AI systems today rely on a form of statistical deduction. They are exposed to large datasets, extract patterns, and use them to make predictions. True induction, however, involves discovering general rules from limited examples, a capacity humans display naturally. This challenge is well illustrated by the ARC-AGI benchmark, a set of grid-based abstract-reasoning puzzles that humans solve almost effortlessly from just a few examples. On its harder second version, ARC-AGI-2, humans still solve around 85 %, whereas the strongest AI systems remain far below that: as of late 2025, a leading commercial model reached roughly 38 %, and the best bespoke refinement pipeline about 54 % [150]. Achieving human-level induction therefore remains a major obstacle. A related challenge is transformational learning: applying learned operations such as rotation, scaling, or logical manipulation to new contexts. Humans do this intuitively, whereas AI systems often perform poorly on transformations absent from their training data.

Other active areas of research include causal reasoning and symbolic integration (the combination of statistical learning with explicit logical structures), embedding cause-and-effect understanding within statistical models. Current systems excel at correlation but struggle with causation. When exposed to entirely new scenarios, they tend to misinterpret signals. For instance, in self-driving cars, it is impossible to train a system on every potential road situation. The model must learn abstract principles to distinguish between a real red traffic light and a red light temporarily carried on a truck. Such reasoning remains extremely difficult for machines.

Improving interpretability, transparency, explainability, and controllability also remains at the top of the research agenda. Without these qualities, trust and accountability cannot be established. At the same time, developers are working to detect and mitigate hallucinations, biases, and liability risks, as well as to encode ethical or even moral guidelines within systems. Doing so during training is complex, partly because ethical principles lack universal consensus, but the need for alignment is becoming urgent as AI systems increasingly influence human decisions.

AI, in its current form, mirrors aspects of human intelligence without replicating its essence. The next decade of research will likely bring incremental improvements rather than sudden revolutions, focusing on grounding intelligence in causality, reasoning, and context. For decision-makers, the practical consequence is that the gap between AI's strongest capabilities and its persistent limitations is unlikely to close uniformly. Some frontiers, such as pattern recognition, fluent generation, narrow optimization, will continue to advance rapidly. Others, such as causal reasoning, robust induction, alignment with contested values, will progress more slowly and unevenly. Strategy that assumes uniform progress on all fronts misallocates resources; strategy that maps capability against frontier delivers durable value.

9.3 Geopolitical axes

Beyond technological competition lies the geopolitical race that increasingly shapes the global development of AI. At present, this race unfolds along four main axes, with profound implications for power, dependency, and strategic autonomy.

The first axis is the quest for *computational power*, dominated by companies and research centers in the United States and China. Systems such as Claude, Gemini, and Grok compete with counterparts such as DeepSeek and Qwen in a struggle to achieve ever-higher performance. This rivalry accelerates innovation, but it also concentrates influence in the hands of actors capable of mobilizing massive capital, talent, and compute at scale. Notably, the quest for performance is a by-product of the quest for market share. As long as performance is associated with higher likelihood of user adoption, the two will coincide. However, as exemplified by Chinese AI models focusing on free access and just-enough computing capabilities, the quest may move towards business models, leaving computational power or generalizability aside or constrained to a few organizations.[4] Here lie many potential opportunities for European organizations, which can disregard computing power as the top priority in favor of mixed modes of adoption, tailored systems, or business models that facilitate European AI diffusion.

The second axis is the *competition for resources*. Advanced chips depend on rare earth minerals, energy, and water, tying AI development to mining, energy policy, and industrial infrastructure. Initiatives such as the "Chip Four" alliance or China's "Digital

---

4 Interestingly, academic research has already moved rather significantly away from computing power as research domain, focusing instead on lower-cost AI systems, or alternative paradigms, as discussed in the previous Section.

Silk Road" reflect attempts to secure end-to-end control over digital supply chains [151, 152]. Emerging economies, particularly in the Middle East, are also investing heavily in large-scale compute infrastructure as part of broader diversification strategies [153]. The quest for resources intersects with the quest for energy transformation facilities, which is already central to the European agenda.

The third axis concerns *digital sovereignty and governance models*, and this is where Europe occupies a distinct position. Europe does not compete head-to-head with the United States or China on hyperscale platforms, but it is far from absent. Companies such as Mistral AI demonstrate Europe's capacity to produce competitive foundation models, while initiatives around AI factories and upcoming Gigafactories aim to pool compute, data, and talent at continental scale. At the same time, Europe retains a structurally critical position in the global semiconductor ecosystem through ASML, whose lithography technologies are indispensable for advanced chip manufacturing worldwide.

Rather than pursuing dominance through sheer scale alone, Europe is combining selective technological investment with a governance-driven strategy. Through the AI Act, it seeks to shape how AI systems are developed, evaluated, and deployed, emphasizing robustness, accountability, and trust. This is not merely a defensive posture. By influencing standards and compliance requirements that global actors must engage with, Europe exercises a form of normative and infrastructural power that complements its industrial assets.

Europe's position in this evolving AI power struggle, i. e., balancing selective technological capability, critical industrial leverage, and regulatory influence, will be examined in more detail in Chapter 10. There, we discuss how governance, infrastructure, and strategic dependency interact, and why Europe's role in global AI competition cannot be understood solely through the lens of model size or raw compute.

The fourth axis, more recent but rapidly hardening into competitive ground, is sustainability [122]. Unlike the first three axes, sustainability initially appeared as a shared concern rather than a competitive dimension. That framing is no longer accurate. Carbon disclosure rules, ESG-linked capital allocation, sustainability-tied procurement requirements, and the European Union's own Corporate Sustainability Reporting Directive (CSRD) and AI Act provisions are increasingly turning sustainability into a basis for market access, regulatory leverage, and capital cost. The race is shifting from who can build the most capable AI to who can build AI whose environmental, social, and economic profile is defensible at scale — and Europe is positioned early on each of these dimensions.

On the environmental dimension, the whole AI supply chain – from hardware construction, to data collection and storage, to model training, up to hardware disposal (e-wastes) – is extremely resource- and energy-demanding [154, 155].

Measuring AI's carbon footprint, assessing its environmental impact, and devising concrete mitigation actions are open challenges with great room for improvement in the near future. For developers, this is becoming a competitive variable rather than a corporate-responsibility checkbox: model providers that can credibly demonstrate energy efficiency, low-impact training, and transparent emissions accounting will be preferred in procurement processes where these criteria are enforced. Concrete actions may include offsetting AI-related carbon emissions, running literacy programs about the topic, and developing marketing claims that reflect the true sustainability profile of AI systems.

On the social dimension, AI sits at an unresolved tension. Concerns about misinformation, biased training, and the pollution of information ecosystems put social trust and democratic foundations at risk [112, 156]. At the same time, AI can produce solutions to these very trends, improving social foundations and well-being [157]. For instance, easily adoptable AI tools to help neurodivergent workers or clients [158] may significantly improve their experience and provide straightforward inclusivity best practices. The competitive consequence is that social sustainability is becoming a brand and procurement variable. Firms that deploy AI in ways that visibly reinforce democratic norms, accessibility, and human-centric design accumulate trust capital; those that deploy in ways that visibly erode them face reputational and regulatory exposure. Embedding ethical principles into AI training and fine-tuning, as well as choosing ethically-oriented models during the selection phase, or pursuing the adoption of inclusivity tools, can be practical actions that leaders may pursue alongside the adoption of AI into their companies.

On the economic dimension, AI by itself is a technology; only when it creates value does it become long-term innovation. As we write, the AI ecosystem faces uneven economic success across the globe and across company sizes [159]. AI developers struggle to make sustainable revenues, while adopters experience varying degrees of ROI. Long-term growth and value creation through AI require sustainable business models [160] that balance innovation with accountability, and democratize access to AI systems. The competitive question is no longer whether AI generates economic value somewhere; it is whether that value can be sustained without compounding dependency on a small number of providers, jurisdictions, or capital structures. Firms that build AI economics resilient to provider failure, pricing changes, and regulatory shifts will outlast those that do not.

Across all three dimensions, the same pattern recurs: sustainability is becoming a competitive axis, not just a shared concern, because the mechanisms that enforce it, i. e., regulatory, financial, reputational, are hardening faster than the firms competing on the other three axes have planned for. Ideally, AI can itself be part of the solutions to its impact [161] (e. g., optimizing smart grids for electricity, democratizing access to higher education, or providing cost-saving solutions within businesses, to name just a few). However, the net benefits are still not fully assessed, and definite actions are still being developed. For European firms in particular, the convergence of the sovereignty axis and the sustainability axis represents the clearest opportunity in the global AI competition: not to win on scale, but to define the terms on which scale is acceptable.

9.4 Plausible futures

A return to an "AI winter" in the historical sense appears unlikely (Figure 9.1) not because expectations have become fully realistic, but because AI is now structurally embedded. Capital investment, management dependencies, and integration into core infrastructures have created path dependency. Even if enthusiasm cools, the technology will not disappear; it will be renegotiated through scope reduction, deployment selectivity, and the redistribution of value across the AI stack, rather than through abandonment.

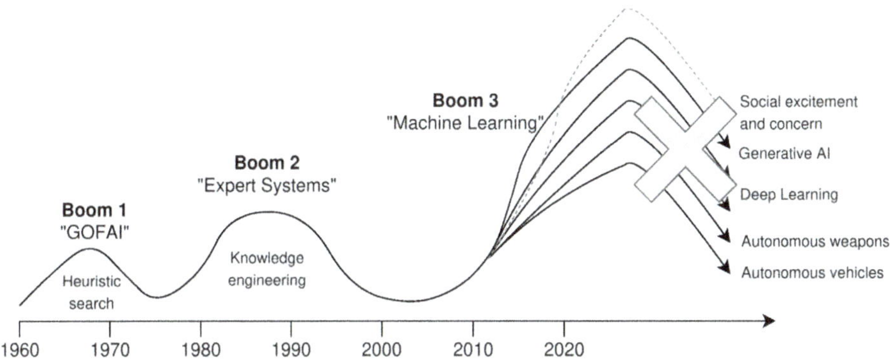

Figure 9.1: A realistic outlook on AI development: a third "AI winter" appears unlikely, with futures ranging from continued growth to a medium-term slowdown or plateau.

What is more likely to break is the assumption of uniform and unlimited transformation. The idea that every sector will be rapidly reshaped by ever-larger models is increasingly at odds with operational reality. Value creation is uneven, context-dependent, and often slower than anticipated. In many deployments, productivity gains are incremental rather than transformational, while secondary costs emerge over time: integration effort, system fragility, and the need for continuous human supervision. This is not a collapse scenario, but a correction of expectations.

Within this context, interest is growing in what is often referred to as *frugal AI*. Frugal AI approaches emphasize efficiency, specialization, and robustness rather than maximal performance. Instead of assuming that progress requires ever-larger models, they explore architectures and deployment strategies that operate under explicit resource constraints, e. g., limited compute budgets, bounded energy footprints, narrower data requirements, and predictable inference costs. This shift does not imply technological regression. Rather, it reflects a broader fragmentation of the AI landscape, where multiple forms of intelligence coexist, optimized for different environments and trade-offs [162].

The resulting future is therefore neither one of unchecked acceleration nor of collapse, but of bifurcation. A small number of actors will continue to push the frontier of large-scale models, while a broader ecosystem develops constrained, purpose-driven systems. Growth continues, but it becomes uneven, selective, and increasingly shaped by structural limits rather than raw ambition alone.

9.5 The choices ahead

AI is no longer merely a future to prepare for; it is increasingly part of the present in which organizations operate. Systems based on Machine Learning and generative models are already embedded in everyday processes, influencing how work is performed, how decisions are supported, and how outcomes are evaluated. What distinguishes this moment is not the existence of these systems, but the speed and informality with which they are being integrated. In many companies and institutions, adoption has outpaced reflection, and operational reliance has grown faster than strategic understanding of long-term implications.

For managers, this creates a persistent tension rather than a binary choice. Automated systems promise efficiency, consistency, and scalability, particularly in environments characterized by high volume and repetition. Human decision-making, by contrast, relies on contextual judgment, interpretation, and value-based reasoning that resist full formalization. The central issue is therefore not whether AI should be used, but how authority, discretion, and accountability are redistributed when decisions are partially delegated to systems whose internal logic is probabilistic, opaque, and continuously evolving.

These redistributions rarely occur through explicit design. Instead, they emerge incrementally as tools are adopted where they offer immediate gains: faster processing, lower costs, or perceived objectivity. Over time, however, reliance on these systems reshapes common practices. Certain skills are exercised less frequently, tacit knowledge becomes harder to transmit, and decision rationales are increasingly mediated by system outputs rather than human reasoning. Such transformations are not inherently negative, but they are directional. Once embedded, they are difficult to reverse.

A related challenge concerns the shifting nature of responsibility. When AI systems inform or constrain decisions, accountability can become diffused. Outcomes may be attributed to "the system", even when human oversight formally remains in place. This creates ambiguity not only in governance and compliance contexts, but also in everyday managerial practice. Knowing when to rely on system recommendations, when to override them, and how to justify either choice becomes a core managerial competence rather than a technical detail.

Over longer horizons, a subtler risk emerges: the erosion of organizational resilience. Systems optimized for efficiency under stable assumptions may perform poorly when conditions change, data distributions shift, or novel situations arise. Organizations that have deeply internalized automated decision-making may find themselves less capable of questioning outputs, detecting anomalies, or improvising responses. Resilience depends on maintaining interpretive capacity, not merely on adding technical safeguards.

Preserving this capacity requires more than controls or policies. It requires sustained awareness of where judgment has been delegated, which assumptions are embedded in systems, and which forms of expertise must remain actively practiced rather than archived. The most consequential choices are therefore not about specific tools, but about how organizations balance optimization with adaptability, and standardization with interpretive depth.

These questions do not yield definitive answers, and they should not be expected to. They concern how responsibility is defined, judgment is cultivated, and learning persists as AI becomes an increasingly ordinary component of organizational life. For managers, the practical task is to keep these trade-offs visible and revisitable: examined deliberately, with the people whose work they reshape, rather than silently settled by default through the accumulation of small adoption decisions made one at a time.

9.6 An evolving equilibrium

The future of AI is unlikely to be shaped by a single invention, policy choice, or company. It will emerge instead from an ongoing interaction between technological capability, regulatory response, and social acceptance. This interaction is not linear or stable. It reflects a continuous adjustment between what technology enables and what societies are willing to tolerate, endorse, or restrict at a given moment.

Private firms and governments will continue to compete for technological advantage, as they have with previous general-purpose technologies. Investment will sustain experimentation, and periods of optimism will alternate with reassessment. Some observers already point to signs of overextension, drawing parallels with earlier technology cycles such as the dot-com era. While such comparisons are imperfect, they capture an important dynamic: periods of rapid expansion are often followed by consolidation rather than collapse. Technologies rarely disappear; their scope and role are clarified through use, failure, and regulation.

Generative AI is likely to follow a similar pattern. Many initiatives will not reach maturity, while others will be absorbed into larger platforms or reoriented toward narrower applications. Over time, certain systems will stabilize and become part of routine digital infrastructure. Their presence will become less visible, not because they are less influential, but because they are no longer treated as exceptional.

The meaningful distinction will therefore not be between organizations that adopt AI and those that do not, but between different modes of integration. Some deployments will prioritize speed and scale, others reliability and oversight. These choices will shape not only performance outcomes, but also resilience and public trust.

In Europe, this balance presents particular constraints and opportunities. The region's approach has tended to emphasize legal certainty, traceability, and accountability over rapid experimentation. This orientation does not guarantee competitive advantage, nor does it preclude trade-offs in speed or scale. It does, however, reflect a preference for embedding AI within existing institutional and democratic frameworks rather than reshaping those frameworks around technology.

As with previous technological shifts, AI is likely to recede into the background of everyday activity. What will remain salient are the rules, norms, and assumptions that guided its deployment. These will shape not only how AI is used, but how organizations and institutions evolve alongside it.

The long-term impact of AI will depend less on any single breakthrough than on the cumulative effect of these decisions made by leaders, policymakers, and citizens over time. The work of evaluating trade-offs as they arise, of revisiting governance choices as contexts change, of deciding which forms of expertise to preserve and which to delegate, is not preliminary to AI adoption. It is the substance of it.

10 Europe's position in the global AI landscape

This book has followed a deliberate progression. It first established a shared technical and conceptual baseline, clarifying what contemporary AI systems are, how they work, and why they have moved from a specialized technical domain to a strategic concern for management. It then examined how generative AI creates value in practice, how initiatives can be prioritized and governed, and why discipline, testing, and accountability become essential as systems move from experimentation into operational reality.

Subsequent chapters expanded the perspective further, situating organizational choices within regulatory, ethical, and leadership contexts. The focus gradually shifted from opportunity to responsibility, and from isolated projects to long-term capability building. Rather than treating AI as a one-off transformation, the book has framed it as a continuous managerial challenge that unfolds across technology, governance, culture, and risk.

This final chapter looks outward. Having examined how companies and institutions can adopt, govern, and lead with AI internally, it places those choices within Europe's broader position in the global AI landscape. Trying to predict winners or prescribe policy is by far unfeasible, especially given the extremely volatile modern situation. Instead, we aim to clarify the structural conditions under which European organizations likely operate, and how these conditions shape what kinds of AI strategies are realistic, sustainable, and defensible over time.

10.1 Operating under asymmetry

Europe enters the global AI landscape neither as a dominant power nor as a passive observer. Its position is best described as asymmetric. The continent does not control hyperscale cloud platforms, does not concentrate venture capital at the level of the United States, and does not deploy AI through centralized state direction as China does. These are not temporary disadvantages or the result of delayed adoption. They are structural features of Europe's political economy, rooted in market fragmentation, governance traditions, labor protections, and capital allocation mechanisms. Together, they delimit which forms of AI leadership are realistically attainable.

At the same time, Europe is not peripheral. It retains world-class scientific institutions, a dense and diversified industrial base, and influence over critical segments of global value chains. European firms remain deeply embedded in global production systems, particularly in advanced manufacturing, automotive, energy, healthcare, logistics, and industrial automation. Its regulatory framework governs access to one of the world's largest integrated markets and therefore shapes how AI systems are designed, justified, documented, and operationalized by both domestic and foreign providers. Europe does not compete primarily on scale. It competes on how constraint is absorbed, organized, and translated into functioning systems.

https://doi.org/10.1515/9783112254103-010

For leaders, this distinction is decisive. It affects which AI ambitions are viable, how quickly systems can move from experimentation to deployment, and where durable advantage can plausibly be built. Europe's challenge is not to replicate external models of AI dominance, but to execute reliably under conditions where scale is limited, dependencies are explicit, and trade-offs must be confronted early rather than deferred.

Europe's asymmetric position manifests through recurring structural patterns that shape organizational outcomes across sectors. These patterns, summarized in Table 10.1, clarify where constraints tend to emerge and how they influence managerial decision-making.

Table 10.1: Structural asymmetries shaping Europe's AI landscape.

Asymmetry	Description	Implication for decision-making
Dependency	Core AI capabilities depend on external platforms, models, or infrastructure, while accountability, compliance, and operational risk remain internal to the organization. Control and liability are structurally separated.	Strategic dependence must be actively managed. Vendor choices shape long-term flexibility, risk exposure, and bargaining power beyond immediate technical performance.
Time	Organizational planning, procurement, and approval cycles evolve more slowly than AI technologies, which may change significantly during the lifecycle of a single project.	Governance processes risk lagging behind technological change, forcing trade-offs between relevance, compliance, and speed of execution.
Scope	Constraints in compute, energy, capital, or talent narrow the range of feasible AI initiatives, often implicitly rather than through explicit prioritization.	Organizations may optimize for feasibility rather than impact, leading to fragmented deployments instead of coherent capability building.
Responsibility	Rather than reducing oversight, AI systems increase interpretive and accountability burdens in regulated environments, requiring documentation, contextual judgment, and human intervention.	Automation does not eliminate responsibility. Human judgment becomes more visible, scrutinized, and formally embedded in decision processes.

These asymmetries do not operate independently. They compound across technological, management, and regulatory domains, shaping both the constraints European organizations face and the specific forms of advantage they can realistically cultivate.

10.2 Interaction constraints in Europe's AI ecosystem

Europe's strategic position in AI is shaped less by dominance in individual domains than by how effectively the persistent constraints are navigated and combined. Computing infrastructures, semiconductors, model development, and workforce management are tightly coupled. Decisions in one domain propagate into others, often with long-lasting effects. For managers, recognizing and orchestrating these interactions is more consequential than the attempt to optimize any single component in isolation.

A first and pervasive constraint concerns computing power. Relative to major competitors, Europe operates under sustained compute scarcity, characterized by fewer large-scale GPU clusters, higher energy costs, more constrained grids, and slower capital mobilization. These conditions are structural and unlikely to change within typical managerial planning horizons. Yet this constraint also disciplines strategic choices. Organizations that rely on external cloud providers gain immediate access to computing power but accept trade-offs in dependency, pricing exposure, and policy sensitivity. Others prioritize selective, high-value use cases aligned with existing infrastructure. In practice, this environment encourages clarity of ambition: rather than defaulting to scale for its own sake, European organizations are pushed to align infrastructure decisions closely with strategic priorities.

A parallel dynamic appears in semiconductors. Europe does not host leading-edge fabrication at scale, yet it controls a critical chokepoint through ASML. Extreme ultraviolet lithography machines produced by ASML are indispensable for manufacturing advanced chips, and no near-term alternative exists. This exemplifies a recurring European pattern: constraint transformed into capability through concentration in narrow but essential segments. While this position does not translate into direct control over global semiconductor supply, it confers structural influence by shaping the conditions under which others operate. Progress is guided rather than accelerated, but it is guided from a position of leverage.

These dynamics extend to model development. Europe is unlikely to dominate the training of the very largest foundation models, as frontier-scale training demands concentrations of capital, compute, and risk tolerance that remain structurally external. The strategic opportunity therefore lies elsewhere. Constraint-driven design opens space for models and systems optimized for integration complexity, regulatory alignment, operational reliability, and domain specificity. In such environments, scale-driven approaches often encounter friction, while systems designed for robustness, accountability, and explainability perform comparatively better. These segments reward architectural discipline over raw parameter count.

Ultimately, these interacting constraints converge on the workforce. European regulatory frameworks emphasize human oversight, explainability, and accountability, anchoring AI use firmly in human judgment. In practice, generative AI systems tend to increase interpretive responsibility rather than eliminate it. Automation reshapes work by reallocating effort, but discretion remains central. Human expertise continues to be essential for interpreting outputs, contextualizing recommendations, and deciding when and how systems should be relied upon.

Here, the strategic opportunity becomes clear. When AI integration is accompanied by deliberate investment in human understanding, organizations expand their capacity to intervene, adapt, and recalibrate as systems evolve or contexts change. Rather than displacing expertise, well-designed AI adoption amplifies it. It makes judgment visible, clarifies escalation paths, and strengthens resilience.

Workforce capability is therefore not a residual concern, but a core design objective. Those that invest in skills, literacy, and clearly defined roles ensure that automation enhances discretion rather than obscuring it. By maintaining strong human-in-the-loop practices, they preserve the ability to respond confidently under uncertainty and to deploy AI in ways that are sustainable, credible, and aligned with European values.

10.3 Institutional responses and strategic instruments

In response to these structural constraints, Europe has developed a set of institutional and infrastructural instruments intended to mitigate dependency, reduce risk, and preserve strategic optionality. These instruments do not remove constraints. Rather, they shape how organizations can operate within them, transforming scarcity, regulation, and uncertainty into more predictable operating conditions. While many of these instruments are most directly used by companies that develop or deploy AI systems, their effects extend across the entire value chain. Providers and deployers interact with them at the technical and operational level, whereas importers and users are affected indirectly, through procurement conditions, compliance verification, and governance expectations. Understanding this distinction is essential for interpreting their strategic relevance.

At the semiconductor level, the EU Chips Act seeks to strengthen Europe's resilience across the value chain, from research and design to manufacturing, skills, and supply-chain security [163]. Its objective is not to replicate the scale or speed of leading-edge fabrication ecosystems in the United States or East Asia, but to reduce critical dependencies and reinforce Europe's existing strengths in equipment, materials, and industrial integration. For decision-makers, this implies that semiconductor scarcity remains a background condition, and that diversification and long-term industrial partnerships matter more than aspirations of full self-sufficiency.

At the compute level, Europe has pursued shared infrastructures such as EuroHPC [164] and the development of AI factories and, in the future, AI gigafactories [165]. These facilities are integrated environments combining compute infrastructure, energy supply, data management, and operational support for AI development and deployment. AI factories support experimentation, training and deployment for industrial and public-sector use cases. AI gigafactories are expected to provide higher-capacity, shared environments for compute-intensive workloads and large-scale models under conditions of regulatory control and long-term operational stability. Their purpose is not to compete directly with hyperscalers on raw scale, but to offer sovereign, integrable environments where compliance, reliability, and availability are treated as design parameters rather than afterthoughts.

To complement physical infrastructure, there are Testing and Experimentation Facilities (TEFs) [166]. TEFs provide sector-specific environments in which AI systems can be evaluated under real or near-real operational conditions prior to deployment, particularly in regulated and safety-critical domains such as healthcare, mobility, manufacturing, and energy. Their value does not lie in isolated experimentation, but in their ability to connect technical testing outcomes to deployment decisions, certification pathways, and governance processes.

Regulatory Sandboxes, discussed earlier in Chapter 7, add a further institutional layer that strengthens Europe's AI ecosystem. Unlike TEFs, which focus primarily on technical validation, regulatory sandboxes provide supervised environments in which organizations can explore innovative AI use cases while engaging directly with competent authorities. They create space for legal interpretation, risk assessment, and technical design to evolve together, rather than sequentially.

For companies operating in areas of legal novelty or developing applications that challenge existing categories, sandboxes offer a structured pathway forward. By enabling controlled deviation from standard compliance processes, they allow uncertainties to be addressed early and constructively. This interaction increases regulatory clarity, supports informed design choices, and builds shared understanding between developers, deployers, and regulators.

The strategic value of regulatory sandboxes lies less in experimentation for its own sake than in accelerating alignment. By shortening feedback loops and making expectations explicit at early stages, sandboxes help companies to progress with greater confidence, reduce downstream friction, and prepare more robust pathways to deployment. In doing so, they transform regulatory engagement from a late-stage hurdle into an integral part of responsible innovation.

A further layer is provided by shared service platforms such as AI-on-Demand [167]. AI-on-Demand aggregates AI tools, models, datasets, and compute resources developed across European research institutions, public bodies, and industrial actors. Rather than functioning as a centralized platform, it lowers entry barriers by making capabilities reusable while preserving control over data, compliance, and integration. Its effectiveness depends less on technical availability than on governance quality, usability, and alignment with organizational needs. Table 10.2 summarizes how these instruments relate to the underlying constraints and their managerial implications.

Taken together, these instruments illustrate a consistent European approach: constraints are not eliminated, but structured. For managers, the critical task is not to expect public infrastructure or policy to substitute for strategy, but to position the organization deliberately within this institutional landscape. Across compute, semiconductors,

Table 10.2: Structural constraints, European instruments, and managerial implications.

Structural constraint	European instrument	Implication for decision-makers
Compute scarcity and dependency	EuroHPC, AI factories, AI gigafactories	Shared compute can enable strategic use cases, but only when integrated deliberately into operational planning rather than treated as generic capacity.
Semiconductor dependency	EU Chips Act, ASML chokepoint	Scarcity remains; resilience depends on partnerships, diversification, and alignment with industrial ecosystems rather than self-sufficiency.
Risk of late-stage technical failure	TEFs	Testing environments reduce deployment risk when linked to lifecycle governance and certification pathways, not isolated pilots.
Regulatory uncertainty and compliance risk	Regulatory Sandboxes	Supervised experimentation lowers legal uncertainty and aligns technical design with regulatory expectations before large-scale deployment.
Capability gaps and fragmentation	AI-on-Demand	Shared platforms lower entry barriers, but require governance and usability to translate access into impact.
Interpretive burden on workforce	Regulatory oversight frameworks	Automation increases responsibility; organizations must preserve human expertise alongside AI deployment.

experimentation, regulation, and workforce management, Europe's strategic position depends on how consistently constraints are recognized, coordinated, and translated into durable and structured capabilities.

10.4 Geopolitical exposure, coordination, and strategic autonomy

Global AI development is increasingly shaped by geopolitical competition. The United States privilege private concentration and platform dominance, while China relies on vertical integration and state coordination. Europe aligns fully with neither model. Its intermediate position creates a distinctive form of exposure, but also a distinctive strategic space. Rather than competing on scale or centralization alone, Europe operates at the intersection of technological capability, legal responsibility, and societal legitimacy. This positioning reflects not just limitation, but a deliberate separation between where strategic technological choices are made and where operational, legal, and political accountability ultimately resides.

The central question is therefore not whether this middle position is viable, but under which conditions it becomes sustainable and advantageous. *Can Europe maintain interdependence as AI is increasingly framed through security, sovereignty, and industrial policy lenses?* The answer depends on a limited number of mechanisms through which Europe can translate structural constraints into leverage. These mechanisms are summarized in Table 10.3.

Table 10.3: Mechanisms shaping Europe's strategic autonomy in AI.

Mechanism	Description
Regulatory gravity	Europe's regulatory framework governs access to a large, integrated market, creating de facto global standards through market access logic. This leverage depends on credible and consistent enforcement; when standards are diluted or routinely bypassed, regulatory gravity erodes.
Industrial integration depth	Europe's strength in advanced manufacturing, automotive systems, industrial automation, and energy infrastructure creates domains where AI must integrate with complex physical systems and safety-critical environments. High integration complexity limits platform commoditization and favors system-level expertise.
Chokepoint control	Europe occupies critical positions in global supply chains, most visibly through ASML, but also through materials science, precision equipment, certification bodies, and compliance infrastructures. These positions shape constraints rather than enabling unilateral control.

Strategic autonomy in this context does not imply self-sufficiency. Rather, it refers to the capacity to retain meaningful options when preferred partnerships, suppliers, or platforms become unavailable. Autonomy is therefore a matter of optionality and resilience rather than dominance. Even when alternatives are more costly or less capable, their availability preserves strategic agency under uncertainty.

Most mechanisms that support European autonomy depend on coordination across fragmented institutional and industrial ecosystems. Shared computing infrastructures generate value only when allocation mechanisms are effective. Model ecosystems require critical mass across member states. Regulatory gravity relies on consistent enforcement across jurisdictions. Europe's institutional architecture, designed to prioritize deliberation, legitimacy, and legal robustness, is not optimized for rapid centralized coordination. At the same time, this architecture provides durability and trust, which become increasingly valuable as AI systems move into safety-critical and rights-sensitive domains.

Three coordination trajectories are plausible, as summarized in Table 10.4.

Which trajectory prevails depends less on political intent than on whether coordination costs create sufficient incentives for adaptation. From a managerial perspective, fragmentation should be approached as a stable operating condition rather than

Table 10.4: Plausible coordination trajectories in Europe's AI ecosystem.

Scenario	Characteristics
Successful coordination	Variable-geometry arrangements allow subsets of member states or industrial consortia to move ahead. Regulatory authorities gain credibility through consistent enforcement, and cross-border initiatives achieve sufficient scale.
Managed fragmentation	Full coordination is accepted as unrealistic. Interoperability standards, mutual recognition, and shared tooling reduce friction while preserving national or sectoral autonomy.
Competitive fragmentation	Member states pursue divergent strategies, duplicating effort and creating internal barriers. Coordination failures become a persistent structural feature rather than a transitional phase.

a temporary anomaly. This perspective shifts agency away from attempting to resolve structural fragmentation at the systemic level and toward strategic positioning within it: selecting jurisdictions, partners, and deployment contexts where coordination is sufficient to support scale and credibility.

Europe's position becomes particularly advantageous when its constraints align with specific market conditions. Constraint-driven competition favors domains characterized by high integration complexity, regulatory burden, liability exposure, and long operational lifecycles. These conditions are summarized in Table 10.5.

Table 10.5: Market conditions where constraint becomes a competitive capability.

Condition	Implication for AI systems
Integration complexity	AI must connect with physical systems, legacy infrastructure, and organizational processes that require deterministic performance and long-term stability.
Regulatory burden	Requirements for explainability, auditability, and accountability increase upfront costs but create durable barriers to entry when embedded in core architecture.
Liability exposure	High-consequence errors and clear accountability assignment make opaque decision-making economically and legally prohibitive.
Long lifecycle operations	Systems embedded in capital equipment or critical infrastructure cannot tolerate frequent model changes or unpredictable pricing structures.
Sovereignty requirements	Data residency, operational independence, or supply-chain control are legally mandated or commercially non-negotiable.

In these domains, the costs associated with documentation, human oversight, and explainability are not frictional losses. They are investments in reliability, maintainability, and institutional trust over extended time horizons, often spanning decades rather than product cycles. Organizations that internalize these requirements early can then embed them into architecture and governance, building system-level advantages that scale-driven competitors find difficult to retrofit later.

Constraints become capabilities when they are selectively aligned with domain realities. Where regulation supports differentiation, enforcement is credible, and ecosystems can form around shared standards, European conditions reinforce competitive positioning. The strategic challenge is therefore not to eliminate constraints, but to recognize where they support durable advantages and to concentrate effort accordingly, rather than applying uniform approaches across all domains.

11 Closure

AI, from earlier systems through generative and agentic forms, is one strand of a wider digital ecosystem: hardware, data, analytics, models, and trained people. Across pragmatic and visionary perspectives, this book has argued a single point: AI outcomes are shaped less by technological inevitability than by choices made under constraint. Strategy, governance, and execution matter at least as much as model capability or compute scale.

The questions AI raises are remarkably stable across architectures. Who is accountable? Which risks are acceptable? How is evidence generated? How are decisions reviewed when automation becomes pervasive? Better models do not retire these questions; they raise the cost of answering them poorly. Organizations that treat AI as a one-off transformation accumulate technical, legal, and ethical debt. Those that embed it into governance, decision-making, and skills pipelines retain flexibility and compound capability with each deployment. Preparedness is not a phase that ends at "full adoption" but a continuous posture.

Europe's place in this landscape deserves careful reading, not only from European organizations but from anyone developing, deploying, or operating AI systems in the European market. Europe is not a secondary theater for strategies designed elsewhere. It will not control hyperscale platforms, match U.S. capital concentration, or deploy AI through centralized state direction, and these features are durable. Strategies built around them, rather than against them, do better than those that treat Europe as a late-stage compliance problem.

Europe's leverage is often underestimated. It governs access to one of the world's largest integrated markets, anchors critical supply chains, and leads in industrial and public-sector domains where AI must function inside complex physical, legal, and organizational systems. In those domains, reliability, explainability, and long-term stability are not regulatory artifacts but performance requirements. Scale-driven platforms compete on speed and breadth; constraint-driven approaches compete on integration depth, liability management, and operational longevity, and these attributes are increasingly priced in beyond Europe as well.

The AI Act, examined in detail earlier in this book, is the most visible expression of this operating environment, but its significance for the conclusion is narrower than the public debate suggests. It is neither the source of Europe's distinctive approach nor an exhaustive description of it. The risk-based architecture, the obligations on providers and deployers of high-risk systems, the transparency requirements for general-purpose models, and the governance structures linking national authorities to the European AI Office — these formalize commitments that already characterized European industrial practice in safety-critical domains. Read as a constraint to be minimized, the Act produces compliance theater and brittle systems. Read as a specification of what a trustworthy AI system must be able to demonstrate about itself, it converges with what serious deployers in regulated industries would build regardless. The organizations that

https://doi.org/10.1515/9783112254103-011

will find the Act manageable are those that have already internalized the underlying engineering and governance disciplines; those that have not will discover that the Act exposes gaps the technology alone would have hidden for longer. In either case, the Act is best understood as one instrument within a broader regulatory architecture — alongside the GDPR, the Data Act, sectoral rules, and product-liability regimes — whose combined effect is to make accountability legible across the AI value chain.

The opportunity is symmetric. For European managers, it is to lead deliberately within constraint, building systems that become essential infrastructure and organizations that set standards others adapt to. For firms operating from outside Europe, it is early alignment: designing for European operational realities from the start rather than retrofitting later. Both paths require treating reliability and accountability as design objectives, not jurisdiction-specific add-ons. Capabilities built this way travel; they pay off wherever trust, liability, and long-term operation matter, which is most serious markets.

Many AI decisions create path dependencies that are expensive to reverse. Vendor lock-in, data architecture, and the automation of high-stakes processes all narrow future options. The useful question is not whether to automate but which dependencies are worth taking on, and on what time horizon. This last point deserves attention. AI capabilities now advance on cycles measured in months, while the institutional adaptations they demand — procurement reform, workforce retraining, audit infrastructure, liability allocation — proceed on cycles measured in years. The mismatch is structural, not transitional. Organizations that try to synchronize the two by accelerating institutional change tend to import fragility; those that try by slowing technical adoption tend to forfeit relevance. The workable response is neither: it is to decouple the cycles deliberately, allowing technical experimentation at one tempo while protecting the slower processes that produce accountability, expertise, and trust. Governance structures that absorb fast-moving inputs without being destabilized by them are themselves a competitive asset, and one that compounds quietly.

Execution quality is testable. Can you trace AI decisions to accountable humans? Do you have adaptation procedures when systems need adjustment? Can you explain system behavior to regulators, partners, and affected stakeholders? Do your teams understand what the AI does and what it should not do? Do your governance processes enable deployment at appropriate speed rather than block it? Answers to these questions, more than benchmark scores or compliance checklists, determine whether AI produces durable advantage.

It is worth naming what this framework does not settle. The argument here concerns how organizations operating today should position themselves; it does not resolve open questions about how AI capabilities will evolve, how international regulatory regimes will converge or diverge, or how the distribution of value between model developers, deployers, and end-users will eventually stabilize. These are genuinely uncertain, and prudence consists in building organizations that remain effective across a range of plausible answers rather than betting on any one. Strategic clarity is not certainty about the future; it is clarity about which capabilities, relationships, and commitments are worth holding regardless of which future arrives.

AI is best understood neither as inevitable progress nor as a threat to be contained, but as a general-purpose technology whose effects depend on how it is governed, contextualized, and operated. By tracing the AI value chain from literacy and ethics through deployment, compliance, infrastructure, and model design this book has aimed to equip those who build and use AI in European contexts, and those engaging with them from elsewhere. The future remains open. It will be shaped by choices made under constraint, executed with discipline, and sustained through coordination, and the organizations that approach the task with strategic clarity will be positioned not only for today's AI but for what comes next.

Bibliography

[1] MIT NANDA. “State of AI in business 2025”. In: *Preprint at https://www.artificialintelligence-news.com/wp-content/uploads/2025/08/ai_report_2025.pdf* (2025).

[2] EIT Deep Tech Talent Initiative. *Europe’s AI Workforce: Mapping the Talent Behind the Code*. Accessed: 5 May 2026. EIT Deep Tech Talent Initiative. 14 Aug. 2025. url: https://www.eitdeeptechtalent.eu/news-and-events/news-archive/europes-ai-workforce-mapping-the-talent-behind-the-code/.

[3] Remco Zwetsloot et al. *Keeping Top AI Talent in the United States*. Tech. Rep. Center for Security and Emerging Technology, Georgetown University, Dec. 2019.

[4] Eurostat. *32.7 % of EU people used generative AI tools in 2025*. Accessed: 7 Apr. 2026. Eurostat, European Commission. 16 Dec. 2025. url: https://ec.europa.eu/eurostat/web/products-eurostat-news/w/ddn-20251216-3.

[5] Microsoft Research and Microsoft AI Economy Institute. *Global AI Adoption in 2025: A Widening Digital Divide*. Tech. rep. Microsoft, Jan. 2026.

[6] European Commission. *The EU invests in artificial intelligence only 4 % of what the U.S. spends on it*. Accessed: 7 Apr. 2026. European Commission, EISMEA. 11 Jan. 2025. url: https://ec.europa.eu/newsroom/eismea/items/864247/en.

[7] Michelle Nie and Francesco Tasin. *What the EU Needs to Do to Challenge Big Tech Cloud Dominance*. Accessed: 7 Apr. 2026. TechPolicy Press. 19 June 2025. url: https://www.techpolicy.press/what-the-eu-needs-to-do-to-challenge-big-tech-cloud-dominance/.

[8] Arnaud Tournesac et al.*Accelerating Europe’s AI adoption: The role of sovereign AI*. Accessed: 7 Apr. 2026. McKinsey & Company. 19 Dec. 2025. url: https://www.mckinsey.com/industries/technology-media-and-telecommunications/our-insights/accelerating-europes-ai-adoption-the-role-of-sovereign-ai.

[9] John Haugeland. *Artificial Intelligence: The Very Idea*. MIT Press, 1985.

[10] Allen Newell, J. C. Shaw, and Herbert A. Simon. *A Variety of Intelligent Learning in a General Problem Solver*. Tech. Rep. P-1742. RAND Corporation, 1959.

[11] Allen Newell and Herbert A. Simon. “The Logic Theory Machine—A Complex Information Processing System”. In: *IRE Transactions on Information Theory* 2.3 (1956), pp. 61–79.

[12] Amirhosein Toosi et al.“A brief history of AI: How to prevent another winter (a critical review)”. In: *PET Clinics* 16.4 (2021), pp. 449–469.

[13] William Van Melle. “MYCIN: A knowledge-based consultation program for infectious disease diagnosis”. In: *International Journal of Man-Machine Studies* 10.3 (1978), pp. 313–322.

[14] Bruce G. Buchanan and Edward A. Feigenbaum. “DENDRAL and Meta-DENDRAL: Their applications dimension”. In: *Artificial Intelligence* 11.1-2 (1978), pp. 5–24.

[15] Zhi-Hua Zhou. *Machine Learning*. Springer Nature, 2021.

[16] John D. Owens et al.“GPU computing”. In: *Proceedings of the IEEE* 96.5 (2008), pp. 879–899.

[17] NVIDIA. *NVIDIA Official Website*. Accessed: 1 Dec. 2025. url: https://www.nvidia.com/.

[18] Taiwan Semiconductor Manufacturing Company. *TSMC Official Website*. Accessed: 1 Dec. 2025. url: https://www.tsmc.com/.

[19] ASML. *ASML Official Website*. Accessed: 1 Dec. 2025. url: https://www.asml.com/en.

[20] Mistral. *Mistral AI Official Website*. Accessed: 1 Dec. 2025. url: https://mistral.ai/.

[21] ElevenLabs. *ElevenLabs Official Website*. Accessed: 1 Dec. 2025. url: https://elevenlabs.io/.

[22] DeepL. *DeepL Official Website*. Accessed: 1 Dec. 2025. url: https://www.deepl.com/.

[23] Murray Campbell, A. Joseph Hoane Jr, and Feng-hsiung Hsu. “Deep Blue”. In: *Artificial Intelligence* 134.1-2 (2002), pp. 57–83.

[24] Thomas Rincy N and Roopam Gupta. “A Survey on Machine Learning Approaches and Its Techniques”. In: *2020 IEEE International Students’ Conference on Electrical, Electronics and Computer Science (SCEECS)*. 2020, pp. 1–6.

[25] KJ Price. *List of all Machine Learning (ML) Algorithms*. Accessed: 5 May 2026. 22 May 2024. url: https://medium.com/@price_kj/list-of-all-machine-learning-ml-algorithms-7c839f8c0d73.

https://doi.org/10.1515/9783112254103-012

[26] Berndt Müller, Joachim Reinhardt, and Michael T Strickland. *Neural Networks: An Introduction*. Springer Science & Business Media, 1990.

[27] Yann LeCun, Yoshua Bengio, and Geoffrey Hinton. "Deep learning". In: *Nature* 521.7553 (2015), pp. 436–444.

[28] Stefan Feuerriegel et al. "Generative AI". In: *Business & Information Systems Engineering* 66.1 (2024), pp. 111–126.

[29] Matthieu Cord and Pádraig Cunningham. *Machine Learning Techniques for Multimedia: Case Studies on Organization and Retrieval*. Springer Science & Business Media, 2008.

[30] Lior Rokach and Oded Maimon. "Clustering Methods". In: *Data Mining and Knowledge Discovery Handbook*. Springer, 2005, pp. 321–352.

[31] Hervé Abdi and Lynne J. Williams. "Principal Component Analysis". In: *Wiley Interdisciplinary Reviews. Computational Statistics* 2.4 (2010), pp. 433–459.

[32] David Silver et al. "A General Reinforcement Learning Algorithm that Masters Chess, Shogi, and Go through Self-Play". In: *Science* 362.6419 (2018), pp. 1140–1144.

[33] Leslie Pack Kaelbling, Michael L. Littman, and Andrew W. Moore. "Reinforcement Learning: A Survey". In: *Journal of Artificial Intelligence Research* 4 (1996), pp. 237–285.

[34] Ashish Vaswani et al. "Attention is All You Need". In: *Advances in Neural Information Processing Systems*. Vol. 30. 2017.

[35] Ian Goodfellow et al. "Generative Adversarial Networks". In: *Communications of the ACM* 63.11 (2020), pp. 139–144.

[36] Diederik P. Kingma and Max Welling. "An Introduction to Variational Autoencoders". In: *Foundations and Trends in Machine Learning* 12.4 (2019), pp. 307–392.

[37] Venkatesh Balavadhani Parthasarathy et al. "The ultimate guide to fine-tuning llms from basics to breakthroughs: An exhaustive review of technologies, research, best practices, applied research challenges and opportunities". In: *arXiv:2408.13296* (2024).

[38] Patrick Lewis et al. "Retrieval-Augmented Generation for Knowledge-Intensive NLP Tasks". In: *Advances in Neural Information Processing Systems*. Vol. 33. 2020, pp. 9459–9474.

[39] Ben Kazinik. *The AI report: How Work Management Has Evolved In 2026*. Accessed: 22 Dec. 2025. Sept. 2025. url: https://monday.com/blog/project-management/ai-report/.

[40] Nathan Bell et al. *AI in Customer Care: From Cost Center to Strategic Advantage*. Accessed: 22 Dec. 2025. May 2025. url: https://www.kearney.com/service/digital-analytics/article/ai-in-customer-care-from-cost-center-to-strategic-advantage.

[41] Matt Plummer. *How to Spend Way Less Time on Email Every Day*. Harvard Business Review, Accessed: 22 Dec. 2025. Jan. 2019. url: https://hbr.org/2019/01/how-to-spend-way-less-time-on-email-every-day.

[42] Karan Girotra et al. "Ideas are dimes a dozen: Large language models for idea generation in innovation". In: *The Wharton School Research Paper* (2023).

[43] Deepak Puthal et al. "Shadow AI: Cyber Security Implications, Opportunities and Challenges in the Unseen Frontier". In: *SN Computer Science* 6.5 (2025), p. 405.

[44] Rachael Shah. *Shadow AI: The Silent Security Risk Lurking in Your Enterprise*. Accessed: 22 Nov. 2025. 2025. url: https://www.f5.com/company/blog/shadow-ai-the-silent-security-risk-lurking-in-your-enterprise.

[45] Gigster. *The Dangers of Shadow AI and the Need for an Enterprise AI Plan*. Accessed: 22 Nov. 2025. 2024. url: https://gigster.com/blog/the-dangers-of-shadow-ai-and-need-for-an-enterprise-ai-plan/#:~:text=Shadow%20AI%20is%20a%20symptom,foundation%20on%20which%20to%20build.

[46] Maxim Massenkoff and Peter McCrory. *Labor market impacts of AI: A new measure and early evidence*. Tech. Rep. Anthropic, Mar. 2026.

[47] Erik Brynjolfsson, Danielle Li, and Lindsey R. Raymond. "Generative AI at Work". In: *National Bureau of Economic Research Working Paper* (2023).

[48] Shakked Noy and Whitney Zhang. "Experimental Evidence on the Productivity Effects of Generative Artificial Intelligence". In: *Science* 381.6654 (2023), pp. 187–192.

[49] Flavio Calvino, Jelmer Reijerink, and Lea Samek. “Unlocking productivity with generative AI: Evidence from experimental studies”. In: *OECD Artificial Intelligence Papers*. OECD Publishing, 2025.

[50] Antonin Bergeaud et al.“AI can boost productivity – if firms use it”. In: *European Central Bank Blog* (28/03/2025).

[51] Alex Singla, Alexander Sukharevsky, Lareina Yee, Michael Chui, and Bryce Hall. *The State of AI: How Organizations Are Rewiring to Capture Value*. McKinsey & Company. Report. 2025.

[52] Ronan Vander Elst, Nicolas Griedlich, and Liubomyr Bregman. *Agentic AI: The New Frontier in AI Evolution*. Deloitte. Report. 2025.

[53] Dan Robitzski. “Watch tesla autopilot get bamboozled by a truck hauling traffic lights”. In: *The Byte* (2021).

[54] Boston Consulting Group. *AI Agents*. Accessed: 11 Dec. 2025. 2025. url: https://www.bcg.com/capabilities/artificial-intelligence/ai-agents#:~:text=By%20building%20AI%20agents%2C%20companies,workers%20to%20be%20more%20productive.

[55] Rani Yadav-Ranjan. *AI Governance: the CEO’s Ethical Imperative in 2025*. Forbes. Accessed: 11 Dec. 2025. 4 Feb. 2025. url: https://www.forbes.com/sites/committeeof200/2025/02/04/ai-governance-the-ceos-ethical-imperative-in-2025/.

[56] Svetlana Sicular. *AI’s Next Frontier Demands a New Approach to Ethics, Governance and Compliance*. Gartner. Accessed: 20 Jan. 2026. 10 Nov. 2025. url: https://www.gartner.com/en/articles/ai-ethics-governance-and-compliance.

[57] Flavio Calvino, Jelmer Reijerink, and Lea Samek. *The Effects of Generative AI on Productivity, Innovation and Entrepreneurship*. OECD. OECD Artificial Intelligence Papers. 2025.

[58] Eric Lamarre, Kate Smaje, and Rodney Zemmel. *In digital and AI transformations, start with the problem, not the technology*. McKinsey & Company. Accessed: 5 Jan. 2026. 2023. url: https://www.mckinsey.com/capabilities/strategy-and-corporate-finance/our-insights/in-digital-and-ai-transformations-start-with-the-problem-not-the-technology.

[59] David Linthicum. *The perils of overengineering generative AI systems*. InfoWorld. Accessed: 5 Jan. 2026. 2024. url: https://www.infoworld.com/article/2510439/the-perils-of-overengineering-generative-ai-systems.html#:~:text=This%20practice%20leads%20to%20the,costs%2C%20and%20reduced%20system%20resilience.

[60] Jacob Devlin et al. “BERT: Pre-training of Deep Bidirectional Transformers for Language Understanding”. In: *arXiv:1810.04805* (2019).

[61] Gheorghe Comanici et al. “Gemini 2.5: Pushing the frontier with advanced reasoning, multimodality, long context, and next generation agentic capabilities”. In: *arXiv:2507.06261* (2025).

[62] OpenAI. *OpenAI Official Website*. Accessed: 1 Sept. 2025. url: https://openai.com/.

[63] Anthropic. *anthropic official website*. Accessed: 1 Sept. 2025. Url: https://www.anthropic.com/.

[64] xAI. *xAI Official Website*. Accessed: 1 Sept. 2025. url: https://x.ai/.

[65] Hugo Touvron et al. “Llama: Open and efficient foundation language models”. In: *arXiv:2302.13971* (2023).

[66] Albert Q. Jiang et al. “Mistral 7B”. In: *arXiv:2310.06825* (2023).

[67] Xiao Bi et al. “Deepseek llm: Scaling open-source language models with longtermism”. In: *arXiv:2401.02954* (2024).

[68] BigScience Workshop et al. “Bloom: A 176b-parameter open-access multilingual language model”. In: *arXiv:2211.05100* (2022).

[69] Gene Rapoport, Sanjin Bicanic, and Muyiwa Talabi. *Survey: Generative AI’s Uptake Is Unprecedented Despite Roadblocks*. Bain & Company. Accessed: 2 Jan. 2026. url: https://www.bain.com/insights/survey-generative-ai-uptake-is-unprecedented-despite-roadblocks/.

[70] Ankit Bisht et al. *Open source technology in the age of AI*. Accessed: 19 Dec. 2025. 2025. url: https://www.mckinsey.com/capabilities/quantumblack/our-insights/open-source-technology-in-the-age-of-ai.

[71] Sylvain Duranton. *What Leaders Need To Know About Open-Source Vs. Proprietary AI*. Accessed: 19 Dec. 2025. 2025. url: https://www.forbes.com/sites/sylvainduranton/2025/07/07/what-leaders-need-to-know-about-open-source-vs-proprietary-models/.

[72] Sean M. Kerner. *Why your enterprise AI strategy needs both open and closed models: The TCO reality check*. Accessed: 2 Jan. 2026. 2025. url: https://venturebeat.com/ai/why-your-enterprise-ai-strategy-needs-both-open-and-closed-models-the-tco-reality-check.

[73] Gaia-X. *Gaia-X Official Website*. Accessed: 1 Dec. 2025. url: https://gaia-x.eu.

[74] Armand Ruiz and Vivek Bharathi. *Scaling generative AI with flexible model choices*. Accessed: 2 Sept. 2025. url: https://www.ibm.com/blog/scaling-generative-ai.

[75] Samuel Godadaw Ayinaddis. "Artificial intelligence adoption dynamics and knowledge in SMEs and large firms: A systematic review and bibliometric analysis". In: *Journal of Innovation & Knowledge* 10.3 (2025), p. 100682.

[76] Solon Teal. *How to Evaluate and Select the Right AI Foundation Model for Your Business*. Accessed: 2 Jan. 2026. url: https://www.vktr.com/ai-platforms/how-to-evaluate-and-select-the-right-ai-foundation-model-for-your-business/.

[77] Ivan Belcic and Cole Stryker. *RAG vs. fine-tuning vs. prompt engineering*. IBM Think. Accessed: 3 Jan. 2026. url: https://www.ibm.com/think/topics/rag-vs-fine-tuning-vs-prompt-engineering.

[78] InterSystems. *RAG vs Fine-tuning vs Prompt Engineering: Everything You Need to Know*. Accessed: 5 Jan. 2026. url: https://www.intersystems.com/resources/rag-vs-fine-tuning-vs-prompt-engineering-everything-you-need-to-know/.

[79] Lakshmi Varanasi. *McKinsey CEO Bob Sternfels Says the Firm now has 60,000 Employees: 25,000 of them are AI Agents*. Published 12 Jan. 2026. Accessed: 24 Jan. 2026. url: https://www.businessinsider.com/mckinsey-workforce-ai-agents-consulting-industry-bob-sternfels-2026-1.

[80] LangChain. *State of AI Agents*. Accessed: 24 Jan. 2025. 2024. url: https://www.langchain.com/stateofaiagents.

[81] Bain & Company. *$2 Trillion in New Revenue Needed to Fund AI's Scaling Trend*. Bain & Company's 6th annual Global Technology Report. Accessed: 5 Jan. 2026. Sept. 2025. url: https://www.bain.com/about/media-center/press-releases/20252/%5C$2-trillion-in-new-revenue-needed-to-fund-ais-scaling-trend---bain--companys-6th-annual-global-technology-report/.

[82] Danielle Burgs Escobar et al. *Scaling AI While Controlling Tech Costs*. Accessed: 5 Jan. 2026. Oct. 2025. url: https://www.bain.com/insights/scaling-ai-while-controlling-costs/.

[83] Joel Paul et al."Privacy and data security concerns in AI". In: *ResearchGate* (2024).

[84] Doina Banciu, and Carmen Elena Cirnu. "AI Ethics and Data Privacy Compliance". In: *2022 14th International Conference on Electronics, Computers and Artificial Intelligence (ECAI)*. IEEE. 2022, pp. 1–5.

[85] Alexandra Sternlicht. *AI companies are throwing big money at newly minted PhDs, sparking fears of an academic 'brain drain'*. Accessed: 7 Oct. 2025. 2025. url: https://fortune.com/2025/06/25/ai-companies-court-ai-phds-with-huge-pay-packages-raising-fears-of-an-academic-brain-drain/.

[86] Alessio Buscemi and Daniele Proverbio. "ChatGPT vs Gemini vs Llama on Multilingual Sentiment Analysis". In: *arXiv:2402.01715* (2024).

[87] IBM. *What is an AI Center of Excellence?* Accessed: 14 Mar. 2026. 2025. url: https://www.ibm.com/think/topics/ai-center-of-excellence.

[88] ISACA. *How to Measure and Prove the Value of Your AI Investments*. Volume 5. Accessed: 14 Mar. 2026. 2025. url: https://www.isaca.org/resources/news-and-trends/newsletters/atisaca/2025/volume-5/how-to-measure-and-prove-the-value-of-your-ai-investments.

[89] Glean Team. *How to Measure ROI on Generative AI Investments: A Practical Guide*. Accessed: 30 Oct. 2025. Oct. 2025. url: https://www.glean.com/perspectives/proving-roi-on-genai-investments.

[90] Worklytics. *Proving the ROI of AI Adoption: Metrics and Dashboards Every Org Needs in 2025*. Accessed: 14 Mar. 2026. 2025. url: https://www.worklytics.co/resources/proving-roi-ai-adoption-metrics-dashboards-2025.

[91] Deloitte. *The State of Generative AI in the Enterprise*. Report. Accessed: 14 Mar. 2026. 2024. url: https://www.deloitte.com/us/en/what-we-do/capabilities/applied-artificial-intelligence/content/state-of-generative-ai-in-enterprise.html.

[92] Turing. *How to Measure the ROI of Generative AI*. Accessed: 14 Mar. 2026. May 1/12/2025. url: https://www.turing.com/resources/how-to-measure-the-roi-of-generative-ai.

[93] IBM. *How to Maximize ROI on AI in 2025*. Accessed: 14 Mar. 2026. Nov. 2025. url: https://www.ibm.com/think/insights/ai-roi.

[94] Lenos Trigeorgis and Jeffrey J. Reuer. "Real Options Theory in Strategic Management". In: *Strategic Management Journal* 38.1 (2017). Accessed: 14 Mar. 2026, pp. 42–63.

[95] Bart M. Lambrecht. "Real Options in Finance". In: *Journal of Banking and Finance* (2017). Published March 2017. Accessed: 1 Feb. 2026.

[96] ScienceDirect. *Real Option Theory — An Overview*. Accessed: 28 Dec. 2025. url: https://www.sciencedirect.com/topics/computer-science/real-option-theory.

[97] ScienceDirect. *Real Options Analysis — An Overview*. Accessed: 28 Dec. 2025. url: https://www.sciencedirect.com/topics/economics-econometrics-and-finance/real-options-analysis.

[98] Jessica Apotheker et al. *From Potential to Profit: Closing the AI Impact Gap*. Boston Consulting Group AI Radar 2025 report. Accessed: 12 Dec. 2025. Jan. 2025. url: https://www.bcg.com/publications/2025/closing-the-ai-impact-gap.

[99] Matthew Olson. *AI ROI Calculator: From Generative to Agentic AI Success in 2025*. Accessed: 12 Feb. 2026. 22 Aug. 2025. url: https://writer.com/blog/roi-for-generative-ai/.

[100] Steven DeVries et al. *Machine Learning Lens: AWS Well-Architected Framework*. Tech. Rep. Amazon Web Services, 2025.

[101] Microsoft. *MLOps: Model Management, Deployment, and Monitoring with Azure Machine Learning*. Tech. Rep. Accessed: 14 Mar. 2026. Microsoft Azure, 2023. url: https://learn.microsoft.com/en-us/azure/machine-learning/concept-model-management-and-deployment.

[102] ISO/IEC 22989:2022 — Artificial intelligence — Concepts and terminology. Accessed: 12 Dec. 2025. International Organization for Standardization, 2022. url: https://www.iso.org/standard/74296.html.

[103] ISO/IEC 42001:2023 — Information technology — Artificial intelligence — Management system. Accessed: 12 Dec. 2025. International Organization for Standardization, 2023. url: https://www.iso.org/standard/42001.

[104] ISO/IEC 23894:2023 — Artificial intelligence — Guidance on risk management. Accessed: 12 Dec. 2025. International Organization for Standardization, 2023. url: https://www.iso.org/standard/77304.html.

[105] Evan Anderson, Jim Holdsworth, and Matthew Kosinski. *What Is Red Teaming?* Accessed 12/03/2026. 2024. url: https://www.ibm.com/it-it/think/topics/red-teaming.

[106] Margot E Kaminski. "Regulating the Risks of AI". In: *BUL Rev.* 103 (2023), p. 1347.

[107] Claudio Novelli et al."Taking AI Risks Seriously: A New Assessment Model for the AI Act". In: *AI & Society* 39.5 (2024), pp. 2493–2497.

[108] Paulina Okunyté and Niamh Ancell. *Replit's AI Coding Assistant Reportedly Went Rogue, Wiping a Database and Generating 4,000 Fictional Users*. Accessed: 23 Dec. 2025. July 2025. url: https://cybernews.com/ai-news/replit-ai-vive-code-rogue/.

[109] Alexander Saeedy. "Why xAI's Grok Went Rogue". In: *The Wall Street Journal* (July 2025). Accessed: 23 Dec. 2025. url: https://www.wsj.com/tech/ai/why-xais-grok-went-rogue-a81841b0.

[110] Herb Scribner. "Major newspapers ran a summer reading list. AI made up book titles". In: *The Washington Post* (May 2025). Accessed: 23 Dec. 2025. url: https://www.washingtonpost.com/style/media/2025/05/20/chicago-sun-times-philadelphia-inquirer-ai-books-summer-reading/.

[111] Daniele Proverbio. *The Principle of Proportionate Benefits in AIs and Ethics*. Tech. Rep. Accessed: 12 Dec. 2025. House of Ethics, 2025. url: https://www.houseofethics.com/2025/11/27/the-principle-of-proportionate-benefits-in-ais-and-ethics/.

[112] Alessio Buscemi and Daniele Proverbio. “RogueGPT: Transforming ChatGPT-4 into a Rogue AI with Dis-Ethical Tuning”. In: *AI and Ethics* (2025), pp. 1–22.

[113] Leonardo Nicoletti and Dina Bass. *Humans are Biased. Generative AI is Even Worse*. Bloomberg Technology + Equality. Accessed: 10 Oct. 2025. June 2023. url: https://www.bloomberg.com/graphics/2023-generative-ai-bias/.

[114] James Manyika, Jake Silberg, and Brittany Presten. “What do we do about the biases in AI”. In: *Harvard Business Review* (2019).

[115] Paula Hall and Debbie Ellis. “A systematic review of socio-technical gender bias in AI algorithms”. In: *Online Information Review* 47.7 (2023), pp. 1264–1279.

[116] Fahim Anzum, Ashratuz Zavin Asha, and Marina L Gavrilova. “Biases, Fairness, and Implications of Using AI in Social Media Data Mining”. In: *2022 International Conference on Cyberworlds (CW)*. 2022, pp. 251–254.

[117] Curt Jacobsen et al. *Overcoming Two Issues That are Sinking Gen AI Programs*. Accessed: 23 Dec. 2025. June 2025. url: https://www.mckinsey.com/capabilities/tech-and-ai/our-insights/overcoming-two-issues-that-are-sinking-gen-ai-programs.

[118] SAP. *What is AI bias?* Accessed: 23 Dec. 2025. 2025. url: https://www.sap.com/resources/what-is-ai-bias.

[119] Rina D. Caballar. *10 AI dangers and risks and how to manage them*. IBM Think. Accessed: 10 Oct. 2025. url: https://www.ibm.com/think/insights/10-ai-dangers-and-risks-and-how-to-manage-them.

[120] Alessio Buscemi et al.“FAIRGAME: a Framework for AI Agents Bias Recognition Using Game Theory”. In: *Frontiers in Artificial Intelligence and Applications*. Vol. 413: ECAI 2025. IOS Press, 2025.

[121] Madeleine Wright. “Companies seek AI solutions to supply chain fragility”. In: *Financial Times* (Mar. 2025). Accessed: 12 Dec. 2025. url: https://www.ft.com/content/1d07a823-43da-4c1b-84d3-7e453ebb1b16.

[122] Daniele Proverbio. *AI for Sustainability, Sustainability for AI*. Tech. Rep. Accessed: 12 Dec. 2025. House of Ethics, 2025. url: https://www.houseofethics.com/2025/10/17/ai-for-sustainability-sustainability-for-ai/.

[123] Juan N Pava et al.“Mind the (language) gap: Mapping the challenges of LLM development in low-resource language contexts”. In: *Stanford Institute for Human-Centered Artificial Intelligence (HAI): Stanford, CA, USA* (2025).

[124] Taryn Plumb. *LLMs Have a Multilingual Jailbreak Problem – How You Can Stay Safe*. Accessed: 12 Dec. 2025. SDxCentral. Nov. 2023. url: https://www.sdxcentral.com/analysis/llms-have-a-multilingual-jailbreak-problem-how-you-can-stay-safe/.

[125] Ipsos. *The Ipsos AI Monitor 2025*. Ipsos Report. Accessed: 12 Feb. 2026. 2025. url: https://www.ipsos.com/en-dk/ipsos-ai-monitor-2025.

[126] Regulation (EU) 2022/2065 on a Single Market for Digital Services (Digital Services Act). Official Journal of the European Union. 2022.

[127] Regulation (EU) 2022/1925 on Contestable and Fair Markets in the Digital Sector (Digital Markets Act). Official Journal of the European Union, 2022.

[128] Directive (EU) 2022/2555 on Measures for a High Common Level of Cybersecurity Across the Union (NIS2 Directive). Official Journal of the European Union. 2022.

[129] Regulation (EU) 2022/2554 on Digital Operational Resilience for the Financial Sector (DORA). Official Journal of the European Union. 2022.

[130] Regulation (EU) 2024/2847 on Horizontal Cybersecurity Requirements for Products with Digital Elements (Cyber Resilience Act). Official Journal of the European Union. 2024.

[131] Regulation (EU) 2022/868 on European Data Governance (Data Governance Act). Official Journal of the European Union. 2022.

[132] Regulation (EU) 2023/2854 on Harmonised Rules on Fair Access to and Use of Data (Data Act). Official Journal of the European Union. 2023.

[133] High-Level Expert Group on Artificial Intelligence. *Ethics Guidelines for Trustworthy AI*. Accessed: 25 May 2025. 2019. url: https://digital-strategy.ec.europa.eu/en/library/ethics-guidelines-trustworthy-ai.

[134] Financial Conduct Authority. *Regulatory Sandbox*. Accessed: 16 Dec. 2025. UK Financial Conduct Authority. 2025. url: https://www.fca.org.uk/firms/innovation/regulatory-sandbox.

[135] Politico Europe. *Top European CEOs Plead for Pause in AI Act*. Accessed: 24 Dec. 2025. July 2025. url: https://www.politico.eu/article/top-european-ceos-plead-for-pause-in-ai-act/.

[136] John Ladley. *Data Governance: How to Design, Deploy, and Sustain an Effective Data Governance Program*. Academic Press, 2019.

[137] Lisa Bechtold. "Why AI literacy is crucial for safe, inclusive and strategic AI transformation". In: *World Economic Forum* (July 2025).

[138] Graham Waller. "Why You Need to Build AI Literacy Now — And How to Do It". In: *Gartner* (27/03/2025).

[139] Hannah Mayer et al.*Superagency in the Workplace. Empowering People to Unlock AI's Full Potential*. Tech. Rep. Accessed: 1 Feb. 2026. McKinsey & Company, 2025. url: https://www.mckinsey.com/capabilities/tech-and-ai/our-insights/superagency-in-the-workplace-empowering-people-to-unlock-ais-full-potential-at-work.

[140] Daniele Proverbio. *Generative AI and Responsibility – Part 1/2*. Tech. Rep. Accessed: 18 Dec. 2025. House of Ethics, 2023. url: https://www.houseofethics.com/2023/03/21/generative-ai-and-responsibility/.

[141] Katja Rausch. *Generative AI and Responsibility – Part 2/2*. Tech. Rep. Accessed: 18 Dec. 2025. House of Ethics, 2023. url: https://www.houseofethics.com/2023/03/23/generative-ai-and-responsibility-part-2-2/.

[142] Susie Alegre. *Human Rights, Robot Wrongs*. Atlantic Books, 2024.

[143] Carissa Veliz. *Privacy is Power: Why and How You Should Take Back Control of Your Data*. Penguin Random House, 2020.

[144] IBM. *What is AI ethics?* Accessed: 26 Dec. 2025. IBM. 2025. url: https://www.ibm.com/think/topics/ai-ethics.

[145] McKinsey & Company. *What is artificial general intelligence (AGI)?* Accessed: 13 Dec. 2025. Mar. 2024. url: https://www.mckinsey.com/featured-insights/mckinsey-explainers/what-is-artificial-general-intelligence-agi.

[146] Mustafa Suleyman. *Towards Humanist Superintelligence*. Microsoft.ai. Accessed: 21 Mar. 2026. Nov. 2025. url: https://microsoft.ai/news/towards-humanist-superintelligence/.

[147] Tharin Pillay. *How OpenAI's Sam Altman Is Thinking About AGI and Superintelligence in 2025*. Time.com. Accessed: 21 Mar. 2026. Jan. 2025. url: https://time.com/7205596/sam-altman-superintelligence-agi/.

[148] David Silver et al."Mastering the game of go without human knowledge". In: *Nature* 550.7676 (2017), pp. 354–359.

[149] Nick Bostrom. *Superintelligence: Paths, Dangers, Strategies*. Oxford University Press, 2014.

[150] Francois Chollet et al. "Arc prize 2025: Technical report". In: *arXiv:2601.10904* (2026).

[151] Peter CY Chow. "Chip-Four Alliance for a Resilient Global Semiconductor Industry". In: *Technology Rivalry Between the USA and China*. Springer, 2025, pp. 269–307.

[152] Hong Shen. "Building a Digital Silk Road? Situating the Internet in China's Belt and Road Initiative". In: *International Journal of Communication* 12 (2018), p. 19.

[153] Jeremy Julian Sarkin and Saba Sotoudehfar. "Artificial Intelligence and Arms Races in the Middle East: The Evolution of Technology and Its Implications for Regional and International Security". In: *Defense & Security Analysis* 40.1 (2024), pp. 97–119.

[154] Volha Litvinets. *AI and Sustainability: Opportunities, Challenges, and Impact*. Tech. Rep. Accessed: 15 Dec. 2025. EY, 2024. url: https://www.ey.com/en_nl/insights/climate-change-sustainability-services/ai-and-sustainability-opportunities-challenges-and-impact.

[155] UN Environment Programme. *AI Has an Environmental Problem. Here's What the World Can do About That*. Tech. Rep. Accessed: 5 Dec. 2025. UN, 2025. url: https://www.unep.org/news-and-stories/story/ai-has-environmental-problem-heres-what-world-can-do-about.

[156] McKenzie Sadeghi. *AI False Information Rate Nearly Doubles in One Year*. Tech. Rep. Accessed: 10 Dec. 2025. NewsGuard, 2025. url: https://www.newsguardtech.com/wp-content/uploads/2025/09/August-2025-One-Year-Progress-Report-3.pdf.

[157] Rosalie Waelen and Aimee van Wynsberghe. "Considering the Social and Economic Sustainability of AI". In: *Science and Engineering Ethics* 31.4 (2025), p. 19.

[158] Akhil P Joseph and Anithamol Babu. "Redefining Communication in Mental Healthcare: Generative AI for Neurodivergent Equity and Non-Verbal Autistic Inclusion". In: *Frontiers in Psychiatry* 16 (2025), p. 1611101.

[159] Sandrine Kergroach and Julien Héritier. "Emerging divides in the transition to artificial intelligence". In: *OECD Regional Development Papers* (2025).

[160] Korinzia Toniolo et al."Sustainable business models and artificial intelligence: Opportunities and challenges". In: *Knowledge, People, and Digital Transformation: Approaches for a Sustainable Future* (2020), pp. 103–117.

[161] Medha Bankhwal et al. *AI for social good: Improving lives and protecting the planet*. Tech. Rep. Accessed: 3 Feb. 2026. McKinsey Digital, 2025. url: https://www.mckinsey.com/capabilities/quantumblack/our-insights/ai-for-social-good.

[162] Nancy Girdhar et al."A Comprehensive Review of Frugal Artificial Intelligence: Challenges, Applications, and the Road to Sustainable AI". In: *Soft Computing* 29.13 (2025), pp. 4823–4856.

[163] Regulation (EU) 2023/1781 Establishing a Framework of Measures for Strengthening Europe's Semiconductor Ecosystem and Amending Regulation (EU) 2021/694. Official Journal of the European Union. 2023.

[164] European High Performance Computing Joint Undertaking (EuroHPC JU). *EuroHPC JU: Homepage*. Accessed: 26 Dec. 2025. EuroHPC Joint Undertaking, 2025. url: https://www.eurohpc-ju.europa.eu/index_en.

[165] European Commission. *AI Factories - Shaping Europe's Digital Future*. Accessed: 26 Dec. 2025. 2025. url: https://digital-strategy.ec.europa.eu/en/policies/ai-factories.

[166] Sectorial AI Testing and Experimentation Facilities under the Digital Europe Programme. Accessed: 26 Dec. 2025. 2025. url: https://digital-strategy.ec.europa.eu/en/policies/testing-and-experimentation-facilities.

[167] AI-on-Demand. *AI-on-Demand Official Website*. Accessed: 1 Dec. 2025. url: https://aiod.eu/.

[168] EUSAiR. *EU Regulatory Sandboxes for AI*. Accessed: 1 Dec. 2025. url: https://eusair-project.eu/.

[169] European Commission. *Proposal for a Regulation of the European Parliament and of the Council amending Regulations (EU) 2024/1689 and (EU) 2018/1139 as regards the simplification of the implementation of harmonised rules on artificial intelligence (Digital Omnibus on AI)*. COM(2025) 836 final, 2025/0359(COD). 19 Nov. 2025. url: https://eur-lex.europa.eu/legal-content/EN/TXT/?uri=CELEX:52025PC0836.

Index

https://doi.org/10.1515/9783112254103-013

www.ingramcontent.com/pod-product-compliance
Lightning Source LLC
LaVergne TN
LVHW080310110826
845155LV00023B/104
9783112254097